HUBERT HUMPHREY
The Man and His Dream

HUBERT HUMPHREY
The Man and His Dream

Sheldon D. Engelmayer
Robert J. Wagman

METHUEN

New York   Toronto   London   Sydney

Methuen, Inc., 777 Third Avenue, New York 10017.

Published simultaneously in Canada by
Methuen Publications 2330 Midland Avenue,
Agincourt, Ontario M1S 1P7.

ISBN 0-458-93450-X
LCCCN 78-58847

Printed and bound in the United States of America

78 79 80 81   1 2 3 4 5

To Jennifer, Malka, Bobby, Juda, Patricia, J.J., and Molly—for whose futures this is all about.

Contents

Acknowledgments

The authors gratefully acknowledge the following individuals, without whom this volume would have been impossible:

Lucianne Goldberg, for her faith in our abilities;

Betty South of Senator Humphrey's office, for her support and assistance;

Elizabeth Towne, for her many hours of slaving over a hot Xerox machine;

Margaret Richards, for Elizabeth Towne;

Mona Marzano and Marc Rangel, for coming to the rescue;

And especially to Carol Ann and Lisa—for their undying patience.

Foreword

Perhaps the most insignificant thing that can be said about Hubert Humphrey's life is that he never became president of the United States.

It is also, perhaps, his greatest tribute.

Hubert Humphrey is one of our nation's immortals. And that can be said of a very few men, indeed. In the early days of the republic, we had many such men: Benjamin Franklin, Samuel Adams and John Marshall were never elected president, but they nevertheless continue to have a profound effect on the course of the nation they helped create. George Washington, John Adams and Thomas Jefferson acceded to the presidency, but they had already established firm footholds on national immortality long before taking the oath of office.

Abraham Lincoln is considered perhaps the greatest of American presidents. But for what would he have been remembered had he not become president? Certainly not for being a mediocre but honest lawyer in Springfield, Illinois.

Woodrow Wilson is regarded as another great president, as is Franklin D. Roosevelt. But would either of them be remembered today had they not risen beyond the governorships of their respective states? That is highly doubtful.

But not Hubert Humphrey. Over the last thirty years, he accomplished more as a senator from Minnesota than most presidents accomplish with the full weight of that exalted office behind them.

Few issues in the past thirty years escaped the Humphrey stamp: civil rights, social welfare, health care, energy, the environment, agriculture, forestry, conservation, national defense, worldwide disarmament, food for peace, the economy.

As Vice-President Walter Mondale once stated: "With any other public figure, you hit upon one subject, analyze what he did, and that's it. There just isn't anyone else whose involvement was so total, whose record touches just about everything that has happened in this country over the past thirty years."

And he did it all without ever having been president.

He could have been—if he had been willing to forego his principles, if he had been willing to let the end justify the means. He could have beaten John Kennedy in the 1960 primary campaign if he had been willing to set morality aside and crawl into the gutter with the Kennedy machine; but he would not do that, and he lost. He could have beaten Richard Nixon in 1968 if he had been willing to stab his president, Lyndon Johnson, in the back; but he would not do that, and he lost.

For Hubert Humphrey, politics was the noblest profession and public service the highest achievement. But it had to be politics with morality, public service for the public good. Principles always came before partisanship and ambition.

Hubert Humphrey dedicated his life to turning his dream of America into the reality of America: an America where people are concerned about other people; where the principles of freedom and citizenship are always held high and never taken for granted; where one person has as much chance as the next to make a better life; where democracy can flourish and grow.

Others have shared that dream over the two centuries of our national life; few, however, have labored as intensely as did Hubert Humphrey to make that dream come true. He achieved much, but a great deal more needs to be done.

What follows is that dream—presented, for the most part, in Hubert Humphrey's own words. It is a challenge to this and future generations to continue the work he has begun until that dream is fulfilled in its totality. To fail to accept that challenge is to fail not Hubert Humphrey, but ourselves.

We do not imply that what appears in this book is a definitive collection of Hubert Humphrey's utterances and writings, for it is not. Nor do we imply that the collection of speeches, letters and articles assembled herein represents the best of Hubert Humphrey, or that he would have chosen as we have; such selection is a matter of personal judgments. But we do believe that what follows accurately portrays what Hubert Humphrey was all about, and does provide the inspiration needed to carry on where he was forced to leave off.

We offer this book not as a memorial to his life, but as a tribute to his immortality. If it inspires just one young person to seek to walk in his footsteps, if it sparks just one idea that moves the world a little bit closer to peace, brotherhood and freedom, it will have served its purpose.

Sheldon D. Engelmayer
Robert J. Wagman

New York
January 1978

Introduction
by Senator Muriel Humphrey

It was July 14, 1948. Democrats from throughout the nation had assembled in Philadelphia for the Democratic National Convention. I had wanted to accompany Hubert, but we had decided that with four young children, including a baby, I should remain at home in Minnesota.

The night before, he had called from Philadelphia to indicate that it was likely he would be presenting to the Democratic Convention the following day his plea for a plank on civil rights.

Because of the warnings from many delegates and some advisers that such a plank would be harmful not only to President Truman in his bid for reelection, but also to the party generally, there was concern whether he should present it.

Hubert and I realized the threat that this action also posed to Hubert's own blossoming political career. But I understood the extent of his commitment to civil rights and shared it. I urged him to give the speech.

As I sat there sewing, the children and I listening intently to the convention proceedings, I still was uncertain what Hubert would do. Would he even be permitted to speak?

Finally, I heard Hubert being introduced to the convention and the presentation of his speech that affected me as it did many others listening around the country. The speech was so moving and beautiful, that I could not hold back the tears, as it conveyed such an essential message for our people.

He inspired me on that occasion, as he did so many, many times throughout our thirty-three years together in public life.

I can't remember when I first heard Hubert speak. My earliest recollections, however, are of his participation in debating activities at the University of Minnesota, and later on at the University of Louisiana where he worked on his Master's degree. Two well-known debating partners during those years were Orville Freeman, who became secretary of agriculture in the Kennedy administration, and Russell Long, who was elected to the U.S. Senate the same year as Hubert.

From the very beginning, it was obvious that he enjoyed speaking and relished the intellectual challenge it presented. His special talent for presenting ideas and proposals was to serve him well during his years as mayor, senator and vice-president.

Hubert always considered his role in public office to involve education and persuasion. His speeches in the Senate and to public audiences were prepared with these two objectives in mind.

Explaining this view to a group of teachers, he once said, "It is the duty of a leader to get just a bit ahead of the people on an issue. And then it is his duty to educate the people. He can't lecture to them or talk over their heads. I try to be a leader by staying just ahead of prevailing public opinion at any time. And I try to get the people interested and involved in an issue, so they will educate themselves."

A good example is the National Domestic Development Bank concept. For over fifteen years, Hubert used every appropriate opportunity to explain the need for such an institution and how it would function. In 1978 President Carter proposed an Urban Development Bank, based on the same concept.

Medicare is another example and there are many others. Medicare was one of the first bills he introduced in the Senate following his arrival in 1949. He discussed the need for such legislation in speech after speech, in city after city. His efforts and those of others finally culminated in the passage sixteen years later, of this greatly needed legislation.

A *Time* reporter, writing about Hubert's desire to teach through his speeches, observed, "Whatever he did, whatever stand he took, Humphrey always wanted his audience, be it one person or thousands, to understand. It was the reason he talked overly long—approaching a subject from the front, the back and every side."

Hubert took chiding on his long speeches with good humor: "I have, in the course of a long public life, sometimes been accused of long-windedness. Part of this I admit derives from a simple love of talk. But part also comes from learning to speak to Midwestern audiences, who actually want to hear a speech of sizeable length.

"Moreover, anyone who has spent a great deal of his or her youth in the formal discipline of debate has been shaped to some degree by the ancient adage: 'Tell them what you're going to tell them; tell them; and then tell them what you've told them.' It's a theory calculated to promote clarity at the expense of patience."

Hubert also felt that his speeches were an opportunity to build enthusiasm and support for public objectives and to remind people of the fundamentals of democratic government to which he had such a strong and lasting commitment.

Themes such as the importance of our Constitution and elective processes frequently were emphasized in much the same style as a history or government professor might use to present such a lesson in the classroom.

With his speeches he challenged his audiences to creative thinking. He didn't tell them what they wanted to hear, but rather discussed what he believed they should be thinking.

For example, despite the opposition of most bankers to the Humphrey-Hawkins bill and economic planning, in his speeches to them during the last years of his life Hubert made certain that they were directly familiar with his proposals in this area, encouraged them to share their opinions with them and sought to convert some among them.

He firmly believed the people wanted leadership from their public officials and that if they knew what needed to be done they would do it. He was delighted to be the catalyst, the advocate, the protagonist, the evangelist for ideas and programs that he was confident had merit.

Just before the 1964 election, a *Washington Post* reporter analyzed his speaking ability in this way: "A power and force beyond words pour out of him when he is on a platform. It is incorrect to identify a Humphrey speech as an 'appearance.' It is a performance.

"He acts out his message with rapidly changing inflections, a vast array of gestures by his hands and arms, and a variety of facial expressions which somehow convey a mood and meaning to the back row of a crowded auditorium.

"One reason for the excitement he can generate in an audience is his spontaneity. Most of his audiences sense that he is giving them something new and exciting. Often his speech to a responsive audience is like an act of love: pain, passion and joy are shared."

As someone for whom extemporaneous speaking did not come easy, I always marveled, too, at Hubert's ability to speak on the spot, to seize and hold an audience without any preparation, to entertain them with wit and candor, and to translate complex material into understandable and colorful language.

After a particularly effective presentation when the audience had responded fully to his oratorical skills, he always was amused by my reaction and would say, "I know that you now want a few words from Muriel."

He particularly enjoyed speaking to young people. His message to them always included an exhortation to get involved in the democratic process.

"Let me tell you," he would say, "politics is just as dirty and just as clean, just as good and just as bad, just as honorable and just as mean as you—as we—the people make it. If you want to make it better, get into it. To put it another way, 'If you're not part of the solution, you're part of the problem.'"

His themes were frequently those of hope and optimism. "I'm one of those who lives by hope," he said. "It's the promise and the hope that inspire me. I'm not a prophet. There are no Humphreys in either the Old or the New Testament. But the future always intrigues me, because that's all that's left."

Because I know how important his speeches were to his efforts in public life and that the messages they convey may be useful to others, I am pleased that this excellent compilation of these speeches is available to those who wish to read and study them—especially the young—some of whom I hope will eventually be considering their own careers in public life.

1

The Past Is Prologue

An Act of Political Courage

In the fall of 1939, Hubert Humphrey went to Louisiana State University for postgraduate studies in political science.

It was to be his first real experience with the Deep South and its overtly segregationist racial policies. Never before had Humphrey come into contact with so many whites who had had intimate dealings with blacks.

He recalls, for instance, one LSU student who talked glowingly of his black mammy, who had raised him and who had been closer to him in his youth than his own mother. Yet this young man held blacks at a distance and upheld the segregationist policies of his region.

Humphrey was appalled by the segregation at LSU, which included separate drinking fountains for whites and blacks.

He had always known of the South's racial prejudices. Seeing them first hand, however, led to an even greater realization: Things were not much better in the North. This was a major revelation for him. His political heritage was rooted in the Populist tradition. Until his journey to the South, he believed that the Populists had steadfastly fought over the years against racism. Now he knew that this was not so.

From that moment on, civil rights on both sides of the Mason-Dixon line became an area of major concern for Hubert Humphrey.

A few years later, as mayor of Minneapolis, he moved swiftly to correct some of the injustices in his city. During his administration, for instance, Minneapolis became the first city in the nation to pass a Fair Employment Practices Act. Mayor Humphrey also established a citywide Council for Human Relations.

Minneapolis was not exactly a bastion of liberal principles, then or now. A friend of Humphrey's, the editor of a black newspaper in Minneapolis, counseled Humphrey to move with moderation. He reasoned that Humphrey stood a better chance to win popular support for his programs if he exercised restraint. But Humphrey believed strongly in civil rights, and moderation, he felt, was not the way to go about it.

As mayor, Humphrey's stand on civil rights brought him to national attention. But his greatest triumph in this area—and it could have been his greatest defeat—was yet to come.

It was the summer of 1948. The place was the City of Brotherly Love, Philadelphia. The Democratic Party was meeting in national convention to choose a presidential candidate to challenge Governor Thomas E. Dewey in the November election.

At the last convention, 1944, President Roosevelt had succeeded in winning a mild civil rights plank in the party's platform. In 1946, President Truman's civil rights commission released a report, "We Hold These Truths," which called for broad-based legislation in the civil rights area.

Southern Democrats, however, were not pleased with these developments. They warned the Democratic leadership that any strong action on behalf of civil rights that July would cause an irreconcilable split in the party.

As it stood then, few people gave Harry Truman much chance of winning the 1948 election. With the Southern Democrats not supporting the party, the chances would be zero. Civil rights, although a strong concern even of President Truman's, would have to take a back seat, the party bosses decided.

Humphrey at the time was contemplating running for the United States Senate from Minnesota. More important, he had his heart set on a leading role in national affairs. He wanted to push for passage of a strong civil rights plank in the 1948 party platform, but he knew what the consequences most likely would be if he did so. Everyone had warned Humphrey of those consequences. He even talked about them with his father and his wife, Muriel. Advocating a strong civil rights plank could very well destroy any chances for election to the Senate and a national leadership role for all time.

Humphrey agonized over the decision for several days. He held many meetings with close advisers. Finally, he decided on a compromise course. Together with Andrew Biemiller, at the time a congressman, he attempted to win passage for a strong civil rights plank in the platform committee, of which he was a member. The Humphrey-Biemiller plank was defeated in committee, 70-30.

This was about as far as it was safe to go politically. He had made his stand and he had lost. But it was done in committee, not on the convention floor. There would be no Southern walkout and the political consequences would not be too catastrophic.

Conventional wisdom, therefore, dictated that Hubert Humphrey stop there. But his conscience and his principles would not let him do so.

As Humphrey recalls it, it was nearly five o'clock Wednesday morning, July 14, 1948, when he finally made up his mind.

That morning, as the convention began its third day, Humphrey walked to the speaker's platform and took a seat, waiting to be called. He was nervous, *uncertain, resigned to defeat. Moreover, he felt as if his entire political future hung in the balance.*

Sitting a few seats away was Ed Flynn, Democratic boss of Bronx County, New York. Flynn was a powerful man in the party and a close confidant of the late President Roosevelt and of Jim Farley. Humphrey approached Flynn almost apologetically. It was as if he were hoping that the Bronx boss could talk him out of making his speech before the convention; as if Flynn could present arguments to Humphrey that party leaders, including Sam Rayburn, and his own close associates had not thought of.

But Flynn, who was by no means a liberal, surprised Humphrey. He told the young mayor of Minneapolis that the party should have acted much sooner on the issue. He promised Humphrey the support of the New York delegation.

Humphrey's courage was restored. Moments later, he rose to address the convention. When he was through speaking, many of the delegates cheered loudly and he knew he would win the plank.

He did—and the Southern Democrats, led by South Carolina's Governor Strom Thurmond, walked out and formed their own Dixiecrat party.

Former Vice-President Henry Wallace had already divided the Democratic Party by splitting away from it and forming his own political unit. Now, thanks to Hubert Humphrey, the Democratic party was split three ways instead of two, with the Dixiecrats running Thurmond for president.

Humphrey knew that this would happen; everyone did. And he knew that if Truman did indeed lose the 1948 election the party would blame Hubert Humphrey, completely oblivious to the fact that no one that summer gave Truman any chance of beating Dewey. It was thus an act of great political courage, one of the finest moments in the life of this great American.

What Humphrey could not know at the time was that, rather than destroy his political future, those few moments before the convention would catapult him to national prominence and prepare the way for all his great achievements over the next thirty years. What he did know was that the future of the nation— indeed, of the whole strife-torn world—depended on all persons being guaranteed equal rights and opportunities. And to him, that was all that mattered.

I realize that I am dealing with a charged issue—with an issue which has been confused by emotionalism on all sides.

I realize that there are those here—friends and colleagues of mine, many of them—who feel as deeply as I do about this issue and who are yet in complete disagreement with me.

My respect and admiration for these men and their views was great when I came here. It is now far greater because of the sincerity, the courtesy and the forthrightness with which they have argued in our discussions.

Because of this very respect, because of my profound belief that we have a challenging task to do here, because good conscience demands it, I feel I must rise at this time to support this [minority Platform Committee report on civil rights]—a report that spells out our democracy, a report that the people will understand and enthusiastically acclaim.

Let me say at the outset that this proposal is made with no single region, no single class, no single racial or religious group in mind.

All regions and all states have shared in the precious heritage of American freedom. All states and all regions have at least some infringements of that freedom. All people, all groups have been the victims of discrimination.

The masterly statement of our keynote speaker, the distinguished United States senator from Kentucky, Alben Barkley, made that point with great force. Speaking of the founder of our party, Thomas Jefferson, he said:

"He did not proclaim that all white, or black, or red, or yellow men are equal; that all Christian or Jewish men are equal; that all Protestant and Catholic men are equal; that all rich or poor men are equal; that all good or bad men are equal.

"What he declared was that all men are equal; and the equality which he proclaimed was equality in the right to enjoy the blessings of free government in which they may participate, to which they have given their consent."

We are here as Democrats. But more important, as Americans—and I firmly believe that as men concerned with our country's future, we must specify in our platform the guarantees which I have mentioned.

Yes, this is far more than a party matter. Every citizen has a stake in the emergence of the United States as the leader of the free world. That world is being challenged by the world of slavery. For us to play our part effectively, we must be in a morally sound position.

We cannot use a double standard for measuring our own and other people's policies. Our demands for democratic practices in other lands will be no more effective than the guarantees of those practiced in our own country.

We are God-fearing men and women. We place our faith in the brotherhood of man under the fatherhood of God.

I do not believe that there can be any compromise with the guarantees of civil rights which I have mentioned.

In spite of my desire for unanimous agreement on the platform there are some matters which I think must be stated without qualification. There can be no hedging, no watering down.

There are those who say to you, we are rushing this issue of civil rights. I say we are 172 years late.

There are those who say, this issue of civil rights is an infringement on states' rights. The time has arrived for the Democratic party to get out of the shadow of states' rights and walk forthrightly into the bright sunshine of human rights.

People—human beings—this is the issue of the twentieth century. People—all kinds and sorts of people—look to America for leadership, for help, for guidance. . . .

I ask you for a calm consideration of our historic opportunity. Let us forget the evil passions, the blindness of the past. In these times of world economic, political, and spiritual—above all spiritual—crisis, we cannot, we must not, turn from the path so plainly before us.

That path has already led us through many valleys of the shadow of death. Now is the time to recall those who were left on that path of American freedom.

For all of us here, for the millions who have sent us, for the whole two billion members of the human family, our land is now, more than ever, the last best hope on earth. I know that we can—I know that we shall—begin here the fuller and richer realization of that hope, that promise of a land where all men are free and equal, and each man uses his freedom and equality wisely and well.

To Show What Life Is For

"I recalled that the poet, Robert Browning, wrote: 'A man's reach should exceed his grasp, or what's a heaven for?'

"We all hope to live that way, though few of us do it very consistently or with very much effect.

"Hubert Humphrey does, though. He lives that way not only to validate heaven, but to show what life is for.

"As a result, his grasp has exceeded even his own wildest dreams. We all know he wanted to be president once. He would have been a good one. But it was never a consuming passion for him. His consuming passion has been to make America a little better, to make the world a little better, to make life itself a little better—and, reaching out for those goals, he overshot this nation's highest office and became instead one of the great world leaders—one of the major moral forces of our time or of any time."

Those words were spoken on the Senate floor on November 4, 1977. They are the kind of words that one would expect one liberal Democrat to say about another—especially after the individual in question had died.

But Hubert Humphrey was very much alive and seated in the chamber, and the man who spoke those words is neither a liberal nor a Democrat. He is, in fact, one of the nation's leading conservative spokesmen and the most recent Republican vice-presidential nominee. And the words Robert Dole of Kansas spoke that day were not mere for-the-record platitudes so common in the Senate of the United States; they were meant to explain why Senator Dole had the month before introduced S. 2169, authorizing the renaming of the new home of the Department of Health, Education and Welfare after Hubert Humphrey.

It was one of the few times in history that a public building had been named after a living public official.

That event was just one of the many tributes lavished on Hubert Humphrey in those final days of his life. Some of them were even more historic—such as the tribute to Humphrey in the House of Representatives on that same November 4, the first time in the nation's history that the lower house paused to honor a living member of the upper chamber.

But, to Hubert Humphrey, Dole's action was the most significant and the most meaningful. "To know that the principles of social and economic justice, compassion, hope and opportunity that have inspired me will continue to thrive and flourish in a building bearing my name is a great gift indeed," he said at the dedication ceremonies.

It is, without doubt, the most fitting tribute to this great American. For Hubert Humphrey was the champion of the poor, the oppressed, the homeless and the helpless; he was the "idea factory" wherein was created much of the social and technological developments of the past thirty years (for which other people often received the credit).

As Senator Dole pointed out to the Senate, there is "a national promise implicit in the very meaning of America and Hubert Humphrey has been diligent—sometimes even obstreperous—in holding America to her promise."

During his sixty-seven years of life, he had been a scoutmaster and a druggist, a student and a teacher, a mayor and a senator, a vice-president and a candidate for president. But above all else, he was a human being in the most noble sense of the term.

While he lived, the Washington press corps liked to say that Hubert Humphrey shed enough tears in his lifetime to cure the drought in Minnesota. But he had an answer for that. "A man who has no tears," he said, "has no heart."

Well, as Arizona's Representative Morris K. Udall told the House of Representatives during its tribute to the senator, "Hubert Humphrey has a heart—and it's as big as the plains of South Dakota."

It was on those plains that Humphrey's heart began to grow and to expand until it encompassed all with which he came into contact.

He was born Hubert Horatio Humphrey, Jr., on May 27, 1911. His father, a Democrat, was a druggist whose family had lived in the United States for generations. His mother, a pretty five-foot-three Republican, was the daughter of an immigrant Norwegian sailor who had come to America's heartland to be the captain of a Mississippi riverboat but wound up a South Dakota farmer instead.

Shortly after he was born, his family moved to Doland, South Dakota, where he was raised and where he went to elementary and high school.

It was in Doland that Humphrey began to learn those things which in later years would give him the drive and determination, the zeal and the compassion that has won him a place in the ranks of the nation's immortals.

From the time he was seven years old, young Hubert would stand for hours behind the soda fountain in his father's drugstore listening to the senior Humphrey expound to friends and customers alike on the various issues of the day. It was from his father, whose hero was William Jennings Bryan, that Humphrey "absorbed a respect for history," as he put it.

"I guess that my interest in public affairs was generated in a family that was proud of its books and particularly by a father who was very well read in biography. . . . [My] father taught me to read biography and I read the Boys Life of Edison, the Boys Life of Lafayette, the Boys Life of practically everybody that ever lived. . . .

"I recall that as a very young man, I was taught by a teacher and father about Woodrow Wilson. . . . Woodrow Wilson, the man of peace; Woodrow Wilson, the man of vision; Woodrow Wilson, who gave his life in that cross-country tour as he fought (and lost the battle) for the League of Nations. . . . So a man's life, a political hero, had an impact on my life."

As a student in Doland's elementary and high schools, Humphrey excelled. "I was expected to do well in school," he recalled some years ago. "In high school, my grades were all A's, except for a B in Latin and a B-plus in Glee Club.

"Yes, I was class valedictorian but there wasn't much fanfare about it at all. . . . It was just sort of expected."

But all that studying, Humphrey recalled, "didn't mean there wasn't time for dreaming a little, too. I can remember sitting in class [and] hearing the whistle of the Chicago-Northwestern train going through Doland. . . . I can remember standing and looking down that track. It was so flat out there that you could see the tracks just fading away out of existence.

"I can remember wanting to get on a train and travel long distances. I remember very well watching the train and thinking about the state capital, and thinking about Washington, and dreaming about that kind of thing."

According to a neighbor of the Humphreys in Doland, the most important factor in Humphrey's life was the influence of his family.

"I think his parents deserve much of the credit," the neighbor, Mrs. Don Wolverton, told the Doland Times-Record in November 1950. "His father's driving ambition to get ahead and burning aspirations for his family must have made a real impression on the boy. But his mother, I believe, contributed just as much in a quieter, less commanding way. Her stubborn adherence to what she believed was right gave him some ideas he shouldn't outgrow—even in politics."

At age eighteen, Hubert left home, now located in Huron, South Dakota, to attend the University of Minnesota, majoring in political science. But the Depression intervened, and soon he had to give up school and return to help his father keep the family business alive.

His experiences during the Depression were to have the profoundest effects on his future course.

"I grew up in a time when. . . the poor were not [those who] had always been poor," Humphrey recalled years later, "but the poor were people [who] once were men and women of substance, of wealth, of middle income, of property— and they were struck down as if they had been rolled over by a mighty tidal wave. I think that that part of history has left its impact upon me and surely has conditioned my politics.

"I will never be able to forget it. I know that out of those days, experiences came. . . that helped shape legislation later on. The Job Corps—I was its original author in the Congress of the United States—[came about] because I remembered the Civilian Conservation Corps and I remembered the young men [who] walked the railroad tracks in the days of the Depression.

"I remember that many of them were considered to be useless and worthless by some of their more fortunate contemporaries, only to have them become generals, and colonels, and congressmen, and governors, and businessmen, and labor people, and labor leaders and professors.

"I have not forgotten. It left a tremendous impact on me. . . .

"I guess it's fair to say that history surely can influence a man in his public utterances and his public life. I recall, for example, that my recollection of history [in the pre-Depression period] is of the Smoot-Hawley Tariff Act. . . . I think that that act had something to do with bringing America to her economic knees and touching off a worldwide depression. Ever since then, I have been a man [who] has advocated not just reciprocal trade but ever more free trade. . . ."

When Humphrey wasn't helping to run the drugstore—which he was able to do after taking a six-month, day-and-night intensive course of study at the Capital College of Pharmacy in Denver, Colorado—he was either working with Huron's Boy Scout Troop 6, of which he was scoutmaster, or going to the dances being held at Huron College.

It was at one of those dances that he met young Muriel Buck and, as he put it, "my life became much more tolerable."

That was in 1932. Four years later, on September 3, 1936, they were married.

Humphrey always had fond memories of those days. "I served as scoutmaster for about three years. During that eventful time, we took into our troop a few boys who today might be labeled juvenile troublemakers. In fact, some of them had been in a little trouble, but they were not bad boys. They simply needed guidance, activity and work. And the Boy Scout troop offered these opportunities. . . .

"Those were days when we took a firmer stand with our young people. I had an understanding with my scouts that we weren't going to have any smoking. So, when I caught several of the boys red-handed, I told them, 'You're through. Beat it!'

"They were the most unhappy boys in the world and they started coming around my home every morning. Finally, they got up enough courage to apologize and we took them all back into the troop—provided they abided by the rules."

As things got serious with Humphrey and Muriel, she became involved in his scouting work, too. "Muriel was always a sort of assistant scoutmaster. Even in those early days before we were married, she encouraged me to carry on my scout work—apparently, she was already learning to cooperate with the inevitable."

Muriel helped her beau with the troop, even, at times, cooking for them.

"They always preferred her cooking to mine," Humphrey once said, "and no wonder. Once, on an overnight hike, I decided to show the boys what a great cook I was. I prepared for them a simple dessert—a sort of pudding of rice and raisins. I recall dropping a rather large portion of rice into a kettle of boiling water. The rice kept expanding. We wound up filling about every container in the camp with rice pudding. From that point on, the scouts of Troop 6 resolved to do their own cooking (or let Muriel do it) and leave their scoutmaster to other chores."

In 1936, however, Humphrey had to say good-by to scouting and to Huron. "Muriel and I had decided to marry and to return to the University of Minnesota to complete my education, which had been interrupted by the Depression."

While Humphrey went to school, Mrs. Humphrey got a job to support the newlyweds. But because that was not enough to cover all the expenses, she also had a side job: She made sandwiches for Humphrey to sell to his fellow students at lunch time.

Once again, Humphrey excelled as a student. He graduated magna cum laude and was a Phi Beta Kappa.

His next stop was Louisiana State University, where he worked to turn his bachelor's degree in political science into a master's.

During the course of his studies, Humphrey reaffirmed his belief in the need to know and understand history.

"I do believe that it is much better to make history than it is to read it, or study it; but I believe with equal fervor. . . that you will really not be able to make much that is worthy of being called history unless you have a sense of history, unless you have the feeling of it."

A man could not live on current events alone, Humphrey felt. "Let a man be ignorant of what his forebears have done for his country and he shall have little love or respect for it."

In June 1940, Hubert and Muriel Humphrey returned to Minneapolis. He was determined to earn his doctorate while teaching. He worked in a local Work Projects Administration educational program at the same time he held down a teaching assistantship at the University of Minnesota and worked toward his doctorate. (It is no wonder that in the early 1960s he would be referred to as the Senate's "perpetual-motion machine.")

In 1942, he became divisional director of training and reemployment for the WPA; in 1943, he was appointed assistant director of the Minnesota War Manpower Commission.

By that time, Humphrey was itching to join up and go to war. But he had been classified 3-A, the classification given to men with wives and children, and the war was passing him by.

If he could not serve his country on the battlefront, he felt, the least he could do was continue to serve on the home front. He dug himself even deeper into his work and soon came to the attention of a group of Minneapolis labor leaders who were looking for a man to run for mayor.

Humphrey took the plunge—and lost. But it was not a horrifying defeat, in the final analysis. A political newcomer, he had only lost by fewer than 6,000 votes. He was determined to try again.

Bitten by the political bug, Humphrey set out to unify the Democratic and Farmer-Labor parties. Only through such unity, he argued, could a successful campaign be waged against the well-entrenched state Republican machine.

He accomplished that goal in early 1944 and it brought him some national exposure; just enough, in fact, to win him the post of statewide campaign manager for Franklin D. Roosevelt's precedent-shattering bid for a fourth presidential term.

Then, in 1945, Humphrey ran once again for mayor. This time, with the support of the Democratic-Farmer-Labor Party behind him, he won handily. Two years later, the voters of the city returned him for another term. But it was a term he would not complete.For the mayor had begun looking beyond the municipality. There was great work to be done out there and he wanted to be a part of it. He made speeches in support of the plan to establish the United Nations, European recovery programs and President Truman's domestic programs.

Most particularly, he began campaigning for a major shift in civil rights policy in the United States. This was his greatest concern in those years and it reflected itself even in his mayoral administration, where he had won city council approval in 1947 for the nation's first municipal Fair Employment Practices Commission.

Then, in July 1948, came his historic speech before the Democratic convention on behalf of a strong civil rights plank.

When Humphrey returned to Minneapolis from the Philadelphia convention, the train station overflowed with well-wishers welcoming back their courageous mayor. That night, a reception was held at a downtown Minneapolis hotel and people began to say that Joseph Ball, the Republican senator who was up for reelection, had better start to fear for his seat.

Before Humphrey went East to the convention, there had been talk about a possible Senate candidacy, but many of the state's politicians were uncertain about the mayor's statewide popularity. They reasoned that he was still a *relatively unknown figure outside of Minneapolis-St. Paul and the south-central part of the state.*

But the civil rights speech in Philadelphia made him a hero throughout the state.

Humphrey himself wanted to make the race. Senator Ball was not terribly popular (or unpopular, for that matter) with the people of Minnesota and the issues in the campaign were, to Humphrey at least, very clear-cut. Ball had voted against the Marshall plan and was a leader in the growing Senate movement toward isolationism. Humphrey was a strong supporter of both the United Nations and the rebuilding of Europe, and he thought the people of Minnesota were, too.

Additionally, Ball had voted for the Taft-Hartley Act and its right-to-work provisions, which Humphrey believed was opposed by many people in the state.

But Ball was not the only candidate he would have to face. Supporters of former Vice-President Wallace also challenged his candidacy. They stood for something Humphrey knew the proud people of Minnesota, despite their isolationist traditions, would never go for: appeasement.

When all the votes were counted, Hubert Humphrey was the winner in a landslide. He had received almost a quarter of a million more votes than Ball and had become the first Democrat in the state's ninety-year history to be elected a United States senator.

In a statewide radio address announcing his candidacy, Humphrey told the voters where he stood:

. . . [Any] man who is a candidate for political office is a part of a common enterprise. And when he declares his candidacy, he joins in a partnership with all the people who share his purposes and ideals.

Your expressions of faith and confidence show that you are willing to join hands with me in this important political struggle.

. . . I have said that I will be a candidate of the Democratic-Farmer-Labor Party for the United States Senate. But I recognize that the issues of this campaign transcend all partisan considerations.

I am a loyal party member but I will not place my party above my country or my principles. The political party is a mechanism for expressing a public policy. The approval of this policy must be voted by the people of all sections and all groups. . . .

Let us not deceive ourselves. No one political party nor any one individual has a monopoly on wisdom or political virtue. . . .

The people of Minnesota have a right to demand that their representatives in Congress protect and advance the legitimate interests and aspirations of all citizens of our state and nation. . . .

The leaders of the third party [the Wallaceites] tell us the road to peace is appeasement. But we have tried appeasement and we know that it will not work. Its leaders criticize every act of American foreign policy but they remain silent about the aggressive acts of Russian policy.

A responsible party must constructively criticize the actions of all nations—even its own.

Americans of every political party dread the thought of a third world war. But most Americans will not lose their heads and run to the camp of the appeasement party nor lose their heads and run to the camp of a war party.

We are ready and we shall always be ready to join in any honest program of world cooperation and world government. We, too, are opposed to any policy of American imperialism. We, too, believe in the century of the common man, but we are not prepared to see the century of the common man become the century of the Comintern. . . .

As a people, we stand at a crossroads of our civilization. What we do in the immediate period ahead will determine whether the world can avert a catastrophic war, or whether we shall create the technique that will bring us lasting world peace. We as a nation must choose between the high road of genuine international organization that will lead to a free and secure world, or the low road of isolationism and narrow self-interest which will lead to world depression and international anarchy.

These are days which demand the most honest, vigorous and intelligent expression from our national leaders. This world cannot be saved by pious-sounding phrases of peace, progress and prosperity. The hope for world peace rests in a meaningful and effective program of action: action in America that develops our human and physical resources; action that insures an ever-expanding economy; action on civil rights that guarantees equality of opportunity; action that builds our national defense—not only in the armed forces, but, more importantly, in the health and welfare and security of our people. . . . Yes, we must have action that embodies within it an understanding that man does not live by bread alone.

The United States Senate, the greatest deliberative body in the world, should echo with the voices of men who fight for the preservation of the great human values of Western civilization. We've had enough of mediocrity and reaction; we need men with a deep faith in democracy and men who understand that democracy is a constant challenge to improvement of our political, economic and cultural institutions.

We cannot look to the past. We cannot, because of partisanship, blind ourselves to the mistakes that we ourselves have made. We must be true to ourselves and true to our faith. To us is given the opportunity to revitalize and rebuild a great, progressive political force.

This is our challenge; this is our responsibility. With a belief, in ourselves, in our people and in the democratic faith by which we live, together we shall go forward to complete this task.

It is in this spirit that I declare my candidacy for the United States Senate.

2

The Freshman Senator

He Was a Comer

There was no question about it. Hubert Humphrey, as his uncle once said, was "a comer."

Of all the freshmen senators who came to the 81st Congress in 1949, Humphrey was getting the most attention. He even made the cover of Time *magazine in its January 17 profile of the Senate's new look.*

To understand just how significant that was, one must consider who else was in that freshman class. Several "new" senators were actually "old" ones who finally managed to get their jobs back, men like West Virginia's Matthew Neely and Iowa's Guy Gillette. Some were men who had made their marks in the House and were now headed for even greater heights in the Senate— Tennessee's Estes Kefauver and Texas's Lyndon Johnson among them. There were even men of the calibre and prestige of the University of Chicago's Professor Paul Douglas.

But it was Hubert Humphrey's face on the cover of Time; *it was from Hubert Humphrey that everyone expected the most.* Time, *in its cover story, referred to Humphrey alternately as "hustling Humphrey," "bustling Humphrey," "ambitious Humphrey" and even "brash Humphrey."*

He was much in demand from the very beginning. Syndicated columnist Drew Pearson invited Humphrey to a party; Edward R. Murrow wanted Humphrey to take part in his radio program; Governor Frank Lausche of Ohio asked Humphrey to address a Jewish Women's Organization in Cleveland.

It was as if everyone had heard Hubert Humphrey, Sr., say after his son was sworn in: "He's going to be a great senator. Maybe he's going to be something else, too."

That kind of attention normally turns a man's head in power-conscious Washington. And it almost turned Humphrey's head, too, until Muriel put him in his place one night. They were driving home from a party and Muriel told him he had to make a choice right then and there. He could either spend his time hobnobbing with the great and near-great in Georgetown or he could buckle down and be a good senator.

It was that kind of attention, too, that got Humphrey into trouble in the Senate right from the start.

The Senate often has been described as "the world's most exclusive club." As Humphrey himself would complain time and again over the next thirty years, it was loaded down with time-worn and antiquated rules, some written and many unwritten. One of the first rules was—and still is—that freshmen senators are to be seen but almost never heard. Their electoral victories guarantee them seats on the Senate floor; but only by learning to "play the game" can they gain entrance to "the club."

Humphrey, however, would have none of it. The world was changing rapidly. A great war had left most of Europe and parts of Asia in ruins; the communist bosses of the Kremlin had begun their campaign to spread the tentacles of totalitarianism throughout the four corners of the globe; their cohorts in the United States were attempting to subvert the progress of democracy in their own country; the world's greatest democracy was still subverting itself by maintaining that some people were more equal than others.

It was a time for leaders, not lackeys. Hubert Humphrey was determined to be a leader.

But the members of the club could not let that happen. They resented the attention being paid to Humphrey and they let him know it. Of all the newcomers, only Humphrey was denied temporary office space before he was sworn in. He was ignored by some senators, rejected by others, reviled by others still. Humphrey recalled, for instance, a remark made by Senator Richard Russell of Georgia as the Minnesotan walked by one day: "Can you imagine the people of Minnesota sending that damn fool down here to represent them?"

"I was crushed," Humphrey would recall in his autobiography. "I wanted to do well, and I knew that my political intensity, my personal enthusiasm needed a friendly environment to blossom. I was not prepared for the rejection by my peers. . . . Never in my life have I felt so unwanted as I did during those first months in Washington. I was unhappy in the Senate, uncomfortable, awkward, unable to find a place. My principles offended, my personality enraged. I wasn't going to change one and didn't know how to change the other."

Still, Humphrey would not give up. He pushed ever onward. And, in his zeal, he nearly destroyed any chance he had of becoming the leader he knew he must be.

Shortly after coming to the Senate, he chose to attack the wastefulness of the Joint Committee on Reduction of Nonessential Federal Expenditures, chaired by Senator Harry F. Byrd of Virginia, one of the highest-ranking members of the club. The purpose of the committee seemed to be to keep unemployment down— among Byrd's family and friends. It meant a lot to Byrd, enough so that he was able to remain chairman even when Republicans were in the majority. It *mattered very little to most senators that this flagrant misuse of government funds was the most "nonessential" federal expenditure of all.*

But it mattered to Humphrey. He put together a strong case and brought it to the floor. That was a big mistake by itself. But to make matters worse, Byrd wasn't even present that day. The next day, about twenty-five senators rose and attacked Humphrey.

The senator had learned his lesson. On the senate floor, at least, he would play by the rules. Off the floor, however, was another story.

There were some "rules" he would not live by, though. There was, for example, the unwritten rule that the only black men allowed in the Senate dining room were waiters and busboys. Humphrey, therefore, took a black member of his staff to lunch one day and ended that rule for all time.

In contrast to the Senate's seeming lack of interest in Humphrey's company during those early months of 1949, it was the obvious desire of people all across the nation to have Hubert Humphrey speak to them. And that made Humphrey very happy, indeed. For it was the people, Humphrey always believed, that made this nation great; it was through the people—and only the people—that democracy would be able to survive the grave tests that awaited it in the second half of the twentieth century and beyond.

It was with this in mind that Humphrey addressed the National Conference on Citizenship at New York City on May 16, 1949:

Lycurgus once said that "Citizens are the best walls of a free city." It is strange how true the words of this great Spartan lawmaker of the ninth century B.C. are today.

Today we live in a world which has no physical barriers. It is a world which can be traversed in a matter of hours. National boundaries are no longer safe. National interest is no longer secure.

In a world such as this, where physical weapons no longer have any meaning, the only dynamic yet constant force upon which a nation can rely is its citizenship.

Yet this thing which we call citizenship is capable of many qualities. Citizenship can be a prison, or it can be a portal. It can enslave man in his loyalty to a totalitarian state, or it can free man through a realization that government and loyalty to a democratic ideal can provide for him the opportunity for individual growth and the expression of individual personality.

The state is an invention of man. It has neither intellect nor conscience nor morals. Yet our world is characterized in the minds of many by a conflict of states one with another.

Why this conflict? Is it sensible that man should allow his own invention, the state, to destroy him and his possessions in conflict? Is it sensible that man should allow a doctrine of citizenship to lead him and his civilization down the road to chaos and to the destruction of that civilization?

It must be, then, that the conflict the world faces is not a conflict between states. It must be then that this conflict has another interpretation.

The interpretation I suggest is that the conflict is one between ideals and ideologists. The state, as an invention of man with no intellect, conscience, or morals, is an inanimate machine. As such, therefore, it relies upon fuel provided for it by the loyalties of citizenship to give it strength, purpose, and direction.

With this perspective, we can better understand the differences between the ideology of democracy and the ideology of totalitarianism. The democratic state is one which is mastered by man; a totalitarian state is one which is master of man. The struggle our world faces is a struggle between both ideologies.

The forces of totalitarianism which we face are not quiet. The very nature of their principles calls for agitation, activity, and fanatic dedication. Their philosophy is not an attractive one.

Man does not willingly submit himself to mastery by a machine of his own creation. Yet the bitter lesson we have learned is that those of us who believe in democracy cannot remain passive in the confidence that totalitarianism has no future because man desires freedom.

Man desires freedom, but man also desires security. Self-government is not a luxury on which men may grow fat and indulgent. Rather it is an instrument by which men can, if they have the wisdom, safeguard their individual freedom and employ that freedom in the pursuit of happiness.

It is true that democracy cannot be defeated in the theoretical struggle of ideologies, but democracy can be defeated by default. Democracy can lose if those of us who believe in it remain indifferent and neglect our personal responsibility for its security and growth.

The strength of totalitarianism lies in the indifference of its people.

Democratic self-government tries its people with a stronger challenge than any other system in the world. Scorning the brutal coercion of totalitarian states, it asks justice and brotherhood of its people; it asks that they cooperate well and voluntarily for their common welfare in order that each may benefit equitably according to his merits.

Democracy is an easy ideology to take for granted. We seldom consider its basic principles in a critical light, in order to formulate our reasons for upholding it.

It is a tragic fact that American youth which went abroad in the Second World War to save democracy was totally unprepared to spread its message of democracy. General [Omar] Bradley, in a recent article, said that throughout Europe, wherever our armies were stationed, the people of Europe were bewildered by our American soldiers who appeared indifferent to the political and philosophical origins and nature of our democracy.

Unhappily, when driven into a corner intellectually, our soldiers were forced to fall back on American wage scales, automobiles, our refrigerators, and eventually and triumphantly on the American bathroom for their defense.

Here then is the danger signal. Here then is an indictment of the indifference which has led our nation to permit this vacuum to remain.

Our democracy is much like a tall stand of timber. We cannot cut from it more than we plant in it without imperiling its survival, and forests like gardens cannot be bought. They must be cultivated by toil and nourished by the sweat of those who would keep them.

We quickly forget that if freedom is to flourish, our society must reexamine its principles of education and rededicate itself to the conviction that education is that strength for freedom of democracy.

It must take strength from the understanding that an educated people is easy to govern, difficult to lead, impossible to enslave. Only the educated man is a free man. . . .

Education as a major social institution is the medium through which citizenship can be translated into loyalty to democratic ideals. Education for democratic citizenship means the practice of democracy. . . .

Education for democratic citizenship in the community means democratic practices in the community, in the homes, churches, businesses, industries, labor organizations, community agencies, patriotic and service groups. It means direct participation in social and civic affairs. It means the training of young citizens with service responsibility in running for office, voting, jury duty, and the study of our institutions.

Education for democratic citizenship means the development of knowledge and the understanding for increased participation in local, state, national, and world affairs.

If America and democracy are to come of age, it means that we must expand our concept of the school to include not merely the formal periods of classroom instruction but also the training of the whole man, the whole individual. It means that our schools must be directly tuned to the need for vocational guidance and aptitude. It means that our schools must relate themselves to the need for psychiatric assistance even on the school level.

It means that our schools must indeed be laboratories for democracy.

A generation ago, Americans had a philosophy of personal and public life which said, "Take care of number one." This idea was very simple. If everyone devoted himself to his own success, if everyone took care of number one, then obviously the sum total of the success of all numbers would be prosperity and happiness for all people. This would bring an end to poverty not only in the United States but everywhere else in the world.

How wrong we were. We were wrong and that philosophy

was doomed to failure because it ran counter to moral law in its glorification of selfishness; its failure was foretold by the teachings of the Bible.

That philosophy is wrong because it ran counter to the democratic principles of human brotherhood, to the declaration that all men are created equal. It was wrong because it ran counter to the true nature of Americanism and American democracy.

It was our country which was the first to present to the modern world a coherent political faith based upon the dignity of the individual, the equality and fraternity of mankind. We were the first to pattern a structure of government and to form a society which denied selfishness as a pattern for behavior, and which emphasized democracy and human solidarity.

This ideology was more powerful than the arms of conquest. This ideology upset thrones in Europe and convulsed a continent. It is now convulsing another.

This ideology put into the hearts and breasts of colonial people, the underprivileged, and the subjected, a consuming desire for liberty. . . .

We never moved a battalion or a regiment, in the eighteenth or nineteenth century, yet the idea of the Declaration of Independence produced the doctrine of the rights of man, the equality of man, and broke the back of oppression and the power of kings.

For a period, we in the United States have forgotten the basic roots from which this democratic idea has come. We forgot that to take care of number one is a principle which runs counter to the principle of human brotherhood and of mutual obligation one to another, which is the basis of democracy.

We forgot and thus failed. Proof of that failure was the frustrating depression followed by a terrible war.

Part of our neglect was translated into an indifference to political life. Why bother with veterans' hospitals, or government research laboratories, or public administration, or public works, or government-paid education?

Yet when depression and war came, the whole science of self-government, the whole process of government which had seemed so irrelevant and so inconsequential to us who thought we had found the golden way, became suddenly the center of our greatest concern. Many of our leading citizens who had never before given a thought to government except as a minor irritant, volunteered or were forced to give up their business to devote themselves entirely to government in order to pull us out of economic havoc and later to win a war.

Let us not repeat the errors of our generation. Instead of "take care of number one" I propose this phrase: "Take care of all." Take care of human brotherhood; take care of democracy; take care of self-government. . . .

We face a crisis. This crisis is not one which military forces alone can conquer, that military forces alone can protect us from. Nor is our crisis of brief duration. Our crisis calls not only for steadfastness and faith but for great skill in self-government. We must summon all of our talents for citizenship, for self-government, for public service.

I am not urging that everyone pursue public service in some form as a life career. Not at all. What I do urge is citizen participation in politics. Only this way can democratic institutions continue to prosper and flourish.

I have stated above that citizenship can be a prison or a portal. Citizenship can confine a man within the narrow limits of the customs and traditions of his own community, or it can make him an active, productive, and responsible part of a political entity much larger than the community with which he has physical contact.

In the Middle Ages, the obligations of citizenship controlled a man's relationship to the city in which he lived. By collaborating with a man from a neighboring city he could be in violation of his citizenship obligations and thus be guilty of treason.

As modern society grew more complex, and as means of communication and transportation cut distances and eliminated frontiers, the concept of citizenship and responsibilities of citizenship has grown and developed.

When the American colonies federated themselves and

formed a United States, citizens of several states expanded their loyalties to include the new federation. A Virginian was no less a Virginian when he became an American.

Today, our concept of citizenship is further. . . expanded because of our realization that democratic citizenship is a loyalty to an ideal and not just to a state. Democratic citizenship is a dedication to the democratic ideal, to the ideal of human rights, civil rights, freedom from insecurity for all people.

Out of every bitter experience of history, out of every tragedy, man learns in his sorrow. Out of the sacrifice of two world wars we again come back to the immortal idea of the one-ness of man, of his essential unity. . . .

Overshadowing and running through the discussion of European federation, alliances and plans for internationalism, there is a rapidly increasing volume of discussion about some-thing called world citizenship and world agreement. The idea of world citizenship is beginning to take form in the minds of men everywhere. The people of the world are coming to realize that they are one, that their interests are one, that our law must be one.

The people of the world are coming to realize—and must come to realize—that if we want a society free of the agonies of war and preparation for war, free of devastation and the fear of tomorrow, then they must accept the principle that every American, every Russian, every Indonesian, every South Afri-can, is in a real though limited sense a citizen of the world, and hence should be subjected to a world law.

Democratic citizenship means a realization that democracy is not a fixed, a static, and an unchanging stereotype, but that it is a vital, dynamic, and constantly growing force. Democratic citizenship must mean concern with the community and, as our community has grown to encompass the world, so must the concept of democratic citizenship grow to encompass the world. . . .

The Enemy Within

Communism dominated much of the political scene—foreign and domestic—in 1949. The Cold War threatened to become a hot one as the Soviet Union continued its step-by-step advance in Eastern Europe while the Communist Chinese set their sights on Asia. In the United States, communist fifth columns sought to spread dissent throughout the land in attempts to capture control of political, social and labor institutions.

To Hubert Humphrey, the battle against communism at home and abroad was a holy war that had to be won.

Others, too, viewed communism as a holy war, though not the kind Humphrey envisioned. For the most part, they were Republicans who were desperately looking for an issue that would topple the Democrats in 1952. Some were Democrats who opposed civil rights (not all from the South) or who wanted to break the backs of organized labor, issues to which the communists paid loud lip-service. Some were members of both parties who did not want to be washed away in the anticommunist tidal wave they saw engulfing the nation.

Ironically, one person who was not part of the red scare rabble-rousers in 1949 was the junior senator from Wisconsin, Joseph R. McCarthy. He was voted the "worst senator" by members of the Senate press gallery, mainly because he spent more time on the telephone with his bookies than he did paying attention to Senate business. He was also a borderline alcoholic, which also did not do much for his concentration. It would be almost a full year before "Tail Gunner Joe" would discover that red was more than just a color.

Humphrey agreed that communism was a serious threat; but to him, the vicious and unrelenting anticommunist smear campaign posed an even greater threat to the American way of life. In the commencement address delivered at Bennington College in Vermont on July 1, 1949, Humphrey warned of the dire consequences if the politics of hysteria continued unchecked.

... It is the thinkers of the world who represent the real strength of mankind. The pages of history demonstrate beyond question that it is the idea, the creative idea, that survives through the ages, and not merely the creative idea, but the new idea—the nonconformist idea.

Who today remembers, except with contempt, the judges

who condemned Galileo, while the name of Galileo rings down through the centuries?

Who today remembers the stodgy conservatives who hounded Byron out of England for his unconventional ideas, while Byron, the poet, sings his songs to all the succeeding generations?

Who today remembers the vicious attacks on Thomas Paine, while Thomas Paine even more securely becomes enhanced among the great men of our history?

And even in more recent times, how seriously do we take those who slandered and libeled and traduced the character of Woodrow Wilson, of Franklin D. Roosevelt, while it is difficult already to remember the names of even their most prominent critics?

It is the nonconformist and creative idea that we need. We are faced in our times with grave new problems. Few of the old answers any longer suffice—we have to find new answers, and that is why we have to encourage bold new thinking by every means.

Those who are behind the current wave of anticommunist hysteria are in reality aiming not only at the real communist menace which exists, but which is relatively speaking insignificant, but are aiming at every manifestation of independent, critical thought. They are aiming directly at precisely the kind of nonconformist, creative thinking that is our country's greatest need today.

Nonconformist, imaginative, creative thinking is needed in politics, in the press, and, above all, in our educational institutions. Education's chief function is to stimulate such thinking and to open the road to intellectual experimentation and discovery.

The continuation and extension of this growth by our academic institutions is crucial to the survival of our democracy. Only by such uninhibited freedom and liberty of education can our society gain the insight and the wisdom and the achievement which the mind has within its grasp to produce for human society.

It is for that reason that it is necessary for those of us who are concerned with the preservation and extension of a democratic society to take note of the evidences of hysteria which are all around us. There is something dangerous and unhealthy in the activities of some individuals and groups who are trying to whip up mass psychosis.

It is true that the symptoms I have described have cause. They can easily be explained. The policy of the Soviet Union since the end of the Second World War, the seizure by communists of control of the satellite states, the revelations made here in the United States in trials and investigations—all these show that there is a real attack on Western civilization and that some part of that attack is affecting our own country. No wonder some people are worried.

When a nation begins to worry, however, it behaves, as *The New York Times* recently said, somewhat like a neurotic patient who exaggerates the seriousness of his ailments, and perhaps invents ailments he really does not have. There are signs that some in this country are losing their sense of proportion.

In the hustle and stir of federal and state un-American activities committees, they act as if there were suspicious characters on every street corner, and an attacker under every bed; we see evidence of anxiety and hysteria in the scores of loyalty investigations that are taking place, in the purge of schools and colleges, in witch hunting and censorship, in attempts to censor schoolbooks, and in hundreds of other manifestations, governmental and popular.

It is not easy to suggest a remedy. We cannot pat a large part of the public on the head and tell it to be calm. What we can do, however, is to make people understand that political illegal acts can be treated like any other illegal acts.

When a crime wave occurs in any city, we do not conclude that the country is going to the dogs. Instead, we urge better police protection and perhaps prompter and sterner court action. but we preserve due process of law.

The same principle can be applied to illegal disloyalty. We

investigate it by orderly means, taking great care to protect the innocent. We can punish it when it is clearly proved.

More than that, however, it is important for the preservation of our liberties that we do not overemphasize the problem of disloyalty. This republic has endured for more than a century and a half. It has survived the great Civil War and enormous social and economic disturbances. Its people are intelligent and well read. There is no danger that they will sell themselves into slavery.

Never before in our history have the American people shown themselves to be as united as in the last decade. As Professor Henry Steele Commager said, it was not always thus. During the course of the Revolutionary War, only about a third of the American people were for the Revolution, a third for the king and a third neutral. During the War of 1812, a large number of our people bitterly opposed the war and actively sabotaged it. During the Mexican War, opposition to the war was widespread and ardent in the North. The internal dissension of the Civil War has still not been forgotten.

Yet it is an interesting fact that we fought all these wars without sedition acts or loyalty oaths.

Today, we are a country incomparably the strongest, the richest, and the best protected in the world. Our nation and our Constitution have withstood the vicissitudes of 160 years. Our people are intelligent and they are moral. They are devoted to freedom.

The real danger we face is that a spirit of fear will produce an atmosphere of timidity and suspicion that will discourage independence of thought, original investigation and association. The real danger we face is that a program of suppression will seriously endanger effective operation of our democracy; will lower the morals of the civil service by putting a premium on conformity and will discourage men and women of real ability from entering government service.

The real danger we face is that a spirit of hysteria will endanger the morale of American science by putting a premium on mediocrity in a field requiring independence, originality, and full freedom of inquiry and communication.

The real danger we face is that a society gripped by fear strengthens the hand of the military in areas traditionally and wisely entrusted to civilian control.

The real danger we face is that freedom of teaching will be imperiled by requiring conformity to standards, by introducing the grave peril of censorship in textbooks and ideas, and drive away from the teaching profession men and women of independent minds.

We must guard lest it create an atmosphere in which teachers find safety not in orthodox ideas, for they will never know fully which ideas are orthodox, but safety in no ideas.

In the end, this can produce a generation taught by teachers who are afraid of ideas. Such people cannot grow up into wise and competent and democratic citizens.

Yes; the real danger we face is that the right and necessity of criticism is threatened.

No government can operate successfully without criticism and no government which censors its critics can get the criticism that it needs. . . .

Our security lies not in secrecy but in the preservation of peace and in the encouragement of free inquiry; our real long-term security lies in perfecting our own democracy.

Even as our society now exists, it is the freest in the world and confers the most benefits on the humblest of citizens. We must make sure that it is kept free and flexible.

Jefferson, in his first inaugural address, said: "If there be any among us who wish to dissolve the Union or change its republican form, let them stand undisturbed as monuments of the safety with which error of opinion may be tolerated where reason is left free to combat it."

The American system is strong enough to stand competition of communism or any other ism. The American people are intelligent enough to resist subversive doctrines.

It may be that we cannot wholly live up to Jefferson's observations, but we can maintain a society in which the activities of those who would be disloyal will be rather an annoyance than a deadly menace. That is where our real security lies.

For our security lies in the democratic philosophy, the democratic way of life and the democratic idea. That is our historical role; that is our historical mission.

Toward Economic Expansion

The reception Hubert Humphrey was receiving throughout the nation soon began to be felt in the Senate itself. The icy wall that kept Humphrey from being accepted into the club began to thaw, and senators from all regions sought him out for help on legislation. For here, they realized, was a man to be reckoned with.

Two such senators were John J. Sparkman of Alabama and James E. Murray of Montana. Together, the three men introduced a bill to provide for a National Economic Cooperation Board, to be composed of representatives of industry, labor, agriculture, consumers and various economic specialists. The purpose of the board was to study the developing conditions in the national economy and make recommendations to promote maximum employment, production and purchasing power.

They bill also proposed assistance to private investors to expand capacity and production wherever necessary; to provide scientific research and advice for the use of small business; and for a study by the Federal Trade Commission of any existing barriers to private investment and production.

Unemployment had reached 3.5 million people. Several million more workers were employed only part time. Many communities across the nation were suffering from severe unemployment.

Two days after his speech at Bennington College, on July 3, 1949, Humphrey appeared with Senators Sparkman and Murray on a nationally broadcast radio program to explain their bill.

Economics can be a dull subject; a piece of economic legislation can be even

*duller. But not when Hubert Humphrey is the speaker. After his two colleagues
had completed their descriptions of the pending legislation, Humphrey issued a
resounding call to arms.*

Charles Parmer. This is Charles Parmer from Washington. As
the Fourth of July 1949 approaches, a new declaration of independence is being formulated—a bill to be introduced in Senate
and House, which may guarantee freedom from want and
misery.

Here, as the week ends, three of our Senate leaders, Democrats all, confer together in the office of Senator John J. Sparkman of Alabama, who for long has been planning such a fight....

Sitting across from Senator Sparkman is Senator James E.
Murray of Montana, who led a congressional delegation on a
mission to the White House a few days ago to inform the
president of their plan. And here is Senator Hubert Humphrey
of Minnesota, who has thrown himself wholeheartedly into the
battle.

I'm glad to tell you that these gentlemen—realizing the
gravity of our national situation—have brushed aside sectional
differences; they present a united front to our common enemy
—national want.

Senator Murray, why do you plan this bill on economic
expansion?

Senator Murray. Our bill is proposed as a means of checking
the development of economic conditions that might result in a
serious recession. In many sections of the country there has been
a general slowing down in industry, and serious unemployment
is found in certain spots. Our program is designed to offset this
unemployment, encourage business and industrial expansion,
provide ways and means of encouraging private enterprise, and
thus avoid any dangerous conditions of unemployment and
business recession.

Mr. Parmer. Are conditions that bad, senator?

Senator Murray. They are not serious at this moment from a

national standpoint, but in particular localities where unemployment has developed, it presents a very serious problem. A
prudent government should not be expected to take steps in any
other direction except to aid in preventing these conditions from
spreading and creating a serious catastrophe. . . .

Mr. Parmer. Now, Senator Sparkman, how much do you
estimate such a vast program would cost?

Senator Sparkman. Well, Mr. Parmer, I don't know that that
could be estimated. You probably have in mind the feature in the
bill in which we recommend a fund of $15 billion. That I think
would be referred to more or less as working capital for all of
these various objectives, and that figure certainly should not be
used as the estimate of the cost of the public-works program. Of
course, we never get through with public works in this country.
The big question is, how much do you want to congest them
in any one particular given period of time?

Mr. Parmer. Thank you, Senator Sparkman. And now,
Senator Humphrey—you, sir.

Senator Humphrey. Mr. Parmer, I. . . look upon the economic
situation that now confronts us, which surely is not alarming
but is one that deserves our consideration, as similar to any
situation that might exist in international affairs.

For example, in 1935 and 1936, we knew that Hitler was a
menace. We knew that he was taking certain steps that were
aggressive and that could cause great trouble. The question at
that time was, should we quarantine the aggressor before he
gets out of hand? Or should we wait until he did—and as we did,
at Pearl Harbor, when everything was out of hand. In other
words, should we take preventive measures to stop aggression
or should we wait until a full-scale war comes upon us?

So we waited for a full-scale war, and we spent not only
hundreds of thousands of lives but billions and billions of dollars,
into the hundreds of billions.

Now, the same thing is true in economics—in our economy.
Should we wait until we have what Senator Murray has referred
to as catastrophe or, back a step, depression; or should we attack
these islands of depression, recession, unemployment, where we

see them? When we see them and at the time that we see them.

I believe in quarantining unemployment; I believe in putting up a public notice that here's a place where we need preventive economic medicine. We need to come in and cure the problem right where we see it, at that moment. . . .

It is like visualizing an attack on the part of an enemy. What are you going to do about it? You have long-range plans.

And. . . the substance of this bill is centered around the very nature of our economy—private enterprise. The independent businessman working with the established institutions of our economic system—in other words, this is a bill that works within the framework of the American economic plan. . . ; a great portion of this bill is dedicated toward strengthening the productive capacities, providing loans and credits and quick amortization of plant. In other words, using American management, American capital, to meet a problem in our own country.

I want to say that there are only two dangers that this nation faces—one is on the outside, from totalitarian aggression, and I think that danger is even less than the danger of breakdown within our own economy. And surely if we can appropriate billions and billions of dollars to stop a potential international aggressor, we ought to at least be willing to make plans—sensible, long-range plans within the American pattern—to stop any kind of economic disaster within our own economy. . . .

We can't have the status quo, Mr. Parmer. Every year we get from five hundred to seven hundred thousand new people in our work force; we have to think of America as a growing country—a young nation still growing and moving ahead and unwilling to stand on past laurels.

Fair Trade and the Fair Deal

Legislation, however, was not enough. Humphrey knew that the only true solution to the nation's economic ills rested entirely with the people themselves. He had to find a way to mobilize the various private sectors of the economy into an integrated, unified army to carry on the economic war he had talked about on July 3.

On September 23, 1949, Humphrey made that point in an address delivered at the 51st annual convention of the National Association of Retail Druggists. His talk was on fair trade but his message ran much deeper. Simply stated, it was: Don't let anyone else decide what is best for you.

Humphrey would use a similar theme time and time again. It is no less relevant in 1978 than it was in 1949.

Our nation and our national philosophy are under attack as never before in our history.

I do not refer at this time only to dangers arising through threats of force. I refer to something equally important—survival of the spiritual factors which go to the essence of the basic political and economic philosophy of our people.

Ours was originally a land where each one of us, our sons and our grandchildren, faced a world full of invitations. Until the Industrial Revolution hit the United States toward the end of the last century, there was practically no business or economic activity which an American citizen could not enter with courage and with hope.

The Industrial Revolution carried with it the dynamic movement of technology and further opportunity for economic man. Yet, with the Industrial Revolution there also came that which we call big business, concentration of economic power and deep problems associated with antisocial economic institutions called trusts and monopolies.

It is in this perspective that I view the problems which small business faces today. I approach this problem not only from an academic viewpoint, but also from the viewpoint of a practicing small-business man. I was brought up in a small-town drug store. My youth was spent working along with my brother and father in what we now think is the best drug store to be found on Main Street of Huron, South Dakota. I maintain my interest in that business and in the problems faced by that drug store and the many hundreds of thousands of small businesses like it in our economy.

I therefore have an intimate knowledge of what we mean by capital, fair trade, and fair-trade laws.

I remember vividly the terrible days of the Depression when I worked behind the counter of our store and saw and felt the effects on our community when large price-cutting organizations moved in on the independent businessman struggling to keep his head above water.

I know the bitter miseries of predatory price competition. It is against this background of experience that I speak of the independent business enterprise.

I suppose it was the Depression and the economic repercussions of the late 1920s and 1930s that molded my economic and political philosophy. It gave me a respect for hard work, ingenuity, and determination. It brought into sharp focus the reality of suffering that comes from unemployment, mortgage indebtedness, irresponsible financial power, wildcat market speculation, and ruinous low prices and degrading low wages.

I learned by experience—cruel, sickening experience—the interdependence of our economy; the relationship between farmer, worker, retailer, wholesaler, and manufacturer. I know by experience and not by theory, that a depressed agriculture, an unemployed labor force spell debt and bankruptcy for business.

I know, by experience and not by theory, the dangers that are ever-present in concentration of economic power, in monopoly.

I know what it means to have banks close their doors, and have no federal deposit insurance to protect the bank account. I know what it means to have unemployed people stand around in a drug store and not to have even an unemployment-compensation check.

I know what it means to have farmers without price supports, fair trade, for their products. I know what it means to see merchant after merchant close his doors only to see the big chain or corporate enterprise survive and preempt the field.

Yes, I think I know what it means to see a nation prostrate and dying while a government of the people, by the people, and for the people does nothing but talk of confidence and prosperity around the corner.

That is why I support a policy of government that seeks to protect the welfare of the people, that joins hands with the people in preserving the institutions of political and economic freedom.

I support a policy of government that believes in fair trade for all parts of the American economy. To me, fair trade means a a fair trade body of rules and regulations that preserves the competitive-enterprise system but removes competition from the realm of unprincipled and vicious practices either by government or by business enterprise. . . .

Free enterprise—yes, individual private enterprise—cannot be based upon the philosophy of greed and selfishness or have as its rules the law of the jungle. Business enterprise has a responsibility not only to itself but to the rest of the community.

It is through government—a free and democratic government—that a just and fair body of rules for the conduct of society is appropriately designed and fairly enforced. . . .

Fair trade in essence means respect for individual rights, the preservation of competition between responsible people and institutions, a society based upon law and order. These should be the objectives of all freedom-loving people in all aspects of our political, social, and economic life. . . .

The basic purpose of American democratic government has been the guaranty of equality of opportunity and the preservation of individual liberty. In simpler terms, that is, in the language of the businessman, fair trade—a guaranty of the opportunity to do business with, to associate with other persons on a basis of fairness and equality, but at all times preserving the differences that come with individual initiative and the development of individual capacity.

There has been a great hue and cry these last few years about the loss of our liberty. . . . Unfortunately, some people look upon liberty and freedom as a license to exploit and to destroy.

The American philosophy of liberty is not merely absence of restraint. More basically, it is the establishment of conditions of fair play and of equality of opportunity that permits an orderly development of society and a development of individual ability for the benefit of the individual as well as the community.

It is for these reasons that we have laws that regulate zoning in cities, that control traffic, that set up standards of public-health protection and sanitary codes.

It is because we look upon liberty as a privilege but also as a responsibility that we have developed laws which regulate our finance, which control and direct our commerce, which protect and develop our natural resources, and which guarantee to the individual citizen his basic rights of free speech, free press, freedom to worship, and freedom to assemble.

Now, some people may call this "statism" or they may even call it "the welfare state." I call it "democracy." I call it responsible government and an orderly society.

It is my observation that the sure path to "statism," the sure road to collectivism, is the failure to recognize the basic needs of our people and the failure to protect and guard the free flow of commerce in an economic system that is based not only upon free enterprise but upon individual enterprise.

I repeat—the heart and core of the American economic system is individual enterprise—the small independent business-man. The threat to that economic system is the ever-growing concentration of economic power and that threat is a real one. . . .

Statism will come to us when business gets so big that it can only be managed and controlled by a government that is even bigger. Just as big business becomes intoxicated with its own power and loses its sense of initiative and imagination and its respect for individual rights, so big government that is designed to check big business can become inefficient, inconsiderate, unimaginative and unconcerned as to individual rights.

Statism in simple terms is absolute power—power has many manifestations. There is political power but the essence of political power is economic power, and it is my considered judgment that if statism comes to this great nation, it will come because those who cry out the most against it at this day are often unaware of the menace of economic concentration and the destruction of free competition. . . .

I believe with a deep conviction in property rights and in private property. I believe in private property so much that I think everybody ought to have some of it and not a few people have most of it. It is in this frame of thought that I rise to defend the fair-trade laws and state categorically that they are a fundamental part of our political and economic freedom. . . .

Fair trade has demonstrated, without peradventure of doubt, over the years of our Depression, war, and postwar periods, that it serves a useful social and economic purpose in the public interest in our free-enterprise economy.

Fair trade has proved itself one of the keystones of our antimonopoly structure; for it has stimulated competition while, at the same time, setting down just rules of competition which eliminated the vicious practices of those who want only free-for-all enterprise and whose textbook is jungle economics.

Under fair trade, the independent retailer has been given the opportunity to earn a livelihood. I say opportunity advisedly; because that is all he has been given. The independent retailer must still earn his living—fair trade does not guarantee it to him. He must know how to keep store, how to buy, how to sell, how to serve his customers. Those who fail in these and in other essentials of retail distribution will surely fall by the wayside; and, indeed, they have. . . .

Let us make no mistake about it, our free enterprise system cannot long endure if economic power is concentrated in relatively few hands. We must have large numbers of businesses, and we must make it possible for men to have a fair chance of success in business enterprise, if we are to avoid the statism about which there is so much fear. . . .

The American heritage of freedom is yours. To perpetuate that heritage by keeping alive a vigorous competitive spirit is your responsibility and the responsibility of every American citizen. Only the will to maintain this spirit can keep it alive.

No amount of law enforcement can preserve this spirit or, without it, maintain a system of free enterprise. Only if you and the American business community are true in act as well as in word to your tradition of freedom, will that freedom be a reality.

Eternal vigilance is said to be the price of political freedom. Without economic freedom the other freedoms, including political freedom, are lost.

This, I submit, is your stake in the competitive system.

Get Involved—Or Else

Labor, like small business, was seriously threatened in 1949, Humphrey believed. The fault, he felt, was at least partially due to political fence-straddling on the part of a fragmented and bickering labor movement.

On October 3, 1949, Humphrey issued a challenge to the American Federation of Labor's 68th annual convention, then meeting in St. Paul, Minnesota. Get involved, he warned, or suffer the consequences.

Labor listened and learned. In the last thirty years, it has become one of the most powerful political forces in the nation. It spends more money and time on political campaigns and lobbying efforts than its national opponent, industry. What they do now is what Humphrey urged them to do then.

. . . Labor's rights are no longer secure merely through the process of collective bargaining. The rules of collective bargaining and the rights and privileges of organized labor are now the subject of legislation and the subject of political determination.

Politics, effective political participation, must go hand in hand with the growth and the development and the maintenance of a strong labor movement in America.

No one is asking anyone any longer in this country of ours, "Are you interested in politics?" The simple fact is you are either interested in it or somebody is going to take the very interest out of you by political action. . . .

We need—when I say "we" I mean every American—needs and welcomes an aggressive, constructive political action program on the part of organized labor.

To hear some people talk and to read the writings of some editorial commentators, one would think it was against the law for a man that carries a union card to even be interested in politics. For years and years in this country, the molders of public opinion, the powers that be who managed the political machines and the major political parties, have told the folks in labor, "You just kind of keep out of our way. We will run this whole thing for you."

They have operated it pretty well—but not for you. They have operated it in behalf of management, of their political organizations. They have too often been what is called the political bosses.

Now, I say we need a constructive and an aggressive political action policy on the part of labor. But I want to make my position quite clear, because all too often we think of these political policies as top-level strategy. Make it crystal clear in your own minds that elections are not won in Washington, D.C. They are lost there, but they are not won there. . . .

Elections are won by hard work and by active participation in every voting precinct in this country. The essentials of a successful political campaign. . . as I see them are the following:

—A program—and I put program first—a program that meets the needs of the people.

—Secondly, candidates willing to fight for the people. We have got too many candidates where you have to fight for them. We need candidates who are willing to go out and fight for you, to fight for the American people.

—Thirdly, there is a need of political organization that belongs to and is controlled by and managed by the rank and file of the people.

—Finally, a clear-cut statement of the issues in language, in the simple language that is understandable by all of the people.

Now, my friends, if you have those ingredients, if you have a program that meets the needs of the people, candidates willing to fight for the people, if you have a political organization that belongs to the people and they are a part of it, and if you have a clear-cut statement of the issues in language that is understandable by the people, I submit to you no one can beat you, no one. There is the essence of success. . . .

Liberal organizations and labor groups have not always set themselves down to the job of effective political action. In some areas, there is a tendency on the part of labor to remain aloof from other groups who have similar objectives, and in some areas there is an outright refusal to join hands with other sections of the labor movement and the liberal, democratic forces. . . . It is going to be a responsibility of the labor movement and of every liberal and democratic organization to forget personal pride, petty differences and to unite behind candidates and around a program. . . .

There is a dangerous coalition in this country. There has never in the history of America been a greater propaganda barrage against the American worker than there has been in the last seven, eight, or nine months.

Ever since the miracle of November 2, [Truman's upset of Dewey] the soothsayers have been concocting some kind of a new witches' brew to pour out to the American people. While we were celebrating and while we were patting each other on the back, the old rear guard was in there plotting and planning every day of the week, getting their machinery ready again for the onslaught.

Humphrey's parents, Christine and Hubert, Sr.

Hubert Humphrey, age three.

Humphrey's high school graduation picture.

Scoutmaster Humphrey.

Muriel Humphrey in 1932.

Christine Humphrey is flanked
by two Hubert Humphreys,
her husband and son.

The University of Minnesota Debating team, 1940. Humphrey is standing
third from left, beside Orville Freeman, on his right.

Right: Minnesota's future senator poses with the state's future governor, fellow classmate and debating teammate, Orville Freeman.

Below: The Mayor at work.

United Press International

Senator Muriel Humphrey

Senator Muriel Humphrey

Left: Hubert H. Humphrey Jr., Minnesota delegate to the 1948 Democratic convention in Philadelphia, talks things over with a delegate from South Dakota, Hubert H. Humphrey Sr.

Below: Mayor Humphrey with his family at breakfast.

Right: In an act of political courage, Mayor Humphrey tells the 1948 Democratic convention in Philadelphia that the time has come to grant equal rights to all Americans.

Below: The mayor campaigns for the Senate.

United Press International

Senator Muriel Humphrey

United Press International

United Press International

Above: A happy Harry Truman, who had recently won an upset victory over Republican presidential nominee Thomas E. Dewey, shakes hands with two other winners: freshman Senator Humphrey and freshman Representative Eugene McCarthy.

Left: Following the death of his father, Humphrey, a freshman senator in 1949, mixes a prescription in the family drugstore.

Right: The Humphreys
used this photo for their
1952 Christmas card
in Duluth, Minnesota.

Below: The Humphrey
family picnic in the
backyard of their Chevy
Chase, Maryland home.

Senator Muriel Humphrey

Senator Muriel Humphrey

There is a dangerous coalition: a coalition that distorts public opinion, a coalition that defies the truth, a coalition that is not interested in the presentation of the truth. It is a coalition of the reactionary element of the press of America.

That coalition is made of the reactionary element of the press, the postwar isolationists, the politically bankrupt leadership. . . of the GOP, and a handful of determined Dixiecrats and the soft-headed confused pinks, along with the outright communists. That is the coalition that faces America.

They are the ones who have lost faith in this country and whose vision has not gone beyond yesterday, who are incapable of facing the problems of today, and who shudder and shake at the thought of tomorrow.

This frustration of political malcontents have set themselves up as a holding company for all and sundry purposes. . . . The only qualification for membership in the fraternal order of frustrated politicians is to be against labor, to be against price supports for the farmers, to be against pensions for the aged, to be against the good life, and God bless you, to be against the welfare state.

God bless you, that's what you have to be. The fraternal order of frustrated politicians condemns our policy at home and abroad in the same wild irresponsible charges. At home, it is the welfare state they are against; and abroad, it is our aid to Great Britain and Western Europe.

Their policy is isolationism abroad and confusion and despair at home, and they have seized upon the concept of one of the most noble, one of the most decent, one of the most worthwhile and blessed words in the English language—they have seized upon the word "welfare," and they have added it to the word "state," and they have tried to make the American people believe that the welfare state is equivalent to purgatory or hell, or is a manifestation of all the human evil that it is possible to conjure.

As one of the men on the other side, I accept that challenge. As one young man, I am prepared to do battle with them on any issue. I am prepared to argue the issues of the welfare state. . . .

Those who are screaming today against the welfare state tell you that you are losing your liberty, that you are being collectivized, that the omnipotent hand of the state is upon you. . . .

Let's go along and take a look at this subject and see who is on the right side. I like to believe in the American Constitution, a great immortal document, and yet those who are opposed to the welfare state are registering their opposition, despite the mandate of the Constitution of the United States of America, where it places upon the government of this country the responsibility to promote the general welfare. And those words are written out in the commerce clause of the Constitution, Article I, Section 9. . . .

Two world wars and a major worldwide depression have not demonstrated to these die-hard apostles of the past that we are living in a changed world. And believe me, we are living in a changed world as the fraternal delegates who are here from the Western democracies of Europe will tell you—not only a changed world but one that was almost destroyed.

My friends in the labor movement, I urge a rededication. . . to the fulfillment of our responsibility for international leadership. . . . If this world is going to be a better world, we are going to help make it that way. If this world is going to collapse in its own evil, in its own misdoings, we are going to be a part of it.

We are not the America of 1800, we are not even the America of 1900; we are the America of 1949 and 1950. We are the America that is the greatest financial power the world has ever known, and believe me, we have to act with a sense of great social responsibility when we hold the money bags of the world.

I don't want my country getting the reputation of pinching the last ounce of blood and the last pound of flesh. We are the greatest industrial power in the world. Our industrial know-how goes on beyond any possible comparison in this world, and with that tremendous productivity that is ours, the skill that we have, we cannot just live unto ourselves. . . .

The very ethics of our religious faith—whether we be Jew, Gentile, Protestant, or Catholic—every moral tenet of our religious faith tells us that we are our brother's keeper, and he who would deny it will destroy himself.

I submit to you also that it is a privilege to help other people. Nothing that we should go around boasting about, but something about which we should be humble. Isn't it wonderful that out of this terrible destruction of World War II God Almighty spared one nation to help its fellow men? Isn't it wonderful that out of the terrible cost and the torture and the suffering of millions and millions of people, one great economy of this world was spared to lift up the level of mankind?

That is our mission. We have a destiny to fulfill, and that destiny is one which should make every American proud— proud that you are an American, proud that you can do something for those who have done so much for us, because every one of us in this room at one time or another was a [displaced person], every one of us at some time or another in the years gone by in our family were immigrants.

Now it is our opportunity to offer the advice and counsel of a great democracy, of a great, free people—not only to offer it, but to share the fruits of our labor, to share our productivity, to be the good Samaritan—and believe me, friends, no one hates a good Samaritan.

But some people hate bill collectors, double-entry bookkeeping artists. So I call upon this labor movement to accept the responsibility for international leadership. The liberal, social, democratic forces of Europe—and by the way, friends, the only hope in Europe are the liberal democratic forces—are looking to us.

The hope of Europe does not lie in the reactionary communistic left. That is the black pit of disillusionment and despair. The peoples of Europe will only turn to that when there is no other place to turn.

The hope of Europe does not rest in the economic or political leadership of the extreme right, and it does not rest in the mollycoddle leadership of those who want to be in power.

It rests with those great forces of the free labor movement, it rests with the forces of the free cooperative movement, it rests with those intellectual leaders of Europe who are attracted to the proposition of human freedom.

And may I say to the American Federation of Labor, God bless you, may you join with those forces as you are doing in saving Western Europe and Western civilization. . . .

The labor movement is one of brotherhood. It is one of sharing, it is one of fraternity. There is no room in the ranks of labor for a political policy that sets labor off from the rest of the community. The political fact of this decade is the recognition of our interdependence, not only our independence, but our inter-dependence—the interdependence of the nations of the world on trade between the nations and world commerce. The political fact of America is the interdependence of the worker and the farmer.

These two great producers of real wealth are the lifeblood of our free economic system. The economic well-being of both the worker and the farmer is the only hope for a prosperous America. . . .

My good friends, an economic breakdown in America as to its effect upon the world situation and the future peace and security of this world would make the atomic bomb that Russia may have look like a firecracker. An economic breakdown in America would destroy the productivity and the prosperity of the greatest nation in the world, of the only nation that many other nations are leaning upon and looking for help.

The greatest contribution that this nation can give to the rest of the world today is a strong, prosperous, enlightened, humanitarian America. . . and those who would seek to destroy us are patiently waiting for us. . . to create our own mistakes and our own troubles.

The aggressor, or the potential aggressor, the foe and the enemy of free America is a reactionary policy at work that does not recognize the needs of the American people, a reactionary, isolationist policy abroad which fails to recognize the basic needs and legitimate rights of their people. . . .

It is our job, . . . to figure out to the best of our ability how we can best prevent the catastrophe and calamity of World War III.

The expenditures for peace are expenditures for the good life, for better men and better women, for healthier and more enlightened children, and I want to see the same determination in our eyes and in our minds and bodies, to win this struggle for a free Europe, to win this struggle for a free Asia, for a free world.

I want every American to dedicate his life and to dedicate his treasure and to dedicate his ability to the crusade for a just and enduring peace, which we can obtain if we but will it, so help me God.

A Political Program for Democracy

Organized labor was not the only group to whom Humphrey had important advice. He also had a few words to say to the nation's two political parties. And he said them before the New York Herald Tribune *Forum on a Political Program for Democracy, on October 24, 1949. But, whereas organized labor heeded Humphrey's words and began a new course, the nation's two political parties have still not caught up with some of the senator's ideas.*

. . . The conduct of public affairs in these crucial days calls for positive direction and responsibility if we are to achieve the promises of the American life at home, and safeguard democracy in the world at large.

What we seek, within the framework of our inherited form of government, is a series of arrangements which will at once promote better teamwork between the Congress and the president, avoid dangerous roadblocks, inculcate national rather than provincial loyalties, and give the spirit of youth a larger place in legislative halls.

Ours is a federal system in constitutional theory, but it is increasingly becoming a national system in actual practice. While we have forty-eight state legislatures, we have one national economic and industrial system.

The trend from state government to national government has been fortified and accelerated by the Civil War, by the onward sweep of science and technology, by the unifying forces of transportation and communication, and by a long series of Supreme Court decisions. The same evolutionary influences are operating in our political system. . . .

One of the articles of our political faith has been our belief in the biparty system. We believe that political parties are the principal instruments of democratic government and that the party which wins a majority of the popular vote should have the responsibility and the power to govern the country. . . .

The American people have long accepted the principle of party responsibility for the conduct of our national government. We must translate that principle into practice.

Each party should be encouraged to reformulate its platform every two years—it might be that national conventions should be held every two years—and the platform should be regarded as commitments by all candidates for office and officeholders of the party.

This would go far to make our congressional elections, as well as our presidential elections, more meaningful to the American people by providing them with an opportunity effectively to choose on basic issues rather than personalities.

American politics should not be a beauty contest or a popularity contest. Policy and issues must be the standards for decisions. Party elections must increasingly become issue elections, otherwise more and more people may lose faith in representative government and become impatient with democratic processes. . . .

With an educated and informed party membership, party platforms on a national level will increasingly come to represent policy decisions made on the local level. It should be the function of the local party membership to express itself on national issues not only by choosing delegates to national conventions, but by making on a local level decisions on national issues which their representatives are to carry forward to the national convention.

Party membership would come to feel that its views and decisions on policy matters have an effect on national party policy decision, and would be an alert and active and responsible membership. . . .

Twentieth-century America is a dynamic society facing complex problems. Our task is to evolve a political mechanism which will utilize the democratic process, place responsibility for action, and maintain an unobstructed connection between the electorate and the elected representatives in government.

Caring about Health Care

By the end of 1949, Hubert Humphrey was established as an up-and-coming member of the "world's most exclusive club." Members of both the House and Senate were beginning to like and respect the junior senator from Minnesota— Even Senator Russell, who had called him a "damn fool." And Humphrey, for his part, was beginning to enjoy being a member of Congress.

At every opportunity, Humphrey would defend the Congress when he felt it had been wronged. In a speech to the Democratic-Farmer-Labor Party's legislative conference in Minneapolis on February 18, 1950, Humphrey attacked press reports that said Congress was "torn by conflict and argument— much talk and very little action" on health-care legislation.

Not true, said Humphrey. Congress had "worked a miracle" and had passed five major health bills in one session of the 81st Congress. Four parts of President Truman's seven-point health program had already gone through the Senate, Humphrey told his fellow Minnesotans.

One piece of legislation that did not pass in 1949 was Humphrey's plan for medical care under Social Security. He would push for the bill for the next fifteen years. When Medicare, as it became known, finally was enacted in 1964, the credit went posthumously to the man "whose idea it was"—John F. Kennedy.

A lot more had to be done in the field of health care, Humphrey told the conference. It would require the help of every American if proper health programs were to be instituted.

I should like to take this opportunity to tell you about what's going on in Washington with respect to the one thing that is more important to you than anything else in the world—your health and that of your family, of your neighbors and of your community. . . .

We have learned that we Americans are a highly mobile people. With no iron curtains or immigration bars between the states, our people by the hundreds of thousands move from place to place throughout the country each year hunting better jobs, seeking greater opportunity, carrying on their business or just looking for rest and relaxation. . . .

Just as our people move about freely and in great numbers, so too does disease disregard community borders and state boundaries. We know that the great cities of the country draw their people from the farms and rural areas of the nation. We know that the health of city workers in large measure determines their ability to earn enough to buy the products of our farms. We know that the nation's wealth depends on its people's health—that, in fact, our health is the basic source of all our wealth.

We know these things and we've learned that, while the job of protecting our health must be carried out at the local level—in the states and in the local community—the states and their local governments cannot themselves finance necessary health measures. Their taxing powers are far too limited. Not even in the case of very wealthy states, can they effectively carry on separate and uncoordinated programs.

We know, that just as disease recognizes no boundaries, recognizes neither state lines nor differences between rich and poor, so too must the battle against illness and disease and against the wrecked hopes and broken homes they leave in their wake, be national in scope. Our country's strength is in the health of our people.

We are all agreed that the Congress should concern itself with health problems. . . . To a great extent, we are also agreed as to what those problems are. Briefly put, they involve problems of preventing disease as well as curing it. Problems of getting enough doctors and dentists and nurses and other health personnel to meet the needs of our people. Problems of having the hospitals and clinics in the places where they're needed.

And, given enough doctors, nurses, hospitals and clinics, the great big problem of seeing to it that people are able to use them—are able to afford their services.

Those are the problems. Throughout the nation and in the Congress there's pretty general agreement on them.

But after we've stated the problems, we've got to agree on solutions for them; we've got to do something about them. . . .

We. . . think that American medical care is among the best in the world. But we know that too many Americans can't afford it under our present system of payment. We want to change not the practice of medicine, but only the way in which we pay for it.

The people of this country are demanding a change and. . . we're going to give it to them. Without your help, we won't do as well and you may inadvertently and unnecessarily suffer. With your help, we should have no problem reaching a solution satisfactory to all.

For myself, for the Congress and for the people of your country, I ask that help. I can pledge you our good faith—completely. Will you extend to us a little?

God, Man and the Hydrogen Bomb

Nineteen days before Humphrey talked about health legislation to his fellow Minnesotans, an event took place that would alter for all time the course of East-West relations and the price of any future global war.

From the moment that Harry Truman, on January 31, 1950, ordered construction of a hydrogen bomb, the world has skirted the precipice of nuclear holocaust. It was no longer a question of whole cities being destroyed; it was now a question of global extinction.

Three days after Truman signed that unfortunate but very necessary order, Senator Brian McMahon of Connecticut, chairman of the Joint Committee on Atomic Energy, graphically described the true meaning of the president's announcement. He then challenged the world to turn from a path toward war and build for peace.

On February 4, a group of twelve of the nation's leading physicists declared that "this bomb is no longer a weapon of war, but a means of extermination of whole populations."

Two days later, on February 6, Senate Armed Forces Committee Chairman Millard Tydings of Maryland urged the United States to call an international conference on world disarmament.

And on February 12, Dr. Albert Einstein, the leading scientist of the day, added his voice. "The idea of achieving security through national armament is at the present state of military techniques a disastrous illusion. . . . Radioactive poisoning of the atmosphere and hence annihilation of any life on Earth has been brought within the range of a technical possibility."

Ten days later, on February 22, Ash Wednesday, Hubert Humphrey offered his "moral alternative to world chaos" in a speech he delivered at Washington Cathedral.

It is with deep feeling of humility that I address myself to the subject of the day—God, man and the hydrogen bomb.

But man cannot escape coping with the harsh realities of international life. Man today spends more of the earth's resources, his wealth, and his genius on preparation for war and the ultimate destruction of human and religious values than he does on the creation of a living society based on the eternal religious principles of human brotherhood.

What the United States, for example, spends each week for military defense is what the federal aid-to-education program proposes to spend for one whole year, or for rural electrification for one whole year.

We meet here today on Ash Wednesday. We, with the millions in Christendom, today enter the Lenten season. We begin the search into the recesses of our own souls; we come to grips with the facts of our own human inadequacy; we come to the ultimate realization that unless man prepares himself to commit an act of faith, he and his civilization may disintegrate....

The threat of physical destruction is obvious to all serious and informed persons. Whatever faith in inevitable progress which those of us reared in the liberal tradition may have had is seriously shaken. Not only is the threat of physical disaster a grave one for the future of mankind, but the chronic threat of war, even without its advent, must inevitably create a state of perpetual crisis and resultant loss of human freedom.

Fear can result in placing the control of man's destiny in the hands of just a few. Decisions in such an atmosphere must give special weight to the advice of those who specialize in violence. Under the stress of continuing war tension, the body politic may well transform itself into a garrison-prison state.

In much of the globe, this process has gone far already. If the crisis continues, the process can appear in every country. Its success may call for no revolutionary seizure of power by totalitarian forces. The process has more in common with man's struggling in a bottomless bog. The hard truth, however, is that while America stands powerful, the idea of democracy which it represents is losing strength in the world....

The fear and mistrust within nations today is too obvious to need documentation. It is that which produces atomic and hydrogen bombs. Yet, in spite of possessing a stockpile of atomic bombs, and spending more than $15 billion a year on military preparedness, many Americans are still insecure.

Here is further justification for further self-analysis and inquiry into better ways of seeking security and peace. . . .

Let us not ignore the deep-rooted contradictions between democracy and totalitarianism of any form, whether it be communist or fascist. Let us never cease expressing our indignation toward slavery, nor our vigilance in behalf of freedom. So long as there is oppression or injustice or totalitarian power in the world, there is conflict.

We must, however, lift conflict out of the realm of war.

Our responsibility is to tell the peoples of the world that we, temporarily the mightiest of nations, are ready to join in an international effort to abolish war. We must resolve to take some of the imaginative daring which we have shown in the physical sciences to start a chain reaction among the peoples and governments of the world against this madness and insanity.

Here lies our strength. With a positive reaffirmation of our democratic faith, with a determination to protect freedom and resist totalitarianism, with an unequivocal declaration in behalf of an international agreement to abolish war and for universal disarmament, America would gain for itself moral supremacy in the world, and recapture, in the eyes of the world, leadership for peace. . . .

History offers many examples of mortal conflicts between great movements which, with the passing of the years and the cooling of passions, have found it possible to resolve their conflicts without war. The conflict between the Moslem and the Christian worlds was finally resolved by the destruction of neither, in spite of the Moslem slogan "Face Islam or die."

Our first concrete proposal to the leaders of the Soviet Union must be to set up a conference on universal disarmament —universal, not unilateral—with international guaranties of security. It is the responsibility of our heads of state to make unmistakably clear to the leaders of the Soviet Union our plans for such a positive proposal and issue an invitation that they join with us in submitting such a proposal to the United Nations.

We must also make it perfectly clear to the leaders of the Soviet Union that the alternative to peaceful negotiations and settlement could well mean turning the world into a battlefield which would make it the graveyard for the human race.

Our proposals for disarmament should include the absolute prohibition of the manufacture of weapons for mass destruction, limited not only to atomic and hydrogen bombs but to conventional armaments as well. We should stand ready to consider practical suggestions as to how necessary supervision and control can be exercised.

We should stand ready to turn over our own stockpiles of destruction to the United Nations as part of such an international agreement and in concert with all other nations of the world. . . .

Our disarmament proposal must also include with it a plea for universal abolition of peacetime conscription. It is unnecessary to train young men and women for war in a world society dedicated to peace.

Such a program to be effective must be accompanied by provisions for a police force to maintain international security. The United Nations must be transformed into an organization capable of enforcing peace under law.

Carrying the banner of such an international program, the United States will find itself in partnership with the entire non-Soviet world. With such a program we present the leaders of the Soviet Union with a challenge. It is a challenge not only to its military power but to its very purposes, which are the ultimate roots of its power.

We would be affirming our faith that in the conflict of ideologies between democracy and communist totalitarianism, democracy will prevail and we would be proclaiming to the leaders of the Soviet Union, "Dare you affirm less for your faith in communism?". . .

With such a program we demonstrate to the Russian people, and certainly to the people of Asia, Africa and Europe, our basic striving for peace, for understanding and for international justice. Let any government who refuses our offer then face the responsibility in the eyes of the peoples of the world for continuing the race of humanity toward destruction.

At this moment in history, the helpless and teeming millions of people, citizens of the world, anxiously look for a declaration of American foreign policy which will provide them with the hope that war is not inevitable and that peace can indeed be a reality for them and their children.

Having offered our willingness to join as partners in the struggle for peace and against the real enemies of mankind—hunger and poverty—we would gain for ourselves the friendship and loyalty of all the peoples of the world.

Here is a moral alternative to world chaos.

People in Politics

The New Deal had created a revolution in the United States. The Fair Deal sought to continue that revolution.

But those who opposed Franklin Roosevelt and later Harry Truman were gaining momentum. They were out to turn back the clock to the way things were before the Great Depression hit.

In Hubert Humphrey's view, they were doing this because the New Deal and the Fair Deal had provided the general public a greater role in the decision-making process, thus posing a serious threat to the special interests.

But the Depression was over. A great war had been fought and won. The people were becoming apathetic again, and in their apathy lurked a grave threat to their hard-won gains.

On April 18, 1950, Hubert Humphrey talked about this threat to a group of people in Richmond, Virginia.

I know that frequently it is difficult for those of you who live in Virginia to realize with how much awe and respect those of us from other sections of America look upon your native state.

I well remember my school days as a youngster in a small town in South Dakota, reading about Monticello and Mt. Vernon, and studying the lives of Thomas Jefferson, James Madison, George Mason, Patrick Henry, and the many other illustrious figures in American history.

I remember my sisters and my brother and myself talking about those early days and about the great state of Virginia with my father.

Later, as a young man in Minnesota and as a student and a teacher of political science at the university there, the picture of Virginia as the birthplace of presidents took shape more clearly....

The great teachers of democracy have taught us that the judgment of the majority of the people is a far better judgment to follow than the judgment of any single minority, whether it be the few who own property or the few who control wealth. They had the faith because democracy to them meant participation by all the people in the political process. And the political process to them meant that the people would rule through their votes, after becoming informed and intelligent through debate and discussion and a free expression of their views.

The development of American history since that early day has been one of broadening and extending democracy. It has been a continuous striving to attain that goal so beautifully described by Abraham Lincoln when he said that ours was to be a "government of the people, by the people, and for the people."

It was striving to make a political reality out of the immortal idea created and championed by that noble Virginian Thomas Jefferson, when he said "all men are created equal, and are endowed by their Creator with certain inalienable rights."

That tradition of human equality, of human brotherhood, and of increasing democracy has been championed in the twentieth century by Theodore Roosevelt, Woodrow Wilson, Franklin Roosevelt, and Harry Truman. It is receiving its greatest expression today in the program and political life of the New Deal and the Fair Deal.

This, my friends, explains the intensity of the opposition faced by the Fair Deal and the New Deal. The people are beginning to express themselves and as they express themselves the few and the privileged who have looked upon political activity and politics as their business and only their business are fighting to maintain their power and positions of privilege.

Make no mistake about it. The programs of the New Deal and the Fair Deal have helped business. Profits are at the highest level that they have ever been in the nation's history. The New Deal and the Fair Deal have been good to them at the same time as those programs have provided for our welfare—yours and mine—and the millions of American farmers, workers, and small businessmen.

There is only one logical reason for their opposition and their bitter hostility to the New Deal and to the Fair Deal. It is their realization that with the New Deal and the Fair Deal they no longer make the decisions; it is the people who make the decisions.

Losing Face

In talking about the Fair Deal to that audience in Richmond, Humphrey also talked about "human equality. . . [and] human brotherhood." In doing so, he had once again showed that principles came before politics where he was concerned.

For Richmond was a part of the South. Its favorite son was Senator Harry Byrd, the darling of the conservatives; the same Harry Byrd whom Humphrey had attacked, only to pay a stiff price. Yet Humphrey had dared to bring up the subject of civil rights in this Southern bastion and in Byrd's own bailiwick, no less.

There was good reason for Humphrey to have civil rights on his mind that day. The Congress was about to take up legislation that would permanently create a federal Fair Employment Practices Commission, which had years ago been established by Executive Order under President Roosevelt. Humphrey very much favored the FEPC legislation, having seen first hand as mayor of

Minneapolis the wonders such a commission could work in the furthering of civil rights.

Several days after the Richmond speech, Humphrey and Senator Spessard L. Holland of Florida, an avowed foe of civil rights, appeared together on NBC's "American Forum of the Air" program. Humphrey's relevant remarks, taken from a transcript of that program, follow.

Here is a country that has in its Declaration of Independence that all men are created equal. Here is a country that has in its Constitution the whole concept of the people, of popular sovereignty, of the people ruling.

Here we are at a point where we have an opportunity to give people a chance—for what? For economic well-being. That is all we have been talking about. We are not talking about social habits or anything else. We are talking about a job.

So what I point out very frankly is that America cannot afford to discriminate against people on the basis of such false factors as their religion—for example, the Catholics, and we discriminate against a lot of them. The Jews, the Mexicans, the Spanish, the Italians, the Negroes—they have been discriminated against in state after state and locality after locality, and forced to take substandard labor when they are equipped to do good jobs. . . .

This is not communism. As a matter of fact, the one thing that is robbing us of our great moral weapon in this world today is the way we treat our minority groups in this country. . . .

[We] cannot afford to have American policy in a critical world situation dictated by the prejudices and the minority prejudices of a group anyplace in this country. The race problem is a fundamental international problem. We are losing face in Asia. We are losing it all over the world. . . .

We are not talking only about constitutional government. . . , we are talking about human rights. In this world today the issue of human rights is the number-one issue. That is what our fight is with communism, which denies human rights.

May I point out that every time Mr. Gromyko or Mr. Molotov wants to put an American representative back on his heels at the United Nations, they do what? They bring up the way we treat our minority groups.

When we proposed, for example, that we investigate the slave camps of Siberia, what was the immediate response? The immediate response was, "Let's investigate the poll tax, the lack of economic opportunity. Let's investigate the lynchings," if you please, "in parts of America."

What did our government representatives say? They said, "If that is the case, we had better have no investigation."

We are not just talking about the South. We are talking about people, American people. We are talking about people who are more American than almost anybody, except the people who came over on the *Mayflower*, almost native Americans. In fact, we are talking about the American Indian, native Americans, if you please.

Discrimination isn't a matter of Louisiana or Florida or South Carolina. It is a matter of Minnesota, North Dakota, New York, and Washington.

As Humphrey had pointed out on the NBC broadcast, opponents were trying to paint the FEPC proposal as communist-inspired, a great way to kill anything in that first year of the McCarthy era. Angered by these cheap tactics, Humphrey denounced such accusations in a speech on the Senate floor on May 16, 1950.

Mr. President, today the senator from Florida has stated to the Senate that this proposed legislation is communist-inspired, that the source of this legislation is the Communist Party.

However, to the contrary, I say that the source of this legislation is the Declaration of Independence, which says that "all men are created equal," and that "Governments are instituted among men. . . to secure these rights. . . [of] life, liberty, and the pursuit of happiness."

Mr. President, during the debate on this measure, when we get away from the present parliamentary maneuvering, I shall quote again, and at great length, from the report and from the hearings of the Senate committee in the 80th Congress and from the House committee hearings in the 81st Congress and I shall recite the testimony of persons of importance who apparently have been influenced by the desirability of the enactment of FEPC legislation.

I mention first some of the great spiritual leaders who have testified in behalf of this legislation. I say it is sheer distortion and adulteration of the facts and the evidence to try to label this kind of legislation as communist-inspired. . . .

Mr. President, for any member of the Senate to try by word or by the inflection of his voice to indicate that this legislation is communist-inspired is, in my opinion, blasphemy, and should be so labeled.

Believe me, Mr. President, there are other arguments than arguments based on rumor or smear or distortion to be made in connection with this legislative proposal. There are other arguments which can be made against FEPC, but FEPC is not to be attacked on the ground of alleging that it is communist-inspired or communist-supported. . . .

I know what I believe to be the truth. I believe that the truth is that in politics in America, when someone wishes to kill a proposal, he merely has to find that the communists have supported it. . . .

Mr. President, I have my own faith, and it is grounded in the Judeo-Christian democracy. If the communists happen to subscribe to it once in a while, I will not leave it. After all, the communists can be right once in a while, I suppose.

Mr. President, the facts in this matter are crystal clear. The facts are that the most responsible, the most enlightened, the most devoted citizens of the United States have appeared before the committees of Congress to testify in behalf of this legislation.

I resent the fact that every time a decent bill comes before the Senate, a bill which has good purposes and good objectives, some senator must drag in the communists.

On that basis, I suppose we will get rid of the American flag because it has red in it.

Mr. President, it is simply ridiculous. . . .

Our Message to Asia

When one considers that Hubert Humphrey very rarely became angry and bitter, the sight of the junior senator from Minnesota strongly condemning those who called the FEPC proposals a "communist plot" is even more striking.

Humphrey's anger, it should be noted, had as much to do with his own views on communism as they did with his strong advocacy of civil rights.

For Humphrey was a strong anticommunist who believed that the communist threat was very real. He also believed very strongly in the American system and felt that, in the long run, it would prevail over the forces of evil, as he once referred to communism.

Humphrey explained this view in a speech delivered on September 14, 1950, on the floor of the Senate.

. . . Like all Americans, the international crisis occupies most of my thinking and energies today. We are required to do what we hoped we might never have to do again—ask men and women to risk and possibly lose their lives to preserve freedom.

The preservation of freedom, however, requires more than military victory. We must convince the populations of the world that democratic ideals mean a fuller and richer life for them than they can achieve through the objectives of totalitarian communism.

It is in Asia that we are weakest—and I want to invite the attention of the Senate to this line—and it may well be in Asia that the future of the peace and the security of the world will be determined.

We are not only weakest in Asia militarily but we are weakest there ideologically. The American people at home understand the nature of the force against which we fight. The American people have had the opportunity to understand what we fight for, since we have for so many years now enjoyed the fruits of liberty and equality. We cannot, however, expect the underprivileged peoples of Asia, who will in the end determine the ultimate resolution of the conflict, to accept our word about the desirability of the world we seek and the validity of the principles we profess.

It is this which primarily concerns me. In other words, Mr. President, good as it is to have a great program of education and of information, such as the Voice of America, it is of great importance also that we understand that the underprivileged peoples of Asia, numbering more than a billion, are somewhat unacquainted either with the material or the political blessings which have made the American nation great. Our job is a tremendous one to explain the practical meaning of the principles of liberty and economic opportunity.

I know that the communists will exploit our every weakness. Falsehood, deceit, conspiracy, are commonplace weapons in the arsenal of totalitarian propaganda.

In our attempt to reach the minds and hearts of the peoples of Asia, we in the United States face a number of problems which the communists have exploited to the great benefit of themselves. . . .

First, the fact that our own colored peoples in some sections of America are relegated to second-class citizenship is so magnified and distorted abroad that the colored peoples of the world mistrust our words of good will.

The second is the fact that we of the Western world are associated frequently with the evils of colonial exploitation.

Third is the fact that any nation blessed with such an abundance of material resources and comforts easily becomes an object of envy and hostility on the part of those not so fortunate.

These factors, distorted and exaggerated by unscrupulous propaganda, place us at a decided disadvantage in the conflict of loyalties. . . .

Our message to the populations of the world, in all conscience and in all humility, should admit our weaknesses and frailties as American citizens. We frequently fall short of attaining our democratic objectives. We cannot deny our failure to achieve full civil rights for all our peoples, but we continually strive for them. . . .

It is difficult to set forth a specific program, equally applicable and equally attractive to all peoples. Democracy is not doctrinaire. We can make clear, however, to the best of our ability, that democracy is the technique by which people can reach their goals of human freedom and human happiness. We can make clear that self-government for all peoples and a peaceful world are our aims. . . .

If we lost this chance in Asia by our failure to adequately express our objectives and to outline a practical program, if we lose this chance, it will make little difference how many men we recruit for the army and the navy.

America does not have the manpower—nor does any other one nation have the manpower in military force alone—to control a billion people in a revolutionary movement in Asia as of this moment. . . .

If we fail in this effort, we shall have lost everything for which we have worked. It is my considered judgment that the peace of the world will not be decided in Western Europe, but that the peace of the world will be decided in the Far East, where we are least prepared, where we are the least understood, where we are the most unwelcome.

Therefore it is important that we mend our ways, that we project a program which is practical and meaningful; that somehow or other we find a bond of understanding and friendship with the millions of people who today are almost within the grasp of the communist conspiracy. . . .

A Tribute to Samuel Gompers

Nothing turned on Hubert Humphrey more than a great American success story. And we would be remiss if we closed this section on the 81st Congress without letting Humphrey say a few words about one of his favorite success stories: the life of Samuel Gompers.

The American success story is usually a story of accumulation of wealth. On this day I want to memorialize a success story of a different sort.

The hero of my success story was born a poor man. And died a poor man—that is, poor in worldly goods.

My man specialized in accumulating ideas and ideals. His all-consuming ideal was the vision of a great American labor movement. And, he lived long enough to see the fruition of that ideal. . . .

History reveals that in no democratic country has unionism had a harder row to hoe. When the forces of law and order, through the injunction and other devices, were not adequate to beat back the efforts of workers to form organizations of their own choosing, some employers resorted to an arsenal of savage tactics—strikebreakers recruited from the boweries and flophouses of the nation, spies hired through industrial espionage agencies, the militia, the National Guard, the tear-gas bombs—all were used in a primitive and savage attempt to keep men and women from organizing into unions.

In spite of this hostile environment, unions grew—slowly, it is true—but they grew with a kind of inexorable recognition of the rightness of their cause.

And if any man has the right to be called the chief architect of a movement as great and as strong as the American labor movement, it is that immigrant lad born in 1850, Samuel Gompers.

For almost seventy-five years before Gompers came upon the American labor scene, national federations had come and gone. The hostility of the environment and, in part, the bewildered idealism of some of the early labor leaders prevented their organizations from persevering.

It was Samuel Gompers who, by studying history and also what was happening around him, developed pragmatically the ingredients of effective labor organization. . . .

Democratic unionism owes much to Samuel Gompers. Gompers' experience in the Knights of Labor had taught him that no overall labor organization was wise enough and strong enough to deal with the infinite variety of problems that confronted unions in our complex industrial civilization. . . .

What was Gompers' essential genius? I think it was his penetrating understanding of the American culture and what a union had to have to survive and grow in that culture.

As an American, I take an enormous satisfaction in the Gompers story because it serves to give additional strength to the American heritage of equal opportunity irrespective of national origin, creed and color.

Sam Gompers had many strains in him. His family origins include German and Dutch influences. Rabbis and merchants are found in the Gompers' lineage. Samuel Gompers himself was born in England and received his first training in a Jewish free school where he learned to read the Talmud.

Upon his arrival in New York, he was thrown in with a circle of German socialists and unionists.

Yet these diverse strains produced through Gompers a form and shape of unionism peculiarly American and integrated in American life as nothing in the past history of labor had been.

The career of Samuel Gompers illuminates the way in which our cultural diversity has been a source of strength in building an effective democracy.

If the labor movement is one of the great pillars of our democracy, and I believe it is, Gompers, as the man who has given it shape, substance and meaning, deserves to be ranked as one of the social architects of our times.

3

The First Term

On the Offensive

When Hubert Humphrey came to Washington for the start of the 81st Congress in January 1949, they called him a comer. Now, as the 82nd Congress was about to open and a crop of new freshmen prepared to take their seats, Hubert Humphrey had begun to arrive.

With four years left to his first Senate term, the man from Minnesota was gaining a reputation as a hard-working, tough-talking senator with a national, liberal constituency.

During the past two years, he had served first as chairman and then as vice-chairman of the fledgling Americans for Democratic Action. He had championed liberal causes both on and off the Senate floor.

He had introduced legislation to abolish the electoral college, to allow for the direct election of the president and vice-president; he had introduced civil rights legislation, challenging both the Democrats and Republicans to live up to their parties' 1948 national platforms; he had introduced economic measures for the benefit of family farmers and small businessmen; he had fought hard for repeal of the Taft-Hartley Act, which was anathema to the nation's labor movement; he had introduced his first Medicare bill.

He had even been chosen to defend the president on a nationally broadcast radio address.

In the first week of May 1950, Republican Harold Stassen, a former governor of Minnesota, engaged in a bitter, personal attack on the administration and on President Truman himself. The speech was carried over the American Broadcasting Company's radio network.

On May 9, 1950, Humphrey used the same microphones to offer Mr. Truman's defense. It was a singular honor rarely bestowed on so junior a senator and it was a supreme compliment, too. Humphrey did not disappoint those who had reposed their confidence in him.

"Last week," the senator told the nation that spring evening, "those of you who were listening to this network were subjected to a most extraordinary attack on the president of the United States. Some of you have been sympathetic to the criticism of Mr. Truman's policies. Some of you may have shut off the radio. But I am sure that those who continued listening were shocked at the type of attack which was made.

"I, myself, was deeply shocked. I come from the state of Minnesota, of which I am justly proud. I am privileged to serve as a United States senator from that state. So it was especially difficult for me to realize that the slashing, irresponsible attack poured out over the air came from a man who at one time had been the governor of my state—Mr. Harold Stassen. . . .

"Effective and constructive criticism is essential to the preservation of democracy. Irresponsible and reckless criticism is destructive of democracy.

"But Mr. Stassen did not criticize—he vilified. Distasteful as his methods were. . . , [we] could have ignored these charges except for one thing: Mr. Stassen represents a pattern of political conduct and political strategy which the disgruntled Republican Party is trying to design out of the rags and tatters of their despair. . . . Their political sideshow has been repudiated. Having nothing of their own to offer the people of this country, in desperation they have decided to try to tear down what Mr. Truman has offered. . . .

"It is imperative that every American identify this Republican strategy for what it is—a strategy to deceive, to confuse, to bewilder and to frighten the American people.

"We have seen this strategy unfold itself under the guise of such terms as 'welfare state,' 'statism,' 'socialism,' 'regimentation' and 'communism.' These scare words have been hurled about with reckless irresponsibility. This is but the beginning of a frenzied effort to stampede the American people into a state of confusion and fear."

Humphrey, of course, was only too right. The Republican Party, out of power since 1933, was desperate. Harry Truman's up-from-the-bottom, experts-be-damned victory in 1948 helped turn that desperation into an obsession.

The party leaders wanted the power of the presidency so badly, they were willing to do almost anything to get it. And they did. They let Joe McCarthy loose on America while they cheered him on from the wings.

Such Republican stalwarts as Senators Everett McKinley Dirksen of Illinois, Owen Brewster of Maine, Henry Dworshak of Idaho, Karl Mundt of South Dakota, Styles Bridges of New Hampshire, Homer Capehart and William Jenner of Indiana, and even "Mr. Republican" himself, Ohio's Robert Taft, helped set the mood for McCarthy's dangerous farce. And, whenever the senator from Wisconsin got into trouble, they were there to bail him out.

McCarthy had only "discovered" communism in January 1950. He was two years away from reelection and, the way his fortunes were going, he was not *exactly a shoo-in. He needed an issue—a really big issue—to even have a chance for a second Senate term. He approached his friends for advice. Soon, he had a mighty nation at its knees, hailing their newfound savior.*

His friends had told him what he should have already known: People were building big reputations calling other people communists—especially when those "other people" worked for the Truman administration. Most notable among the anticommunist crusaders, he was told, was a young California congressman named Richard Nixon. Why didn't McCarthy take a crack at it, too?

The commies-under-the-covers crusade had been gaining momentum since the end of World War II. First, there had been the concessions made by President Roosevelt to Stalin at Yalta in early 1945. Obviously, some people said, these concessions were communist-inspired. That meant that communists were alive and well and living in the State Department. The unmasking of Alger Hiss (who was dumb enough to trap himself and smart enough to dupe liberals into making him a martyr) only "proved" that point, since Hiss was at Yalta with Roosevelt.

Then came the fall of Chiang Kai-shek's regime to the forces of Mao Tse-tung. Once again, the State Department's closet commies were to blame. It did not seem to matter that Chiang's repressive and corrupt regime had played a major role in the communist victory; it was the smear that counted.

The China Lobby helped to perpetuate the myth and the charges, although rooted in reality, grew louder and louder and wilder and wilder. One member of the House of Representatives on January 30, 1949, for example, rose to bitterly denounce the administration. He lamented the fact that "a sick Roosevelt, with the advice of General [George C.] Marshall and other chiefs of staff, gave the Kurile Islands, as well as the control of various strategic Chinese ports. . . to the Soviet Union." Marshall had been army chief of staff at the time of the Yalta conference; between 1947 and 1949 he served as secretary of state and was Truman's emmissary to China before the communist victory. As such, he was a favorite whipping boy of the witch-hunters.

The congressman waxed eloquent as he castigated "the indifference, if not the contempt, with which the State Department and the president [Truman] treated the wife of the head of the Nationalist government, who was then fighting for a Free China, Madame Chiang Kai-shek. . . ." This, the congressman declared, "was the final chapter in this tragic story."

The young member of the House told his audience, "We must search out and spotlight those who bear the responsibility for our present predicament." One of the ironies in this call for yet another witchhunt was the setting of the speech: Salem, Massachusetts, where they used to make a practice of hunting witches and then burning them at the stake.

"Our policy in China," declared the congressman, "has reaped the whirlwind. . . . So concerned were our diplomats and their advisers, the [Owen] Lattimores. . . , with the imperfections of the diplomatic system in China after twenty years of war and tales of corruption in high places, that they lost sight of our tremendous stake in noncommunist China."

McCarthy, in testimony to a Senate committee two years later, charged that Lattimore was the number-one Soviet spy in the United States. Several days later, he insisted that what he meant to say was Lattimore gave bad advice to the State Department; nothing more. McCarthy got the whole idea from this and similar speeches.

"What our young men saved," the young congressman passionately concluded, "our diplomats and our president have frittered away."

Of course, Republicans were almost expected to say such things in 1949. It had become the party line, so to speak. But this congressman was no Republican. He was, in fact, a Democrat from a prestigious New England family with a long history of service to the Democratic Party. His father had served in the Roosevelt administration as head of the Securities and Exchange Commission. He himself had eyes on a seat in the Senate and beyond.

So, if John F. Kennedy could say the kinds of things that Richard Nixon was saying, why couldn't Joe McCarthy pick up the ball, too—and run even farther with it? (Only after McCarthy was long gone from the scene did Kennedy seek to associate himself with the enemies of McCarthyism. Fortunately for his career, the future president was in the hospital on the day the Senate voted to censure McCarthy, and he was not forced to make the choice he had so carefully avoided until then.)

On February 12, 1950, a little over a month after finding his big issue, Joe McCarthy appeared before the Ohio County Women's Club in Wheeling, West Virginia. His subject: the "Communist Conspiracy."

There was only one problem. As someone who only just learned that such a conspiracy existed, he did not know too much about it. So he searched the Congressional Record, found a couple of Richard Nixon's speeches there, changed a few words every now and then ("espionage agents" became "spies," etc.) and proceeded to wow the women of Wheeling.

One thing Nixon's speeches did not contain, however, was the grabber, the gimmick that would give McCarthy national headlines. He found that, too, in the Congressional Record. It was a June 1946 letter from then Secretary of State James Byrnes (a former senator himself) stating that, of the 3,000 government employees who wound up in the State Department after their wartime agencies went out of business, a careful screening process had recommended that 284 not be permanently employed. Of those 284 persons, 79 had been fired and the rest were kept on pending the results of further screening.

That meant that 205 persons who failed to meet the standards during the original screening process were still in the State Department in June 1946.

Another item McCarthy found in the Congressional Record involved a security leak at the State Department (the Amerasia Case), in which 108 employees were investigated. According to the item McCarthy read, 57 of these employees were still at the State Department in 1948.

McCarthy had found what he needed. His only problem now was which figure to use: 205 or 57? To this day, no one really knows what he decided.

According to a rough draft of the speech which McCarthy handed over to radio station WWVA in Wheeling, the senator made the following charge during his speech:

"While I cannot take the time to name all the men in the State Department who have been named as members of the Communist Party and members of a spy ring, I have here in my hand a list of 205 that were known to the secretary of state as being members of the Communist Party and are still working and shaping the policy of the State Department." (Emphasis ours.)

In his speech to the women, McCarthy claimed later, he actually used the number 57, saying that 205 was a typographical error.

Needless to say, most of the 205 in the WWVA copy were no longer with the State Department in 1950; the same was true for the 57. Nor was what he held up to the audience really a "list," at least as far as anyone can determine. (The Wheeling Intelligencer insisted that McCarthy had used the number 205 during the speech; the senator conveniently "lost" the list upon his return to Washington as well as the "final draft" of his speech.

McCarthy had played the numbers game and had won. In succeeding *days, he managed to avoid challenges that he produce his evidence. Instead, his charges grew and so did his popularity. It seemed that everytime someone sought to corner McCarthy, he would counter with a new, more ridiculous charge, like the one about Lattimore.*

The public, unfortunately, was buying it, lock, stock and laundry list. After all, responsible politicians from Richard Nixon to John Kennedy to Robert Taft had been saying all along that there was something wrong with the way the State Department had been playing up to the communists. There had to be more than just faces that were red down there in Foggy Bottom.

The Gallup Poll soon showed that at least 50 percent of the American people thought Joe McCarthy was doing a fine job. More joined the bandwagon every day.

Republicans who had kept their distance from McCarthy tried to get their pictures taken with him. Democrats, who in normal times would have moved heaven and Earth to force McCarthy to put up or shut up, suddenly shut up themselves. Only a few—a very rare and special few—had the courage to stand up to McCarthy early in the game.

Hubert Humphrey was one of those men. In speech after speech, on the floor and off, he challenged McCarthy to produce the list, the speech, the names—whatever he could find that would prove the charges which were undermining the government in a far more effective manner than anything the communists could do.

Exactly one year after the Wheeling speech, on February 12, 1951, the issue still remained unresolved. The numbers game was still Topic A and no proof had been forthcoming. McCarthy's popularity was still growing. To be anti-McCarthy was now a dangerous thing.

Humphrey was a staunch anticommunist and he had fought communists wherever he found them. He even went looking for them, albeit in a responsible manner. But McCarthy had taken the smoke of the communist conspiracy— there was plenty of it, too—and turned it into a raging fire that was threatening to destroy both government and society.

In an act of political courage (which by that time had become almost commonplace for Humphrey) the senator rose to address his colleagues on that Lincoln's Birthday. He never mentioned McCarthy by name, however; he had learned from his attack on Senator Byrd that one never used a senator's name if it could be avoided. In this case, it could be. Everyone already knew it.

. . . Without looking into the merits or demerits of what has transpired during the past year, I wish to say that the greatest tragedy that can befall the cause of human freedom in this critical hour of world history is to undermine faith in representative government, to undermine faith in the elected representative of the people, and the apparatus of government which serves our nation. . . .

It appears to me that fear and suspicion is growing throughout the country. American freedom cannot live in an environment filled with suspicion, and American political institutions cannot live in an environment filled with fear.

It is true of those of my colleagues with whom I have talked about the matter that, unfortunately, much of the mail received from home during the past year has indicated that there is doubt and great suspicion in the hearts and minds of thousands and thousands of people.

It is true that the attack of the junior senator from Wisconsin has been very effective politically, but it has been very unfortunate morally, and in terms of the preservation of free institutions.

I have no doubt that politically, speaking in terms of elections, it has been a powerful and perhaps successful attack, but I think what is more important to keep in mind is not whether this kind of attack is successful politically, but what it means in the long run, for the solvency, the security and the stability of free political, economic and cultural institutions.

Unfortunately, it seems to me, there is today a psychosis of fear in our nation, at a time when our people should be imaginative and creative, at a time when we should have people in government who are trying to think out new answers to meet new problems.

I would say that it is a tragedy that members of the Senate permitted this to happen.

Many letters have come to my office on this subject. Last evening I took home with me between two and three thousand letters which have come to my office in the last few weeks on the issue of foreign policy. In many of the letters I read of the lack of trust and lack of faith in our secretary of state, in our president, in our government, arising from charges made on the floor of the United States Senate.

The question before us is a simple one, as was the question a year ago—namely, are there 205 communists, known to the secretary of state [Dean Acheson], in the State Department? If 205 is the wrong number, the next question is, are there 57, or are there 7, or are there any?

If the charges are not true, then I suggest that someone should refrain from further comment about the alleged subversion in this government, because the best way in the world to break down the spirit of the American people and their morale, the best way to destroy the faith of the American people in the entire mobilization program, the best way to sell out this country to the communists, is to make false charges—any kind of false charges, whether false charges of corruption or subversion or whatever else it may be.

Mr. President, this is a time when we need to believe in democracy. Our procedures should conform to the democratic spirit.

No one in the world has a greater responsibility to live and breathe for democracy and to do his utmost to make it work than the members of the United States Senate or of the House of Representatives. . . .

We are the ones who at this hour should lead in asserting a steadfast belief in democracy, and we should do so by exercising leadership, both political and moral.

So let me suggest to the senators on both sides of the aisle that charges be documented so that they will be able to stand up in a court of law. If there is no such evidence and such documentation, the charges never should be made, because to destroy faith in our goverment is to strike a blow deep in the heart of freedom; and to destroy the name of a man is to perform the most immoral, un-Christian, indecent act which possibly could be done, for, Mr. President, after all, the name, the reputation, and the character of a man are his most precious heritage. . . .

Anticommunism Is Not a Dirty Word

Challenging McCarthy, however, was not enough. Certainly it was important to prove that McCarthy and his cohorts were a pack of irresponsible, cruel and evil men. But it could not be done at the expense of fighting communism.

For there was a communist threat and it had to be beaten back. Communists, for instance, were trying to take over labor unions. Humphrey, a member of the Senate Labor Committee at the time, held hearings to expose the plots and plotters.

Communists were also trying to put on a benevolent face by advocating such issues as labor reform, civil rights, health care, and the like—issues with which they could gain supporters but for which they had no real concern.

The international communist conspiracy had to be stopped—and that had to be done in a responsible manner by responsible people. But just as his repeated challenges to McCarthy had gone unheeded, so for the most part did his pleas for a responsible anticommunist crusade. No liberal wanted to be associated with an issue that Joe McCarthy had anything to do with.

In 1954, when "McCarthy was at his raging peak," as Humphrey later described it, the senator from Minnesota sponsored a bill designed to take the communist conspiracy out of the hearing room and put it into the courtroom, where evidence could be weighed, accusers confronted, witnesses cross-examined, guilt or innocence determined by a jury of twelve citizens who were not out to build their political reputations.

The bill made membership in the Communist Party a crime. Anyone accused of being a communist could sue for libel if the charge were false.

Every constitutional safeguard possible was included in the bill so as not to violate anyone's legal rights. For the Senate's conservatives, the bill was too liberal; they voted it down in favor of a harsher measure introduced by Senator Pat McCarran of Nevada. For the nation's liberals, the bill was a dangerous blow to civil liberties; some never forgave Humphrey until the day he died. It was just enough to cost Humphrey the presidency fourteen years later.

Humphrey, of course, knew the risks, as always, but his political fortunes were not important; the country's fortunes were. He knew the risks, but he still introduced the bill; he still challenged McCarthy at every opportunity; he still challenged liberals to take back the anticommuism crusade and put it into responsible hands.

One such challenge to the nation's liberals came on May 23, 1953, at the sixth annual convention of Americans for Democratic Action, in Washington, D.C.

To understand the courage Humphrey showed, consider this: Ten months later, Edward R. Murrow had condemned McCarthy on his nationwide "See It Now" television show. Following the program, CBS News anchorman Don Hollenbeck said on camera that he agreed with Murrow. The hate mail Hollenbeck received and the unrelenting newspaper campaign against him finally drove him to suicide.

Here, in part, is what Humphrey told the ADA in May 1953.

Those who believe in the democratic faith—in its traditional rights and liberties, responsibilities and privileges—can never cease in their struggle against communism.

Democracy and totalitarianism are mortal enemies. It is to us to be the brave and the strong. It is our privilege and sacred obligation to be the champions of liberal faith, and never to compromise our principles with the subtle but ruthless foes of human liberty.

We must be ever on guard. The modern totalitarian is a cunning and devious character. The strategy and the tactics of this worldwide communist conspiracy shift and change constantly. . . .

Our society is deeply concerned about communism—and rightfully so. There is no greater threat to our political and moral standards. There is no greater threat to the peace of the world and to the hope and future of all mankind.

ADA came into being in 1946 and 1947 because it was so concerned about communism—and rightfully so. The mainstream of American liberalism has been fighting bolshevism and communism ideologically and politically before many of the self-styled anticommunists of today were even aware of the nature of the threat. And they have been doing so without adopting the methods and attitudes of totalitarianism. . . .

The American liberal community, acting in partnership

with the New Deal and Fair Deal, worked to strengthen the fabric of democracy by knitting and weaving into a pattern a program of improved educational facilities, better housing, human equality, health care, insurance, abundant public power and many other programs.

These bold and progressive policies have so effectively strengthened our democracy and economy that the threat of political communism in the United States is at an all-time low. The Communist Party is shrinking to a noisy and neurotic group of politically ineffective diehards.

With this emphasis on deeds rather than words, American liberalism succeeded in virtually destroying the appeal of communism as an internal political threat to the democratic institutions of the United States. But in this emphasis of deeds rather than words, we allowed others to usurp for themselves the title of anticommunism. Knowing as we do that the most effective anticommunist program is a prodemocracy program, many American liberals tended to shy away from the oversimplified use of the term "anticommunism." Thus, we abdicated the term and the title to the irresponsibles.

This has created serious problems for us and for the nation. It has allowed the irresponsibles to distort the meaning of terms and the meaning of truth by identifying communism with its archenemy, liberalism. And it served to identify in the minds of too many American people anticommunism with irresponsibles who had no real understanding of communism, and hence could not effectively oppose it.

The fact that men in the United States Senate who assume for themselves the mantle of anticommunism can ask our nation to abandon its allies and go it alone is a sign of the political immaturity and political danger of abandoning anticommunism to those who have no real understanding of its operations.

The challenge to the liberals of today is to once again reassert the initiative in developing, fostering and strengthening a program of anticommunism and a program for democracy which is mature, realistic and effective. . . .

Leadership calls for courage, integrity and determination.

The liberal opposition today is determined to put aside partisan politics in support of a mature program which understands the nature of communism and is prepared to meet its threat to democratic institutions and to the democratic way of life.

The president can have our support for his foreign policy as that policy is stated in his speeches. He will not have our support, however, for the foreign policy represented by some of his spokesmen in the Congress and too frequently represented in the deeds of those who claim to represent him.

If the president places the unity of his own party as the number-one objective of his administration, then the kind of leadership that the democratic world needs today will not be forthcoming.

Party unity within the Republican Party on the issues of foreign policy can only come at the cost of a positive and effective foreign policy. The president must be willing to pay the price of alienating the irresponsibles of his own party in order to rally the support of the American people and of the Free World.

This is not too dear a price for so important a cause. The unity of a political party is, indeed, a little thing as compared to the unity of free men in their struggle against the oppression of totalitarian power.

Therefore, tonight, let us dedicate ourselves to a program of enlightenment—enlightenment as to the nature of communism and its threat to the world. But equally important, enlightenment as to the true meaning of democracy and the hope that it offers to the world.

Hackneyed as the expression may seem, this is the time for greatness. We can survive with no less.

Cockeyed and in Reverse

To Hubert Humphrey, there was something terribly wrong in the world. The warmakers were hailed as the harbingers of peace while the peacemakers were condemned as the spreaders of war; the slavemasters were looked upon as the champions of liberty while liberty's children were thought of as oppressors; the true imperialists were cloaked in the mantle of people's liberation while anti-imperialists were portrayed as land-grabbing, power-hungry despots.

It was a world where good was bad and bad was good—and it should never have been allowed to happen. Line up communism and democracy side by side, Humphrey would often say, and compare the two. Then you will see which was the force of evil and which the force of good.

True, there were flaws in the democratic system; that was so even in the United States. But those flaws can be corrected by the people in a free and open society. The people have very little to say about anything under communism, much less about correcting flaws.

That is what Humphrey meant when he told the ADA in May 1953 that what was needed was "a program of enlightenment." It was an old theme for him by then, but it was one of which he never tired for as long as he lived. It made no sense, he said, for the United States to allow the communists to make political points throughout the world by calling America's virtues their own and ascribing their evils to America.

There was a right way and a wrong way to fight communism, Humphrey often declared. We were fighting it the wrong way—and we were losing. If we would only fight it the right way, he said, communism would not stand a chance.

Humphrey explained this position to the Senate in a March 22, 1951, speech.

. . . Mr. President, I wish to direct my remarks today to what we have been doing in terms of informational and inspirational leadership. I do so because something has happened which is almost incredible and unbelievable.

Let me point out what I mean. We have a great nation, the

United States of America. The nation is predicated essentially, through its history, on great religious and spiritual resources. The whole early history of America relates to religious freedom and the spiritual strength of our people.

The Mayflower compact, Thanksgiving Day, the Declaration of Independence—everything one can think of in the history of this nation from its very beginning has a great spiritual aspect to it.

Our nation has based its entire system of government and philosophy of life upon Judaic-Christian principles. They are the principles which are found in the Old Testament and in the New Testament.

I think it is very fitting and important that on the day before Good Friday, in this holiest of holy weeks, which will be climaxed on Easter, we should give consideration to our spiritual resources and heritage.

These principles include not only humanitarian service, but a recognition of the dignity of man and his right to life, liberty, and the pursuit of happiness. These Judaic-Christian principles are based upon the principle of peace. . . .

On the other hand, there is the communist or totalitarian philosophy. The whole principle of this philosophy is force, brutality, and enslavement. It is a philosophy that repudiates honor, dignity, kindness, love, and peace. Totalitarianism is organized war. It is planned force. It is the very antithesis of the Judaic-Christian ethic. All sensible people know this.

And yet, Mr. President, international communism has appropriated for itself the honor of being the disciple of peace. To be sure, that is a travesty upon words. In religious terms the anti-Christs have, in their hypocrisy, taken on the mantle of Christians. The persecutors are now posing as the liberators. The modern slave traders appropriate to themselves the honor of emancipators.

This is so incredibly paradoxical that it shocks one's intelligence.

Why do I say this? Because I have been watching the developments in the international conferences. Yesterday's newspapers reporting on the deputy foreign ministers' meeting told a recurring story. Mr. Gromyko, the representative of the Soviets, grabbed the headlines by proposing disarmament under international inspection. Yet some of our colleagues in this body. . . and many others have called upon our government to state our purposes, objectives, and goals, and to be the agent of peace in the world. They recognize, as I do, that we must have strength and security, which can come at this hour only through certain defensive measures.

Our government has been asked to dramatize once and for all that we are not interested in planning for war, but that we appeal to the peoples of the world for peace.

If there is anything that anyone in the world wants today, it is peace. . . . How has it happened that the Soviets have been able to assume the initiative? The Soviet system is a complete repudiation of the hope of peace. By its philosophy, its government, and its practices it denies every principle of peace. Then, how does it get the headlines in behalf of peace?

It seems to me that this is the result of a failure on our own part to understand the mainsprings of our own philosophy. We have placed the emphasis not on our strength—which is humanitarianism, kindness and peace—but upon that which we abhor: namely, force, war, and power.

The whole world seems to be cockeyed and in reverse. Those who by their history and tradition are the peacemakers are now being branded in many areas of the world as warmongers; and those who by their own words and their own history are the true warmakers are taking upon themselves the role of peacemakers. . . .

The people of the world are confused by our objectives. Where are we heading? What is the purpose of all this sacrifice, and all the military and economic mobilization?

The American people want to know the same. It is here that we are weak. Not only do the people in other lands have uncertainty as to our goals and ultimate objectives, but our people at home are bewildered and confused. . . .

Apparently, we have not made it abundantly clear that our

entire mobilization is for defense. . . . We do not seek war; we seek peace. We strive to expand the area of freedom.

How do we state our objectives? First. . . , we must educate our people and the people of the world as to just what communism is, how it operates, how it grows. Once we have done that, we need to get at the roots of the disease, not the symptoms. The symptoms are aggression, pressure, tension, unrest, violence. But the roots of communism, the soil in which it grows, the seeds from which it springs, are poverty, injustice, frustration, fear, malnutrition. . . .

I think it would be a tragedy if we permitted the communist disciples of brutality and of fear, war and violence, to run around with the olive branch looking like peacemakers. In fact, it is something which I think borders on the extreme of hypocrisy and of paradox.

Here we are in this holiest of holy seasons; yet we, the people of a great nation, as well as the people of all Christendom, are permitting the communist leaders who have denied the existence of God, who do not believe in humanity for humanity's sake, to parade as the friends of freedom.

This is something that goes against my grain. I speak out in protest. I think it is time that those of us who say we believe in freedom and democracy should act in accordance with our belief.

A Matter of Civilian Control

Hubert Humphrey had called those who helped create Joe McCarthy and who continued to give him life the "irresponsibles."

For the most part, they were good men and loyal Americans, as equally dedicated to democracy as Humphrey was, even if they did not share his views of what democracy should be. They were men like Senator Robert Taft and House Republican leader Joe Martin. But they allowed partisan considerations to lead them into those irresponsible acts which nearly tore a great nation apart. The greater the specter of domestic communist subversion, they theorized, the better the chances to uproot the Democrats from the White House they had held since 1933.

These men acted on political impulse while casting aside logic, reason and good old common sense. They considered only the short-term benefits without ever looking beyond to the long-term effects of their actions.

Nowhere was this more evident than in their reaction to the dismissal of General Douglas MacArthur by Harry Truman on April 11, 1951.

When Truman, "as president and commander-in-chief of the United States military forces," acted to replace MacArthur "as Supreme Commander, Allied Powers; Commander-in-Chief, United Nations Command; Commander-in-Chief, Far East; and Commanding General, U.S. Army, Far East" at the height of the Korean War, it had nothing to do with subversive elements in the administration or with Truman's suddenly going soft on communism.

It had everything to do with the survival of a system of government established by the Constitutional Convention of 1787.

It was the president, with the advice and consent of the Senate, who set the nation's foreign policy; it was the president, as commander-in-chief of the armed forces, who decided when and how those forces would be used. No other person— and certainly no military person—had the right to usurp those powers.

But that was what MacArthur had tried to do. He had attempted to usurp the powers of the president of the United States and he had to be stopped. Truman was forced to act. MacArthur was out and the country, it seemed, went wild.

The general, corncob pipe at the ready, returned to the United States to an unprecedented hero's welcome. State legislatures and city councils passed resolutions condemning Truman; telegrams poured into Washington by the thousands each day, calling the president names and demanding his removal from office; four times the amount of ticker tape was showered on MacArthur's head in New York as was tossed on Dwight Eisenhower a few years earlier; the Gallup Poll showed that 69 percent of the American people were four-square behind MacArthur. The rebel general was even invited to address a joint session of Congress on April 19, eight days after his removal.

Most politicians from both parties joined in the praises that were heaped on MacArthur; few bothered to consider that just maybe the nation owed Harry Truman a tremendous debt of gratitude. And for good reason: It was considered political suicide to be found in Truman's corner on this one.

Hubert Humphrey was one of those who saw the MacArthur firing for what it was and, political consequences be damned, he made it very clear where he stood.

Humphrey jumped right into the fight without even bothering to wait for the furor to die down first. The following remarks were made by Humphrey in St. Paul, Minnesota, on April 14, just three days after MacArthur's dismissal had been announced.

. . . The real issue involved in the president's dismissal of General MacArthur is one basic to American constitutional government. The president, under the mandate of our Constitution, is commander-in-chief. The president, under the political tradition of our republic, is responsible for foreign policy.

It has been a basic principle of representative government that the military is subordinate to the civilian. The military officers and services are the servants of the republic, not the master. The action of the president is within the tradition of American constitutional government.

The issue is: Shall military commanders dictate and formulate American policy or shall they carry out that policy? In this instance, the issue was even more broad because the military action in Korea was not only an American action but one under the overall supervision of the United Nations.

President Truman, as all presidents before him, demanded that foreign policy be established by the elected representatives of the people, not by any one or a few generals, able as they may be. Once we lose civilian control over foreign and military policy, then we lose the fabric of our democracy.

In dismissing General MacArthur, President Truman had no other choice. The general—a brilliant and able military leader, a great man in his own right and by his own record—openly disagreed with our government's policy and with that of the United Nations. He disagreed with the recommendations of the secretary of defense, General Marshall and the Joint Chiefs of Staff. No government can exist so divided in policy since no government can be guided by two inconsistent foreign programs.

General MacArthur, as an individual, has a perfect right to disagree with our government's foreign policy, but as a general subordinate to his commander-in-chief, he has neither the right nor the prerogative to formulate and attempt to carry out his own program and to disregard the program established by the government.

While I have a high regard for General MacArthur and his abilities, I am not prepared to accept his judgment over that of the president, the secretary of state, the overwhelming majority of the representatives in the United Nations, the majority in Congress, the secretary of defense and the combined chiefs of staff.

It should be clearly recognized that the bold statements of General MacArthur were causing great concern in other nations and among our allies. . . .

The Dignity of Man

Communism was the big issue during Humphrey's first term and he was as determined to make the best use of it as he was to do battle with it.

There were other issues that needed consideration—important issues like health care, civil rights, labor relations, unemployment, fair trade, and the like. But his colleagues—particularly the conservative ones who generally opposed such legislation anyway—felt that anything that did not have to do with the battle against communism was not worth bothering about.

So Humphrey turned the tables on them. In speech after speech on issue after issue, the man from Minnesota invoked the anticommunist crusade to win support for one piece of legislation after another.

On June 25, 1951, for example, Humphrey rose to introduce his civil rights package for the year. In effect, he told the senators as he placed the bill before them, there was no better weapon with which to fight the forces of depravity than the passage of a bill designed to promote human dignity.

Mr. President, once again I stand before this great democratic body, the United States Senate, to make a plea for an end to discrimination against American citizens because of their race, religion, color, or national origin.

Again I ask the Congress for action on a legislative program for human rights, and I humbly join with a distinguished array of my colleagues in presenting such a program.

I do this today for a reason. I do this today rather than tomorrow or last month or a week from now because it is essential to dramatize, in every way we know how, the historic importance of the anniversaries which this day represents:

—One year ago today, the communist forces of North Korea invaded the Republic of South Korea.

—Ten years ago today, the first national Fair Employment Practices Committee came into existence by Executive Order of our late president, Franklin Delano Roosevelt.

The relationship between these two events is an important one for us to understand. This relationship affects the very roots of our national security.

We have been drawn into a global struggle against the communistic and totalitarian forces of Stalinism. All over the world, from central Europe through the Near East and into Asia, we stand opposed to a ruthless group of men who espouse doctrines denying the dignity of men and their right to develop to the best what is within themselves.

The North Korean attack on South Korea, on June 25, 1950, represented an attempt by the totalitarian world to begin its program of world conquest by the use of force. Our support through the United Nations in resisting the communist invaders in Korea has symbolized our resolve to resist communist attack wherever it may occur.

Thus, on both the military and political fronts, we stand as opponents of communist aggression.

However, it is on the political, or in a more comprehensive sense, the ideological front that we are weakest. The conflict with Stalinism is not merely of a military character. Equally important, it is political or ideological in nature.

Ideologically, as the great protagonists of democracy and freedom, we stand opposed to those doctrines which enslave and reduce men to mere machines. We believe in the inherent dignity and worthwhileness of man, that man is an end in himself, that only in a genuinely free society can man attain his true nature.

We believe that, given equality of opportunity, each individual irrespective of color, religion, national origin or race, can realize his true self. These are the great values for which we are currently engaged in the struggle against communism.

Yet, while we may be winning the conflict in military terms, I believe—and this is a view supported and confirmed by the observations of many—that we are losing ground on the ideological front. We are in danger of losing the political and ideological fight for many reasons, but I believe that the most important of them lies in the fact that there are occasional practices at home which conflict with the values in which we believe and which we are trying to spread abroad.

Newspapermen, travelers and others who have visited many areas of the world report that communism at present has its greatest appeal in those areas of the world inhabited by dark-skinned peoples. These areas—Africa, the Near East, Southwest Asia, Asia itself—house two-thirds of the world's population, a population which, in the main, is non-Caucasian. Needless to say, China is already gone and sections of Southeast Asia may be on the way.

To these people our exhortations about democracy and equality of rights seem hollow and empty; they are not taken seriously. How can they be? They point to the peoples of dark skin such as Negroes, Oriental-Americans, Mexican-Americans, Indians, and others who all too often are treated as second-class citizens right here in the United States. They do not have equality of opportunity—for jobs, for education, for medical care, for housing.

While much has been done in the past decade to guarantee these rights to all Americans, there is much that has yet to be done. The extent to which these things are not done does irreparable harm to our international policy.

Soviet propagandists point daily to the discrepancies between the American theory of democracy and its practice at home. . . .

While these statements are distortions, particularly because they leave the wholly false impression of unbridled discrimination in America, nevertheless the fact that discrimination against our colored citizens exists at all makes it difficult for the United States to refute absolutely the statements made by the Moscow radio. . . .

Soviet propaganda has done an effective job of putting American democracy on the defensive. It seems to be a sad commentary that Americans have to be apologetic for the weaknesses in our great democracy, that so far we have been unable to face the Soviet propaganda machine squarely, disproving absolutely the statements which it makes. . . .

Mr. President, we spend a great deal of time in America and elsewhere in the world pointing out that the United States is a democratic nation. Let me say right here that there can be no legitimate question that this is a true and accurate statement. America is a great democracy, as any fair and observant person will know who goes into its highways and byways to talk to its people and to observe its activity.

The people of America believe in freedom—believe that all alike should have the opportunity to develop themselves in the manner in which they choose and to the degree which is within them.

These are not idle words or false words or half-truths. They are words that reflect the fundamental attitude and deep feeling of those who live within the confines of the United States and who know what it means to be part of a society which is based on these values.

Deep within the individuals who make up our democracy lies a sense of justice which no one who has any understanding at all of what this means can disparage or treat lightly. . . .

It is only in the Congress, particularly in the Senate of the United States, that the area of civil rights progress in America is ignored.

It is altogether fitting and proper that on this day of commemoration and anniversary, the Senate of the United States may make itself again aware of the need to face up to its responsibilities. In the interest of the continued free existence of our nation, we must blunt the criticism leveled against our country and, indeed, use our dedication to civil rights as a weapon to turn against the enemies of the free world.

For all these reasons, we have chosen this day to present to the Congress a program for civil rights fully consistent with the traditions and wishes of the American people. . . .

The "Little People"

For some reason that defies comprehension, we ordinary mortals who must toil for our daily bread are called the "little people," the "common people," and so on.

The obvious implication, of course, is that we are unimportant (except at election time) and whatever attention is paid to us by those of greater stature and station is truly more than we deserve.

But not as far as Hubert Humphrey was concerned. The United States was the "little people," and their needs came first.

Quite naturally, lots of politicians were like that. Those "big issues" that benefited the "little people" translated into "lots of votes." Befriending the common horde was politically wise.

But again, not as far as Hubert Humphrey was concerned. If there was a wrong that needed righting, he would set about righting it even if no one asked him to and if no one even cared. Take, for example, a bill he introduced in the Senate in June 1951, designated S. 1575.

Some months ago I was disturbed by a decision of the Supreme Court ruling that because of a legal technicality, the widow of a Navy petty officer was required to start all over again in her once-successful effort to win a $1,365 lawsuit against the Navy. That legal technicality came about through no fault of her own but was related to the fact that the Navy had appointed a new paymaster general and her court papers had failed to name that new appointee.

The Supreme Court, of course, undoubtedly ruled in accordance with the proper interpretation of the law. It is not for me to take issue with that. It does appear to me, however, that it would be most unfair to allow a statute to exist on the books which would interfere with the application of justice. A person who deserves a judgment on the basis of the merits of the case should not be prevented from receiving judgment simply because the holder of office who is nominally being sued as a representative of the government has been succeeded by another official.

The bill, which I introduced today, is designed to correct that inequity by amending the United States Code to provide that when a government officer dies or otherwise ceases to hold office and is a party to legal action, he shall be deemed to have been substituted by his successor.

Union for Survival

McCarthyism and communism were not the only important issues that had to be confronted in the early 1950s. There was the war in Korea, the dawning of the nuclear age, armament and disarmament, a divided Germany, economic reform, electoral reform, the influx of immigrants to the United States and European recovery.

European recovery was of major concern to Humphrey. He was a strong supporter of the Marshall Plan—President Truman's massive program to rebuild what World War II had destroyed—but he knew that was not enough. No amount of money, no amount of aid could possibly do the whole job. What was needed was a joint effort on the part of the Europeans themselves; not each country working independently of the other, but working together in a common effort with a common purpose.

Humphrey did not originate the idea, but he did support it. And so did the Europeans. To many of them, a United States of Europe was the best way to rebuild after the ravages of war, to safeguard against a future war and to present a unified front against possible Soviet aggression.

The Schuman Plan was a step in that direction. On May 9, 1950, French Foreign Minister Robert Schuman proposed a common market for coal and steel in Europe. The plan, Schuman suggested, would forge an organic link between France and Germany, Europe's traditionally bitterest enemies. And it would join the nations of Europe in a limited economic union that would pave the way for even greater things.

Great Britain decided not to take part, but six other countries—France, West Germany, Italy, Belgium, the Netherlands and Luxembourg—in 1951 signed the Treaty Establishing the European Coal and Steel Community. The treaty went into effect in July 1952. It was the beginning of what five years later would become the Common Market.

In February 1952, Humphrey offered his views on the Schuman Plan in an article in Europe Today and Tomorrow; International Bulletin of the European Movement.

I think it is generally accepted that Americans have a great stake in Western Europe. We are bound to this strategic and historic area by ties of family, custom, law, economies, and politics.

Even those who by their words and actions seek to isolate America from the Western European area find it impossible to ignore the close bonds between our peoples.

The policy of our government. . . places us in intimate association and partnership with the Western European countries. Whether we like it or not, their problems are ours. Our actions influence their political and economic policies. Their accomplishments or failures either strengthen or weaken our position. We are as one, bound together in a common purpose for the foreseeable future. It is because of this evident fact of partnership, formalized by the North Atlantic Treaty Organization and. . . other policies and programs, that every American must take a keen interest in the Europe of today and tomorrow.

It is imperative that Americans and Europeans alike recognize the nature of the menace that seeks to destroy them, namely, totalitarian communism. Whether we like it or not, Russia has integrated her empire into one political and economic unit. She has done this through force and brutality, but she has done it. She brings to bear upon Western Europe and the Free World the full weight and force of this tremendous empire under one command and with one objective.

It appears to me that you cannot defeat a totalitarian monster by having uncoordinated, fragmented, separate and distinct independent political and economic units.

Western Europe is potentially much stronger than the Soviet system. Western Europe, plus the United States, is immeasurably stronger in terms of industrial capacity, natural resources, and the skill and ability of its people than the Soviet satellite system.

But we are not arguing theories, nor can international communism under the direction of the Kremlin be defeated or checked by the eloquent logic of sound theory. The Soviet system represents power, the power of military might, industrial production, and the power of an idea.

This power faces to the West as well as to the East. It presses hard upon the countries of Western Europe. It is a power mass pressing upon a loosely knit coalition of independent nation states—independent and relatively uncoordinated economic systems.

This is the *realpolitik* of Western Europe. These are the real facts of the political realities of the European continent. On the one hand, there is a regimented, organized, disciplined and directed power. On the other, there is a free, disorganized, disunited and semicoordinated group of nations. . . .

Europe has made great strides since the end of World War II. Here is an area that was devastated by bomb and fire, its communication system wrecked, its capital dissipated, and its resources exploited and severely damaged. This was the picture of Europe at the end of World War II. It was to this set of circumstances that American economic aid was directed.

The rehabilitation of Western Europe is truly miraculous. Out of the ashes cities have been rebuilt. Industry is back into production. The people are at work. But there is something wrong and that something must be corrected unless the investment which America and her partners in Western Europe have made to date in European recovery is to be lost. . . .

Europe needs a new deal, but that new deal will not come about by slavish adherence to the economic practices of the past and pagan worship of the legal fiction of national sovereignty. If Western Europe is to lift herself out of the quagmire of political and economic distress, she must unite. . . .

The balance-of-power technique of nineteenth-century diplomacy worked fairly well because it was accomplished by balancing off a number of independent nation states. This situation no longer prevails. Eastern Europe is in the Soviet empire, united, integrated and under the direction of the Kremlin. Western Europe finds herself divided and sick. . . .

Political federation will not come about quickly in Europe nor should it be expected to. . . . Boundaries and borders mean something in terms of emotion and prejudices. But European federation can get started if Europeans will but let it. . . .

Possibly, the answer is to approach the problem of European federation and economic integration piecemeal or even on a functional approach. For example, the Schuman plan. Here we see the possibility of economic integration in an area of industry that is basic to Western Europe, namely, coal, iron and steel. The Schuman plan is a beginning, and a significant one, to economic integration. It can be followed by other plans and proposals. I think it is safe to say if France, Germany and the Benelux countries can agree upon an international authority to govern steel and coal production, that something new has happened in Europe.

In the realm of political federation, while it may not be possible to get a United States of Europe, it is possible and probable to create a European army. This would truly be significant. It would represent the surrender of sovereignty where sovereignty means the most, namely, the right to raise an independent army. If the European army idea proves successful, it will surely act as a stimulus to further federation.

It is from these functional beginnings that economic and political federation will grow. It is to these projects, such as the European army and the Schuman plan, that all emphasis must be directed.

It would be too much to expect that all of Western Europe would unite into one nation state, but it is not too much to expect, nor is it impossible to achieve, that the people of Western Europe will give up their national sovereign right in certain fields of endeavor so as to provide for the common defense and to promote the general welfare. . . .

If this is accomplished, we Americans will see a Europe that is revitalized. It will become as it was once before—a land of opportunity. The people will again share in the fruits of their labor and production. It is to our advantage. It is to the advantage of the whole Free World that every effort be made to accomplish the integration and unification of Western Europe.

The Need to Stay Strong

Another important issue that needed to be confronted, in Hubert Humphrey's view, was the need to keep pace with—indeed, keep ahead of—Soviet military armaments development.

That was not being done in the early 1950s, however. Isolationist elements in the House and Senate fought back efforts to increase defense expenditures for research and development.

Air power was one example. The Air Force had asked for $725 million for research and development in its 1953 budget. Despite the vigorous arguments of Undersecretary of the Air Force John H. McCone (a future director of central intelligence), the Defense Department's Research and Development Board cut the figure to $580 million. The House of Representatives then cut it to $525 million. The Senate Committee on Appropriations wanted it reduced even further—to $247 million—almost a third of what the Air Force had asked for. At the same time, the committee slashed $78 million from the Army's budget and $115 million from the Navy's.

The Soviet Union, on the other hand, was on a crash military development program. Its gross national product in 1951 had been less than $75 billion, as opposed to the almost $320 billion for the United States. Yet it outspent the United States to produce the tools of war.

In 1952, for example, the Soviets had 20,000 land-based aircraft at the ready—twice as many as the United States. It also had another 20,000 planes in reserve. The cumulative production of Soviet tactical aircraft in the period between 1947 and 1951 was double that of the United States.

Clearly, Humphrey told his fellow senators on June 30, 1952, cutting the budget any further than the House had already done was as close to national suicide as any nation could come. What was needed, he told them, was restoration, not reduction.

Mr. President, the whole war in Korea tells us this sad story. The MIG-15 jet fighters over Korea have proved Russia's ability to produce high-quality aircraft for modern war; and the MIG is merely a sample of that ability. Nor should it be a secret that a new long-range bomber of original design was sighted over Moscow last summer. These are fantastic new developments.

Russia's output of thousands of MIG-type aircraft, her airfleet of 20,000 land-based combat aircraft in organized air units—twice as many combat aircraft as we have in our Air Force and naval aviation units combined—plus another 20,000 planes in reserve, all add up to the fact that Russia has mastered mass production techniques, which we have considered to be the elusive property of the Free World. . . .

The Soviet Union has been working upon new long-range bombers. There is evidence of radical new developments in jet night fighters. Neither development is beyond the capability of the enemy, for Russia has proceeded with an uninterrupted air power research and development program ever since she acquired a number of German aeronautical experts, some of the world's finest, as war booty in 1945.

Our own Air Force research and development program, on the other hand, has been spotty.

During the period from 1947 to 1949, for example, the Air Force gave up, because of lack of money, fully half of its existing research and development projects. Not one new aircraft or guided-missile project was undertaken from 1947 to 1949. This is a matter of official record.

As I inquire into the facts behind this situation, I find that the Air Force requests for research and development funds have been cut back repeatedly at the Defense Department level. . . . As the result of this. . . , several important jet-engine and guided-missile projects will have to be postponed or delayed.

I ask any member of this body, what evidence is there that would lead us to believe that we can afford to postpone guided-missile and jet-engine development projects? We ought to be putting on the steam, putting on the pressure, rather than minimizing or reducing our efforts.

I am concerned about this state of affairs. I am worried especially about our guided-missile program. Russia inherited, or took by force, German missile experts who, in 1945, already were ten years ahead of America in this vital field of development. I do not like to contemplate the prospect of long-range Russian missiles carrying atomic explosives. I am not convinced that we are keeping pace with this threat. . . .

We are taking a risk with our security, our preparedness, which cannot be justified in face of the facts of Soviet power or Soviet pressure. The international situation calls for us to speed up our preparations, not stretch them out. . . .

We must also face the threat of defeat without war—well within reason in this age of power politics. This threat has been referred to as "atomic blackmail." I think the term is well chosen. It describes a state of affairs in which the communist aggressor forces the opposition little by little to her side.

Knowing that the United States will not strike first, the Soviet Union could apply an atomic squeeze on the fringe nations and on our present allies. She would be free to consolidate her gains as she went along, and deal directly with the United States on her own good time. . . . World balance of power would shift from the Western democracies to the Soviet Union and her satellites. At this point, Russia would have less, rather than more, reason to engage in all-out war. . . .

To scoff at danger can be very popular at times. It reassures the timid; it justifies the do-nothing; it frees the prudent from the necessity of making sacrifices.

But to scoff at danger when danger is real is the height of foolhardiness. It can be fatal, not only to the scoffer but to those lulled into a state of self-satisfied complacency by his words of disdain. It can be fatal to a whole nation.

Whatever anyone may say to the contrary, the danger posed to the existence of this country by the Soviet Union is terribly real. To ignore it would be not only to invite, but virtually to make certain our destruction.

The object of the Soviet rulers is to destroy the United States. This is no secret, confirmable only by an undercover pipeline into the Politburo. It is a well-advertised fact. . . .

In our pursuit of a balanced national budget, we must ask ourselves how important that budget will become if, by virtue of it, we lost world balance of power to communism.

In protecting the taxpayer from waste in the military establishment, we must also protect him from the greatest waste of all—war.

In our reluctance to disturb the civilian economy with military production, we must recognize that nothing would disrupt this economy quite so much as a few well-placed atomic bombs. . . .

Let us never look back upon this moment in 1952 and conclude that, through lack of foresight, we failed to provide the means for advancing toward the goal of the century—peace with honor.

Toward a Better Life

Hubert Humphrey was also concerned with the development and improvement of the nation's resources—another area where Senate budget cutters regularly had a field day.

As the 82nd Congress prepared to adjourn in July 1952, shortly before the opening gavels of the two presidential nominating conventions, Humphrey told his fellow senators that, come January, he would be back, "greatly interested in the appropriations and authorizations of the Congress" in this area.

. . . Mr. President, we have a job to develop the resources of America. In recent days, the president has called attention to the importance of saving, to the American economy, our minerals, our oil and all the great substance with which God has blessed this nation.

That is something which alarms every member of Congress. Our job is to find new materials, new energy and new resources for America. We are using them so rapidly that we must do something to save them for future generations.

It is the job of the Congress to legislate and not to listen to the writers who talk about the pork barrel, and not to listen to those who are not willing to spend a dime for improvement.

We have been told by certain sources that we should not spend for the improvement of the nation, that we have got to dissociate expenditures from investments.

They do not tell the truth. It is not an expenditure to improve rivers; it is not an expenditure to develop the great resources involved in our river system; it is not an expenditure to find new ores and new metals; it is not an expenditure when we appropriate for research to improve the health of the people and to build new industries and new areas of activity.

I, for one, refuse to believe that the money we have spent for the resources of the people is an expenditure. It is a prudent and wise investment. It represents the cooperative effort of the American people to raise the economy of the nation to higher levels.

The reason why the economy of America is where it is today is because we have gone into those areas which have been at times classified as marginal areas, and we have made them productive. We have reforested our land. We have spent money to make money.

But, more important, we have spent money to make a better life for our people.

That is the program to which I dedicate myself, and I am not going to be intimidated one little bit by budget pinchers and by modern Scrooges who are opposed to spending some of the money of the United States to develop more money.

America stands for capital investment and the improvement of the material and human resources of the nation. The sooner the Congress of the United States makes up its mind to march forward with this program, the better off we shall be.

It represents democracy, a better country and a better people.

A Question of Corruption

Americans had little faith in politicians in 1952. They have very little faith in them today, for that matter. And this bothered Hubert Humphrey a great deal. Especially in election years—and 1952 was an election year.

One of the reasons Americans believed their politicians were corrupt was obviously because some of them were corrupt, and those who were not often covered for those who were. This was especially true in the legislature.

But it was not just the fault of politicians, Humphrey believed; the people get what they pay for. If they do not want to take a more active role in government through the electoral process, they should not expect to have the kind of men and women in government that they would like—and need—to have.

Humphrey addressed himself to this on many occasions. One such occasion was an article Humphrey wrote for the Annals of the American Academy of Political and Social Science *in March 1952. Portions of that article are reprinted in the first of the two excerpts which follow.*

Another problem adding to the peoples' disaffection with politicians was campaign financing. More and more money was being spent on political campaigns and the money was coming, not from the people, but from special interests who hoped to influence the politicians they were helping to advance. This was particularly true of the presidency.

To this end, Humphrey introduced a resolution on July 5, 1952, calling on the Committee on Privileges and Elections to investigate the preconvention expenditures of the presidential aspirants in both parties and to recommend effective remedies if they were warranted. In the second excerpt that follows, taken from a letter Humphrey wrote to Committee Chairman Guy M. Gillette of Iowa on July 1, the senator explains the need for such an investigation.

It would not be until after the excesses of Watergate and Richard Nixon that Congress would do anything about this problem. And yet, ironically, that same Richard Nixon gave the Congress ample reason to take the necessary steps to curb campaign financing abuses in 1952. Shortly before the election that year, the New York Post *revealed that the California senator and Republican vice-presidential nominee had a secret fund to which private sources had contributed and from which he paid his personal expenses.*

One can only speculate whether Watergate would ever have happened if the Senate had done what Humphrey had asked it to do twenty years earlier.

It has become almost a truism today to equate politics with corruption. Nor is this a new phenomenon in our society. . . .

The National Opinion Research Center discovered that five out of every seven Americans believed it impossible for a professional politician to be honest, and only 18 percent of America's parents were willing to let their sons enter political careers.

This is a revealing if startling commentary on the public attitude toward politics.

American public office has little tradition of honor behind it. In part, this can be traced back to the axiom: "That government is best which governs least." Americans have habitually ignored the government as much as possible and too frequently left office-seeking to those who stood to gain personally from it. Too many people still cherish this early, idyllic concept of the government—or act as if it were still attainable.

At bottom, the solution to the problem of corruption in legislative bodies lies in an alert, participating and interested citizenry. Public opinion must not wait for the disclosure of glaring transgressions before rousing itself to action; it must constantly support men of integrity, ability and candor.

Only the active participation of a large portion of the electorate in political activity—through the medium of political parties—can supplant the power of organized pressure groups on the one hand and backroom politics and personal favoritism on the other.

When the people leave politics to be the plaything or special interest of a few, the public can expect that it will be played with and serve the special economic and political interests of the participants.

Democratic or representative government is everyone's business if it is to be an honorable pursuit. If the people want clean and honest government, the minimum price is an active and continuing interest in political parties and political processes.

Blaming the public for complacency does not solve our problems. Legislative bodies have all too often tolerated corruption in their midst. Even where flagrant violations of law have been proved and the miscreants jailed, too frequently no disciplinary measures have been taken.

In this vein, it should be pointed out that men who stoop to smear tactics, demagoguery and general confusion of the issues in order to gain public office cannot be expected to change suddenly once they are sworn in. They cannot be trusted with the government of this country or any of its states.

While most of the responsibility for correcting such abuses is upon the public, legislative bodies themselves should also act. Callous disregard of the intelligence of the public and the integrity of political office should be punished by voters and legislators alike. . . .

The usual American remedy is "there ought to be a law." Yet the law cannot deal effectively with every range of human activity. Many of the ethical questions cannot be solved by legislation; remedies must instead be sought in a new consciousness of the dignity of public office and a higher sense of civic duty.

All of us, as citizens, can achieve this through awareness of the difficulties and active support of all efforts to raise legislative standards. . . .

Dear Mr. Senator: I am introducing a resolution calling for an investigation by your subcommittee of the campaign expenditures of the various presidential candidates of both parties. I am suggesting an immediate investigation because I believe that you and your committee can restore a sense of sanity and responsibility to American political life. Candidates for the presidency and their supporters are leveling serious charges against one another of political deals and manipulation based upon financial considerations. These charges are serious because they threaten the nominating processes in American political life. . . .

This problem is serious because of its effect on the integrity of our political campaigns. We must have a study made as to the actual cost of the national campaign for the presidency. It is important that we know whether the expenses of such a campaign will be so large as to make the presidency unattainable for any other than the wealthy or those whom the wealthy support. This problem is particularly significant in the light of the many suggestions which are today being made for a national presidential primary.

Many Americans, furthermore, are seriously disturbed by the charges of political deals, "stealing" of delegates, "smear literature," use of patronage, and the like, being made today by many of the presidential candidates and their supporters. If these accusations are true, we are witnessing a degradation of the nominating process. This can result in an increasing public cynicism about politics, and if the trend is not stopped will, in fact, mean that we have allowed a price tag to be placed on the presidency.

The vote in a democracy is priceless. It is the most sacred heritage of the American people. We must be vigilant in our determination to preserve the electoral process from being put up for sale. . . .

One of the most effective weapons by which to preserve the integrity of our democratic electoral system is truth and full disclosure of all the facts. The American public is entitled to know the sources of campaign funds being raised by candidates for public office. . . .

The truth is not complicated. The American people deserve the truth.

Keep Open the Door

In May 1952, Congress passed the McCarran-Walter Act, one of the most restrictive immigration bills ever to be enacted. President Truman wasted little time in vetoing the bill, but his veto was overridden; McCarran-Walter became the law of the land.

To Hubert Humphrey, the bill was an abomination. It was diametrically opposed to everything the United States stood for, he argued, and therefore he was diametrically opposed to it.

He explained some of his reasons for opposing the McCarran-Walter Act in a speech to the Brooklyn Division of the American Jewish Congress on January 28, 1953.

. . . Whether we trace our ancestry to the *Mayflower*, whether we are Sons or Daughters of the American Revolution, or whether we personally stepped ashore in 1900, in 1925, or in 1945. . . , in the historical perspective, we are all new Americans.

All of us came here as refugees from the Old World, seeking a new home and new opportunity in America. All of us made our contribution to the development of this country.

But ever since the creation of our republic, there have been some people whose position on immigration has been: "Thank God we are here. Now let's bolt the door."

But that view, ladies and gentlemen, is not the prevailing view in America today. It is not the view of the President's Commission on Immigration, which recently reported to the country after an exhaustive study of immigration problems. It is not the view of scores of fraternal nationality, patriotic and religious organizations in America, and it is not the view of our Jewish synagogues and our Protestant and Catholic churches. . . .

The spirit of America, the spirit of our people, and the spirit of our religious traditions rejects the notion that there is room for discrimination and bigotry in our immigration laws. . . .

I am aware of the unfortunate fact that most of the people to whom you would have wanted to extend a helping hand, people kept out of this country in the '30s by the national origins principle, are now dead, the victims of the most horrible crime against humanity.

The whispering campaign of the bigots that the fight

against the McCarran Act is a Jewish fight, designed to bring in more Jews, is, therefore, as untrue and unjustified as are all similar campaigns.

In fact, even insofar as the displaced persons legislation was concerned, that was not a Jewish fight. Only 18 percent of all the displaced persons who came into the United States were Jewish.

Here again it is clear that to raise the Jewish question is untrue and unjustified. I must say that I was very sorry and shocked to see such a campaign reach the floor of the Congress. . . .

What hardly any of us clearly anticipated during the fight against the McCarran bill was the sudden stepping-up of officially sponsored anti-Semitism in the Soviet sphere. As of today, we still don't know how far that ruthless group in the Kremlin intends to go. But we must face the brutal fact that if it will serve their purposes, the men responsible for Katyn will not bat an eyelash at creating another Auschwitz. . . .

It is to enable us to cope with sudden emergencies of this nature and to help us make our contribution to the solution of world population problems, that we oppose the rigid, racist national origins principle. . . .

You know that the fight for better immigration legislation did not end when President Truman's veto of the McCarran Act was overridden. The fight is continuing and I am certain that as time goes by an even greater portion of the American public will become aware of its dangers and inequities. I am happy to join with you in the necessary program to educate the public.

The Human Factor

There is an old maxim: "Ours is a government of laws, not of men." This, according to Hubert Humphrey, has been interpreted by many to extract the human factor from government.

But this was wrong, he felt. He would argue, as did Samuel Johnson, that "the law is the last result of human wisdom acting upon human experience for the benefit of the public."

It is "this human quality," Humphrey would often say, "which is the chief characteristic of law in a democracy" and which "irrevocably distinguishes it from law within a totalitarian society."

On June 5, 1953, Humphrey expounded on this theme at the 84th annual convocation of the National University Law School.

. . . The human element is ever-present in the legal processes. There can be no government of laws except through men.

The assumption that the human factor does not enter into decision-making and that, in fact, every decision is in some mystic sense contained in the Constitution, or some other form of organic law, is the fiction which is contrary to actual practice and understanding. . . .

It is imperative in a democracy never to forget that public office is of necessity held by mere men who, of course, have human frailties. It is only in a system where government officials are deemed to be semigods that freedom disappears.

Men in public life must, therefore, be constantly subject to criticism if liberty is to prevail. To say that our government is not only a government of laws but is also a government of men is, therefore, to strengthen the fabric of our democracy.

Let us have a government in which personal prejudices and predilections are reduced, but let us never have a government without the human factor. . . .

Government of necessity must be "administered by men

over men" and not just by an abstract mystical concept of law. Thus, if we are to have "good government" we must have "good men." Our democracy, therefore, can live and survive only to the extent that our government of laws is rendered strong and administered by the right kind of men.

All of you have completed a duly accredited study of legal cases, legal history, legal doctrine and legal analysis. You are about to belong to a noble profession. It is an ancient profession. The ancient Hebraic Talmud says: "God created the law before He created the world."

As lawyers, you will be held in high esteem by your neighbors and by the people in your community. . . . Your judgment on matters not related to the law will be valued by your fellow citizens. . . .

You, therefore, have a great responsibility. You have a responsibility to be men and not just lawyers. You have the responsibility to introduce the human factor into your lives, into your experiences, into your training and into your judgments.

In a word, you are "citizens" in the broadest sense of that term. Do not, I pray, allow yourselves to become specialists alone.

We are living today at a time when men's tempers are frayed and their patience is at a low ebb. The civilized world faces constant threats of violence from the right and violence from the left. Men are proposing desperate measures, the consequences of which are to destroy the values of civilization and destroy the gains which science and learning have brought about through the development of the free intellect.

It is the duty of men, it is the duty of citizens in a democracy, to see that the blindness of desperation does not prevail. You are in a sense, as you enter the profession of law, inheritors of our modern life. . . .

In a world filled with storms of passion and hysteria, we must guide a steady course, and by precept and example in our policies at home and abroad give faith and courage to those who journey with us. Our destination is a just and enduring peace. We can seek no less.

This is not a task for the timid and the old in spirit. It is a task, rather, for the bold, for the young in heart, for those who seek a new and better life, as you and I do this evening. It is no accident that the founders of our nation were, in the main, young men, young primarily in spirit, and some young in years.

The qualities of leadership require enthusiasm, warm hearts, and cool heads, and freedom from imprisoning dogmatism, capacity for freshness, insight, unflagging industry, and intense ardor—with patient determination.

These are the qualities required for leadership in a democracy. They are, in the main, qualities for leadership in a Free World.

We have provided that leadership—we have the capacity to continue to provide that leadership. Whether we succeed depends on all of us. . . .

"We Are Sitting Ducks"

With the advent of the nuclear age, much attention was devoted—and still is—to developing first-strike capabilities, defense systems and retaliatory weapons. Little consideration was—or is—given to an area of equal importance: civil defense.

This, to Hubert Humphrey, was just plain stupid. In the 1952 hydrogen-bomb test, an area of 33 square miles was totally destroyed. Severe to moderate damage covered over 154 square miles, while light damage was recorded over a 314-square mile area.

And that was just one hydrogen bomb. By 1954, the period of American thermonuclear monopoly was gone. The Soviet Union had successfully tested its first thermonuclear device with results which "made the 1952 explosion almost of pigmy proportions," as Humphrey told the Senate in July 1954.

With that kind of destructive capability in the hands of the enemy, Humphrey argued, greater attention must be given—and more funds expended —for civil defense.

According to the 1950 census, 40 percent of the population of the United States and over 50 percent of those employed in manufacturing lived in only forty cities; 30 percent of the population and 40 percent of those involved in manufacturing lived in only fifteen cities. What an inviting target for enemy bombs; and the government was (and still is) ignoring it.

In early 1954, the Civil Defense Administration conducted a nationwide mock attack, carried out by 425 "enemy" planes with targets in sixty-four cities (including the key cities referred to above). The result of the "attack": 70 per cent of the "attacking force" got through U.S. defenses and were able to drop their "atomic bombs" on their prescribed targets. Almost 9 million people were "killed" during the "attack," and over 4 million were "injured."

President Truman had recognized the problem in 1952. He had asked Congress to allocate $600 million for civil defense in fiscal year 1953 and an additional $150 million for fiscal 1954. Congress rejected it out of hand. For fiscal 1954, for example, it authorized a civil defense allocation of only $74 million.

President Eisenhower went Congress one better in his fiscal 1955 budget request: only $68 million for civil defense!

Humphrey called this "the height of stupidity," and no wonder. For, as he told the Senate on July 14, 1954, "We are sitting ducks!"

. . . The policy of the American government has been a constant search for peace and for means to avert war. If, however, war should come—and we must always project our planning and our thinking upon that terrible eventuality—and if our country should be attacked, then our civil defense will become the business of all Americans, for the American public will have to take the final steps to insure its own survival.

The business of the government in the essential enterprise of civil defense is to provide knowledge, planning and direction so that our people can take steps to protect themselves. . . .

I emphasize this point because today very few voices are being raised in the United States in terms of the defense of the people of the United States. We spend billions and billions and billions of dollars to build up what we call our security forces, and we spend billions of dollars for research and development to perfect weapons which can deliver lethal destruction. Yet. . . , there is no one who today can assure Americans that our cities are safe from attack.

It is perfectly obvious that the weapons of mass destruction which have been created are not weapons for the traditional battlefield alone, but are weapons to be used against mass concentrations of people. They are essentially weapons for use against civilians, and I wish to emphasize the fact that the hydrogen bomb, its cobalt partner, and its atomic junior partner, are essentially weapons to be used against helpless civilians, not against military objectives in the traditional sense. . . .

I say it is the height of stupidity, it is the culmination of a complete denial of responsibility to ignore the fact that the enemy is going to place bombs of destruction on American cities if ever there is trouble.

When we have a policy of massive retaliation as an announced public policy of the nation, we can rest assured that the men of the Kremlin, who are not detoured or held back by any moral scruples—there is no Christian compassion in their hearts —are planning a policy of massive retaliation, too. . . .

We are sitting ducks. We are more exposed to attack than were the people of Nagasaki and Hiroshima. We blindly pursue our course and talk about security and defense. I go back to my original premise, that the thermonuclear weapons, the hydrogen bombs and cobalt bombs, are not solely weapons in the military sense. They are to be used against industry, transportation and civilians, and the destruction would be fantastic. . . .

Foresighted, intelligent civil defense legislation, now, is not too much to expect from Congress when the demand is made in behalf of an American public faced with the dread prospect of vaporization.

I want the word "vaporization" to ring out through this chamber.What we are talking about today is not society being able to pick up the rubble after the bomb has exploded because there will not be any society. We are talking about the kind of destruction which is beyond human comprehension.

It is in this spirit of urgency and deep concern that I have addressed myself to a topic which apparently has no political appeal and which is of little or no national interest. But I want to be on record now, as a member of the United States Senate, as saying that the government has been derelict in its responsibility for the protection of the public and the safety of the American people.

A defense structure has been planned which provides a defense in conventional military terms without any thinking having been done to provide an appropriate organization for the protection of the civilian population.

"Of Service to Mankind"

On July 30, 1953, Hubert Humphrey delivered a moving eulogy to a great American and a great Republican senator, Charles W. Tobey of New Hampshire. We include it here because it sums up the qualities Hubert Humphrey most admired in his fellow human beings, qualities which he himself had in abundance.

To those of us young and new in public service, Senator Charles W. Tobey was a great friend, and the nature of his spirit carried that friendship from his soul, and anyone privileged to share it, found there strength and guidance.

Charles Tobey liked to help other people. That is a simple quality, but it is a wonderful one. He liked to help people, because I am sure that in his life he found times when he needed help.

Once I heard a man of great wisdom say that people can never know what it is to sorrow until sadness and grief have come to their families. People can never know what it is to have sympathy until they have been in need of that consoling and healing emotion from others.

I feel certain that Charles Tobey knew all those things, because he lived a full life.

I think it can be best said that Charles Tobey was a good man. He was a decent man. It is not necessary to say he was smart or intelligent. This is readily accepted and understood. The world is filled with such people. But what the world needs is men of decency and goodness. Charles Tobey was that kind of man.

He was a brave and courageous man. His enemies knew it, and the forces of evil and sin, which he fought against, realized it.

Charles Tobey was a great man, great not only as a scholar and a philosopher, but also great because he was a man in the best sense that God Almighty could create.

He was an honorable citizen and a fine public servant. Charles Tobey was an inspiration to young and old alike. His life served to remind the young that political participation and public service can be and should be honorable pursuits. Thank God for that inspiration at a time when far too many people are skeptical and cynical about public service.

The life of Charles Tobey reveals to those who are in the twilight of life that man's spirit can ever be fresh, vigorous and useful; that chronological age has nothing to do with the beauty, liveliness and a youthfulness of spirit which God keeps alive.

So I say the spirit of Charles Tobey lives on. His is a spirit that is to be found wherever there is a struggle for righteousness over the forces of evil. His is the spirit of love conquering hate; of compassion for those who are in need. His is the spirit of the kindliness of the good Samaritan. . . .

Charles Tobey was a builder. He was a helper. To him brotherhood was not simply a word. It was a testimonial of faith in God's children, created in the image of their maker.

That is why Charles Tobey believed in human dignity and practiced it. He believed in God's finest creation—man. He believed people should be free—free to grow, free to develop, free to create.

To Charles Tobey, democracy was not politics alone. It was a spiritual faith, and his political life was motivated by that faith.

Finally, I believe those of us in the Senate and throughout America, who have so much to learn as we live, can look upon the life and works of Charles Tobey as representing America at its best; the kind of America we love and revere, and to which we pay tribute by our patriotism and our devotion.

His was a life of industry, of progressive thought and of worthy deed, a life of service to mankind. . . .

4

The Loyal Opposition

The Road to Leadership

When the 84th Congress convened in January 1955, Hubert Humphrey was more than just a "member of the club;" he was slowly rising within the ranks of its leadership.

The past three years had been eventful ones for him. He had begun to play a major role in foreign policy and he had been the subject of vicious attacks from the right and the left. He had even had his first taste of presidential politics.

As 1952 began, the Democratic Party once again appeared badly split over Harry Truman. Tennessee's Senator Estes Kefauver, for one, made it abundantly clear that he would go after the party's presidential nomination that summer, even if it meant meeting Truman head on in a fratricidal collision. He would enter the presidential primaries, he said, and, if necessary, fight for the nomination all the way up to the floor of the Democratic convention.

Hubert Humphrey, however, had great faith in Truman's abilities as president. To him, the president represented "the best in our democratic traditions" and deserved renomination and reelection.

"In him and through him," Humphrey said in 1952, "the American people have realized to the maximum the American objective of democratic government, 'a government of the people, by the people and for the people.'"

As Humphrey saw it, "Mr. Truman became president of the United States at a time when our nation was thrust into the role of world leadership.

"His was the responsibility for making decisions, the burden of which had implications more vital, more pressing and more awesome in their effect on the peoples of the world than any which have devolved upon any other living American.

"He has been called upon to make decisions with regard to the atom bomb, the Potsdam Conference, the conference of the United Nations at San Francisco, the threat of communism to Greece and Turkey, the Marshall Plan, the Point 4 Program, the North Atlantic Pact and the resistance to communist aggression in Korea.

"In my judgment, these decisions have given the world a hope for lasting peace and for the survival of human dignity in our civilization."

Kefauver's plan, therefore, could deny the United States the benefit of Truman's leadership in the four critical years ahead. To begin with, Humphrey reasoned, Kefauver might actually win enough delegates to enable him to beat

Truman in a convention floor fight, assuming Truman ran. And even if the president did win renomination, the party might be too divided to take on the opposition. For this time, the most likely nominee was not the twice-rejected Thomas E. Dewey, but "Mr. Republican" himself, Senator Robert Taft of Ohio.

Humphrey meant all the things he had said about Truman since coming to the Senate in 1949—enough, in fact, to gamble with his own future in order to protect Truman's. He decided to enter the Minnesota presidential primary as a favorite son candidate against a possible Kefauver bid. He made no secret of the fact that he was in the race merely as Truman's surrogate in the state.

Humphrey never thought he could actually lose the primary; after all, it was his state and he had ended the Republicans' ninety-year hold on Minnesota's Senate seats by a resounding victory four years earlier. But that conviction was not held by many of his supporters. They argued that to make the race and lose to an outsider, even someone as prestigious and well-known as Kefauver, who had gained a national reputation as the first chairman of the Senate Committee to Investigate Interstate Crime, would be to risk trouble in his 1954 reelection effort.

Humphrey weighed the pros and cons for several days. Finally, he accepted the risks and announced that he would indeed run in the Minnesota presidential primary. Kefauver thereupon backed out of the state and the delegates were Humphrey's to command.

Shortly thereafter, however, Truman decided he had had enough of Washington, its politics and the "great white prison" that was the presidential mansion. He yearned to return to private life in Independence, Missouri. He would not, he told a Jackson-Jefferson Day dinner audience on March 29, be a candidate for reelection under any circumstances.

Now Humphrey had to decide what to do with his twenty-six delegates, who were committed to him on the first ballot in any case. A number of Democrats began talking about possible bids for the nomination. Kefauver, of course, had announced back on January 23 that he was in the race to stay. With Truman out, he saw no reason to change his plans. Powerful Democrats like James Farley and United Mine Workers president John L. Lewis were pushing for Vice-President Alben Barkley, who was then seventy-four years old. New York's W. Averell Harriman and Georgia's Senator Richard B. Russell also entered the contest.

Truman, meanwhile, was trying to convince Governor Adlai E. Stevenson of Illinois to make the race.

Humphrey, too, felt Stevenson had a great deal to offer to the America of the 1950s. But Stevenson kept insisting that he would not enter the race, although he declined to say that he would not accept the nomination, if offered. And anyway, Humphrey felt it was too early to commit himself openly for the Illinois governor. Instead, he decided to help play a role in shaping party opinion regarding the kind of nominee the Democrats should select.

On March 31, two days after Truman's announcement that he would not be a candidate for reelection, Humphrey rose on the Senate floor to offer his views:

"The decision of President Truman to leave the White House next January," Humphrey said, "presses upon the American people a great responsibility to choose a successor worthy to carry on in the traditions which he has advanced."

It was not for him to offer advice to the Republicans, Humphrey said. "I do, however, have some words of counsel for those within my party who offer themselves to be standard-bearers of the Democratic Party in the forthcoming presidential elections."

Harry Truman, Humphrey said that day, "is beloved by the American people because of his candor, honesty, frankness and principles. He received the support of the American people because he represented in the minds of the American citizens the bold principles of the New Deal and the Fair Deal.

"The Democratic Party has a responsibility to choose for. . . president and vice-president of the United States candidates willing, eager and determined to carry on in those traditions. . . ."

The candidate, Humphrey declared, must remain "faithful to a Democratic Party political platform committed to the foreign policy of the administration and to a domestic program of parity and progress for agriculture, full and equal civil rights for all, public power. . . , development and conservation of our natural resources, free collective bargaining and defense mobilization."

That, said Humphrey, "is our record. . . . Democrats [should] embrace that record, hold their banners on high, carry forward that record to the American people, and let the people judge it on the basis of accomplishments."

As the July 21 convention date neared, Kefauver seemed to be steamrolling his way to victory. California, Illinois, Massachusetts, Maryland, Nebraska,

New Hampshire, Oregon, South Dakota and Tennessee all fell to the senator in primaries. In addition, he won half of the Ohio delegation and a portion of the Florida contingent. He had also won the presidential preference primary in Pennsylvania.

The Republicans, too, were involved in a bitter struggle between Taft, representing the forces of retrenchment and isolationism, and General Dwight D. Eisenhower, who supported Truman's basic policies regarding European recovery. Eisenhower managed to beat Taft on the convention floor just eleven days before the Democrats were to meet. Senator Richard M. Nixon of California was nominated as his running-mate.

At the Democratic Convention (which, like the Republican one before it, was held in Chicago), Stevenson reluctantly agreed to make a last-minute bid for the nomination. All the intraparty bitterness of the last few months exploded on the floor on July 25 as supporters for each of the major candidates and those of the minor ones battled it out. Kefauver took the first two ballots easily. On the third, however, Stevenson emerged as the leader and delegations began switching their votes to him.

The next day, Senator John J. Sparkman of Alabama was chosen by acclamation for vice-president.

Humphrey plunged head-on into the Stevenson-Sparkman drive. Nevertheless, he began to have some minor misgivings, mainly because of the way the Democratic nominee was treating the man who had been pushing him to take the nomination in the first place. Stevenson and his campaign staff were keeping Harry Truman at arm's length.

Eventually, Stevenson's people called upon the president for help and Truman gave it his all. But nothing helped. In November, the Eisenhower-Nixon combination, with a healthy 6-million-vote margin, brought the Republicans back to the White House for the first time in twenty years.

As Humphrey himself noted years later, Eisenhower's victory turned out to be a good thing for him and for the nation. In his 1976 autobiography, Humphrey wrote, "It is a simple fact that the election of Dwight Eisenhower permitted substantial defusing of the explosive nature of American politics."

The reason was simple: With a Republican running the government, the Republican Party could not long continue to point the finger of suspicion at government actions. The power-hungry "irresponsibles" who had allowed Joe McCarthy to run unchecked now had the power they had for so long sought;

now they had to pull in the reins on the witch-hunters. "His mere election," Humphrey wrote, "drained the boil of irascible partisanship."

As for his own career, Humphrey recalled in 1976 that "it was probably helpful not to be aligned with the party in power. As loyal opposition, I could look at government, and my own role, from a little distance."

It also meant that Humphrey would soon begin to have some input into the conduct of the nation's foreign relations.

Eisenhower's election tossed the Democrats out of more than just the White House; Republicans now controlled both houses of Congress as well. That meant that the various committee chairmanships would go to Republicans in the 83rd Congress.

Eisenhower had chosen such men for his cabinet as Ezra Taft Benson (secretary of agriculture) and George Humphrey (secretary of the treasury), but they were overshadowed by the presence of John Foster Dulles, whom Eisenhower had chosen to be secretary of state.

The minority Democratic leadership feared that Dulles, together with men like Taft, Homer Capehart, William Jenner, William Knowland, Styles Bridges and John Bricker, would turn the nation "into a tory island of isolation and simplistic anticommunism," as Humphrey recalled in 1976.

Alexander Wiley, however, did not share the views of his fellow Republicans, and he would chair the Senate Foreign Relations Committee in the 83rd Congress. The trouble was that Wiley was a politically weak man and the Democratic leadership felt a few strong and outspoken Democrats could keep the Republican chairman in line.

Shortly before Eisenhower's inauguration, therefore, the Texas Twosome —House Minority Leader Sam Rayburn and Senate Minority Leader Lyndon Johnson (who was elected to the post while in his first term)—called upon Humphrey and Senator Mike Mansfield of Montana to accept assignment to the Foreign Relations Committee.

Mansfield accepted right away. For Humphrey, however, going on Foreign Relations meant giving up two other committees on which he served and which meant more to the people of Minnesota: Agriculture, and Labor and Public Welfare. (The Republican victory had forced a cutback in Democratic Senate committee assignments from three to two. Humphrey was also a member of the Government Operations Committee, another important post which he was determined not to give up, particularly because its new chairman was Joe

McCarthy. That meant that both Agriculture and Labor had to go if he took the Foreign Relations seat.)

Rayburn and Johnson argued with Humphrey and, at length, prevailed. The Democrats, they told him, needed forceful men on the Foreign Relations Committee at such a critical time; they needed leaders and not followers, and Humphrey was a leader. It was too good an argument for Humphrey to ignore. He exacted a promise from Johnson to get the next available seat on Agriculture, which was vital to his reelection chances in 1954, and took the Foreign Relations post. (Johnson kept his promise when, on the death of North Carolina's Clyde Hoey in May 1954, he reassigned Humphrey to Agriculture.)

Despite the fact that Humphrey's star kept rising (or, perhaps, because of it), the senator from Minnesota came under vicious attack from both the right and the left during his first term.

Those on the right tried to paint him as a communist. But that was too obvious a lie: If anything, Humphrey was more anticommunist than even McCarthy, although in a democratic, more constructive and certainly more responsible way. So they attempted to picture Humphrey as a corrupt politician, a man on the take. That course, too, was soon abandoned. Try as they did, they could not find anything corrupt about him.

The communists, however, were not that easy to get rid of. They were masters of the big-lie technique—say something often enough and loud enough, and sooner or later someone will believe it. They turned the technique on Humphrey in a nationwide campaign to discredit the senator, who was engaged in a continuing struggle to purge communists from the nation's unions and keep them out.

The campaign carried on by the communists against Humphrey sometimes bordered on the lunatic; often, however, it went way over the line. A sampling taken just from 1952 alone more than adequately demonstrates the nature of the communist campaign.

In the Union, *the publication of the Mine, Mill and Smelter Workers, Humphrey was often pictured as a tool of big business. "The men who sell Wheaties comprise the board of directors of General Mills, the grain monopoly of the Morgan empire," one* Union *article went. "Wheaties is just one of their products. Gold Medal flour is another. Humphrey another."*

The article went on to accuse Humphrey of donning "sackcloth and ashes" and performing "an act of contrition to the white supremacists" of the South.

According to the New York Daily Worker, *"The real forces back of 'liberal' Minnesota Senator Hubert H. Humphrey's move for more legislation to thought-control unions is the National Association of Manufacturers. . . ."*

The American Communist Association's ACA News *reported that Humphrey was sponsoring congressional efforts to pass "even more repressive laws than the present Taft-Hartley slave-labor act."*

The International Longshoreman and Warehouseman's Union publication, The Dispatcher, *accused Humphrey of working "for the express purpose of outlawing labor unions. . . ."*

In a publication called March of Labor, *Humphrey was compared to Louisiana's late Kingfish, Huey Long. "While Humphrey has cloaked himself in a toga of liberalism, the masquerade is not so effective in Minnesota, where they know him. Once you get into Humphrey's own back yard, you find too many skeletons buried there. . . . The 'liberal' Humphrey is exposed as just another Wall Street tool when you shovel aside the oratory and get a peek at his record. . . . He has supported the McCarran Act and concentration camps."*

Big business, of course, looked upon Humphrey as "the enemy." Civil rights was then and always remained one of his most consuming passions. The Taft-Hartley Act was considered by Humphrey an abomination to be eradicated from the nation's lawbooks. And elimination of the McCarran-Walter Immigration and Naturalization Act was one of Humphrey's major causes. None of that, however, stopped the communists' big-lie campaign.

It got so bad at one point, in fact, that one of Humphrey's colleagues, Senator Wayne Morse, rose to his defense in a 1952 speech to the Senate. Morse, incidentally, was then a Republican.

"For many years now," Morse said, "Senator Humphrey has been the subject of much hostile comment among those totalitarians in our society who would destroy our democratic principles in favor of a dictatorship. Both fascists and communists have seen fit to list him as one of their enemies. I know that he is proud of the distinction. He can take pride in the fact that he has been an active and effective opponent of communism and fascism. I believe the intensity of the totalitarian opposition to him is evidence of that effectiveness.

"To the best of his ability, he has attempted to undermine communist influence in his state of Minnesota and in his political party while he was mayor [of Minneapolis]. And he is proceeding to the best of his ability to undermine communist influence in the nation and in the world through his activities as United States senator. . . .

"Irrespective of the fact that the senator from Minnesota belongs to the Democratic Party, so far as I am concerned as a Republican, I think I would be derelict in my duty as a member of the Senate if I did not. . . speak out in defense. . . of Humphrey's statesmanship. . . . [If] people would only go to the record, the senator from Minnesota would need no defense. But the sad thing is that in these days of hysteria in American politics, too many of the people in our country have come to accept the smears as the truth."

The charges went on and on and on. But the people of Minnesota did not buy them. Hubert Humphrey was reelected by a 162,000-vote margin in November 1954.

As the 84th Congress got underway in January 1955, the Democrats were once again in the majority (by one vote, owing to Senator Morse's defection to them) and Humphrey was looking ahead. In one year's time, he would make a convention-floor bid for his party's vice-presidential nomination, which he would lose. In five years time, he would run for the party's presidential nomination, and he would lose again.

But, while such thoughts undoubtedly entered Humphrey's mind in 1955, they were not the dominant ones; nor would they ever be. For these were perilous times for the world, in Humphrey's view, and they called for dramatic, innovative action. Politics would have to play second fiddle to responsible leadership.

And Hubert Humphrey was that leader. Over the next four years, he would introduce various bills promoting civil rights, creating what he called a "Peace Corps" staffed with young Americans, establishing Food for Peace and Health for Peace programs, setting up an Arms Control and Disarmament Agency, introducing a Medicare program under Social Security—in fact, every major piece of social and technical legislation which would move the nation forward toward a New Frontier and for which others would seek to assume the credit in the eyes of history.

One of Humphrey's major priorities in his second term was developing programs designed to promote peace—not merely by stabilizing the cold war with the Soviet Union, but by winning it.

He outlined his views in a July 11, 1955, speech delivered in Hamilton, New York, to the Seventh Annual Foreign Policy Conference sponsored by Colgate University.

. . . This term *foreign policy* has always disturbed me. The word *foreign* has a negative meaning. It indicates something apart, different, unusual.

I suggest that our relationships with other nations are no longer something apart from our everyday life. Nor should these relationships be different from our domestic policy. I prefer to recognize our relationships with other nations as an international policy, a policy of interdependence rather than a foreign policy. . . .

Foreign policy seems to suggest the nineteenth century, the era of colonialism and imperialism. International policy speaks of the twentieth century. It has its roots in the United Nations, in a spirit of interdependence without sacrificing national independence. . . .

Fortunately, we have learned that national independence can be sustained and made meaningful only by a recognition of international interdependence. It took us two world wars and a worldwide depression to have this fact driven home. . . .

I wonder sometimes if we have forgotten the terrible destruction of World War II. Not only were things ruined and demolished, but human spirit was almost destroyed. Established social patterns were uprooted, millions of people were wandering on the roads, dying in prisons and concentration camps.

All of this was but only yesterday. Fear and frustration stalked the land. The political and economic climate was ripe for demagogues, dictators and opportunists. The forces of communism moved in, backed by the power of the Red Army.

It was this unhappy event that compounded the problems and difficulties which faced mankind after this most hideous of all terrible wars. It was almost beyond human capacity to rebuild a war-weary world. But to this awful burden was added the even more intolerable burden of resisting and defeating the inroads of communist imperialism and subversion.

It is nothing short of a miracle that the areas of human freedom are as great as they are. . . .

Not because of plan or design, but simply because we were the only nation with the resources and the strength, we were compelled to meet and challenge this evil force. . . . We were not prepared by experience or expert knowledge. But we did not shrink from the ordeal. . . .

Within a few days, the leaders of the four great powers will be meeting in Geneva. Surely this is the most significant meeting of recent years. . . .

I think we would all be misguided if we expected sudden and spectacular results. The cold war has been very cold a long time and it is going to take more than a brief ray of sunshine to thaw it out. But the fact that there is a meeting is a good sign. If it does nothing else but to cause us to reexamine or reevaluate every facet of our foreign policy, it will be well worth the effort. . . .

Any step in the direction of relaxed tensions must be welcomed by us and we should lead in this effort, making it ever clear to the simplest soul in the far corners of the world that the nation of Washington, Jefferson, Lincoln, Wilson and Roosevelt is a nation of peace, of freedom, of compassion and justice. . . .

This is no time for timid souls. This is the time for men of imagination, courage and daring. The peoples of the world are weary of the constant threat of nuclear war, and particularly when that threat keeps coming from us in the strident voices of small men. The peoples are looking for a clear and challenging political faith that will arouse them to self-determination and liberation from both political and social tyranny. The toxin of fear has run its course.

A tired and suffering humanity seeks the nourishing food of applied idealism.

This is to our advantage. We are not warriors in the strict interpretation of the word. Our history is traditionally one of an expanding democracy—the fulfillment of equality of opportunity, the relation of human equality of law in the social order, and the dedication to a rising standard of living for all. It is these very virtues that fit the present world sense.

It is time, therefore, that we walk confidently in the stature, strength and competence that our history and our present circumstances verify. In a world that is desperately in need of capital, we have the greatest capital resources among all nations. In a world where people are anxious for the blessings of science and technology, we are richly endowed with these blessings. In a world where the majority of people are ill-housed, ill-fed and ill-clad, we are privileged to have an abundance of food and fiber and the knowledge of scientific progress for health and shelter...

The time is ready for us to dedicate our talents, our resources, to winning the cold war, not just stabilizing it.

Specifically, I suggest, first, we join with the spirit of nationalism that grips the underdeveloped and underprivileged countries. Remind these people that we too are the children of self-determination, of revolution, and of a will to freedom and independence.

Second, respect the so-called neutralism of newborn nations, and make it clear that we understand their neutralism to be one predicated on independence, self-determination and self-government. . . .

It is time we recognized that power is more than armaments and wealth. Power is people and ideals—people who aspire to freedom and dignity; ideals that make possible an enlightened and civilized society. . . .

A Matter of Preservation

People and ideals, an enlightened and civilized society. These were the things Hubert Humphrey's dreams were made of. His whole life was dedicated to the proposition that a better world awaited mankind if only it would dare to seek it out.

Part of that better world, he knew, depended in great part on preserving some of the treasures of the world mankind was already in: the wilderness areas where one could enjoy God's wonders unobscured by billboards, where one could frolic in the sun amid trees, flowers, mountains and wildlife without being assaulted by the ever-present signs of "progress."

In July 1955, one of Washington's most beautiful recreation areas, Rock Creek Park, was threatened by plans to run a highway through it. "Not only the people, but also the squirrels, will be scared away as the big, high-powered vehicles travel through the park," Humphrey said at the time.

Humphrey was disturbed by this development and, although there was little he could do about it, he could put the Senate—and the nation—on notice that this type of "progress" had to stop. And that is what he told the Senate on July 20.

. . . I appeal to the Senate to be the guardian and custodian, faithful at all times, of these great resources, the great recreational resources of America—the parks, the playgrounds, and the refuges for game, fish and wildlife. We have so little of them left.

It has been the privilege and the pleasure of Mrs. Humphrey and myself, and of our children to travel extensively throughout our country by automobile. . . .

When I observe the tremendous number of people who go into our national parks; when I consider the yearning of millions and millions of people in the cities for places to go to fish and camp, to have a few nights and days out in the open air, away from the smoke and the smog and the hubbub of traffic and industry; it is nothing short of shocking to me that Congress seems to be so complacently unconcerned. . . .

It seems that every time we have developed a beautiful place or an area dedicated to the enlargement of man's spirit and soul, someone has to ram in a hamburger stand, a truck stop, a filling station, or a big highway.

I thank God that we were able in Minnesota, by federal law, to establish a wilderness area known as Quetico-Superior National Forest. One does not go into that area by plane or automobile; he must go in by foot, by canoe, or by portage. Once inside, he is in an area which is as much a virgin part of America as was America itself on the first day this continent was discovered.

We need some places like that in the nation. When I see the limited, petty, little amounts we appropriate for our Park Service, I wonder sometimes if we have lost our sense of values. We are willing to appropriate more money to study, for instance, hoof-and-mouth disease, which, of course, is important; and money to study the habits of beetles, which may be important; but we always hesitate to appropriate the money we should allow to really do something about people's living conditions. These great recreational facilities are of great importance.

I know the Senate is conducting investigations into juvenile delinquency. That is quite a big subject, but I guarantee that one way to help solve the problem is to provide decent living conditions in homes, in the cities and in the country, which will give the people a spirit of inspiration rather than of degradation.

If we permit a policy to be continued which carves up the great recreational resources in this country, we will not have enough jail space to take care of the people who will get out of hand, and to take care of mental cases.

The greater, the stronger and the richer this country becomes, the greater the speed and tempo, the more recreational facilities are needed. And I am not talking about night clubs. I am talking about places where there are oak trees and pine trees, places where there are little rivers and creeks, hills and valleys, stone and sand, grass and flowers. . . .

In the Lion's Den

The communists had tried to paint Hubert Humphrey with the brush of big business. Some even charged that the National Association of Manufacturers was the real power behind Humphrey.

This, of course, was just what the NAM was not. The NAM was not a supporter of Humphrey or his brand of "politics for people." It supported restrictive labor legislation such as Taft-Hartley; Humphrey opposed such laws. It opposed extension of fair trade law; Humphrey more than just supported such laws, he proposed them.

But, if he were to see the legislation he proposed and/or supported turned into law, he would need the support of at least a portion of big business.

For that reason, Humphrey was always eager to accept speaking engagements before audiences comprised of executives of industry. He enjoyed going into "the lion's den" to explain his positions and seek support.

Such an occasion arose on December 7, 1955, when he was invited to address the Sixtieth Congress of American Industry.

. . . I have great faith and confidence in the political judgment of the American people, and the economic know-how of American industry.

I believe in free and open competition in the marketplace of commodities, as well as in the marketplace of ideas. Political and economic freedom cannot endure long without the free exchange of ideas and material goods.

A balanced and orderly free society, however, requires not only competition, but cooperation, between the individuals and segments of that society. This cooperation must embrace not only private individuals and institutions, but also embrace the institutions of government. . . .

Government—federal, state and local, and I include all three levels—can act as a creative force, either through positive action or by negative and restraining influence.

Fortunately for the American people, the Constitution of the United States places a direct responsibility on the government to promote the general welfare. That general welfare relates to the economic welfare of each and every citizen.

The first obligation of government is to be just—to assure equal opportunity for all. With this moral requirement of justice and equal opportunity, it has been necessary in the past, and it will be necessary in the future, for government to use its powers to curb the private exploitation of our human and natural resources, to regulate commerce in the interests of fair and honorable competition, and to assist the underprivileged and those who are the victims of economic and social injustice.

There are those who term such action by government as interference with free enterprise. I respectfully suggest that they are either unmindful of the constitutional requirements of the government to promote the general welfare, or have willfully and wrongfully interpreted the rules of free enterprise to be synonymous with the code of the jungle.

Freedom is not license, nor is enterprise exploitation.

Free enterprise is a constructive force. It has a social obligation as well as a profit motive.

A political democracy or a constitutional republic cannot long endure when the social and economic needs of the citizenry are sacrificed or ignored. For that reason, the political requirements for prosperity must, above all, include social justice and equal opportunity. . . .

Legislative policies of the past twenty-five years have greatly assisted in building a strong base for the American economy.

This is a mass-production economy and mass production requires mass consumption.

This is a consumer's economy, and it can expand and remain prosperous only so long as it is geared to maximum purchasing power.

Every segment of the economy must be afforded an opportunity to share in prosperity. . . .

Health, welfare and education of our American citizens is basic to a dynamic and expanding economy. It would be shortsighted to seek a material prosperity in which such basic human needs were brushed aside.

There are often costs to maintaining full prosperity.

Yet, there have been and still will be far higher costs to industry as well as consumers for failing to maintain reasonably balanced growth in our economy. . . .

The question is not so much how much we spend or what

tax adjustments we make to insure prosperity, but rather that we do the right thing early enough, and on a large enough scale, to obtain the results we need for our balanced objectives of maximum employment, maximum production and maximum purchasing power.

In summary, the key to the success of any of these political requirements for prosperity is a constant alertness, a boldness of vision that refuses to be satisfied with any goals of the past as being satisfactory goals for the future, a determination to act aggressively and quickly on any of these related fronts when action is needed, and a willingness to accept change when change is called for rather than be chained to any dogma of the past.

Jews Are People, Too

Anti-Semites who are about to begin spouting forth their venom-dripping phrases of hate usually begin by saying, "Some of my best friends are Jewish."

Hubert Humphrey said that many times—only he meant it. Some of his best friends were Jewish. He always felt a special kinship to Jews in his adult years, although it is doubtful that he ever met one while he was growing up.

In one of his final meetings with President Carter, for example, Humphrey told the president that there were "just a couple of things that I may be slightly prejudiced on": organized labor and the American Jewish community. In September 1977, Humphrey told a basically non-Jewish, all-labor audience: "[The Jews] have been my friends and, please, don't ask me to do anything that would betray their legitimate interests and their deep concern over their role in the American life. . . ."

The following speech, delivered to the Senate on February 17, 1956, is self-explanatory. The situation to which he addressed himself, unfortunately, still exists twenty-two years later.

. . . [Present] Arab policy in the Middle East has had an intolerable and discriminatory effect on American citizens of Jewish faith. These American citizens have been refused entry and travel visas in certain Middle Eastern countries. Even members of the United States armed forces and government officials have been subjected to this discrimination.

Airlines have been compelled to drop Jewish personnel if their routes cross Arab countries. Neither Iraq nor Saudi Arabia permits Jewish passengers to land on their territory.

I am talking about American citizens, Mr. President.

In Saudi Arabia, the American government is compelled to arrange that there should be no Jews in the personnel, civil or military, which we send to that country.

Mr. President, we are condoning that kind of discrimination. If we permit this kind of violation of American privileges and rights as citizens to take place in any country, the next thing to happen will be that they will select some other national group which is no longer permitted to enter the particular country with which we may do business.

I wish to repeat, Mr. President, that in Saudi Arabia the American government is compelled to arrange that there shall be no Jews in the personnel, civil or military, which we send to that country. Furthermore, neither Iraq nor Saudi Arabia permits Jewish passengers to land on their territory—American citizens, Mr. President.

Mr. President, no foreign government has the right to discriminate between one American passport and another. Has our government protested to the governments concerned? Has it pushed its protests with vigor and persistence. . . ?

I ask the government of the United States, I ask the secretary of state, to give us a clear, definable, unmistakable, understandable expression of the foreign policy of the United States in the Middle East. . . .

I should like to get the answers to those questions. I think we are entitled to know them. I may say that I am rather discouraged in having to play the part of detective to learn what our government intends to do. . . .

It is about time the government of the United States made up its mind as to what our policies are, and what policies are to be pursued, and then to take into its confidence the appropriate committees of Congress with respect to the nature of those policies. . . .

I trust we shall not constantly have to be engaged in argument and debate over matters which should be settled peaceably, with understanding, and, I may say, with full co-operation between Congress and the executive branch.

Prelude to Little Rock

Events were taking shape in 1956 that would bring about the most serious confrontation between the federal government and the states since the end of the Civil War.

The Supreme Court of the United States, on May 17, 1954, had unanimously struck down the separate-but-equal doctrine that had been the law of the land ever since 1896, when an earlier Supreme Court declared the doctrine constitutional in the case of Plessy v. Ferguson.

In 157 decisions since 1896, the high court had reaffirmed its view that the doctrine did not deny citizens their rights as long as the various states maintained truly equal segregated public facilities.

But, in Brown v. Board of Education, *that decision was unanimously overturned. Separate-but-equal was dead and buried and segregation with it, the court declared. The Fourteenth Amendment, which prohibited states from denying "to any person within its jurisdiction the equal protection of the laws," automatically invalidated any laws which sought to do otherwise.*

Voices of anger and defiance rose from the South. Seventeen states and the District of Columbia maintained segregated public school systems in fact and in law. Four states, while having no such law on their books, nevertheless maintained segregated school systems. Georgia's Governor Herman Talmadge and Louisiana's Governor Robert Kennon openly vowed defiance of the law.

But there were also voices of moderation and reason heard in the South. Governor James F. Byrnes of South Carolina, for example, regretted the decision but declared that order must be preserved at all cost.

For a while, the voices of moderation prevailed. The South decided to sit tight while the administration in Washington decided what course to take to enforce the historic decision.

But the Eisenhower administration moved slowly and cautiously, thus inadvertently giving the militant forces an opportunity to incite the people of the South to defy—by whatever means necessary—the order they hated so much.

Finally, on May 31, 1955, the Supreme Court could wait no longer and took matters into its own hands once again. Segregation must be ended in public school systems and integration made a fact "with all deliberate speed," it said. Still, the Eisenhower administration did nothing.

Then, on March 12, 1956, a "Declaration of Constitutional Principles" was issued by nineteen U.S. senators and seventy-seven members of the House of Representatives, representing eleven states. In that declaration, the signers pledged "to use all lawful means to bring about a reversal of this decision. . . and to prevent the use of force in its implementation." (Emphasis ours.)

What this meant was that the South would do everything in its power to prevent enforcement of an order of the Supreme Court. It was the old doctrine of interposition brought to life again.

A year and a half later, on September 2, 1957, Governor Orval Faubus of Arkansas moved in units of the Arkansas National Guard to block integration of the all-white Central High School in Little Rock. Twenty-two days later, on September 24, President Eisenhower ordered one thousand paratroopers attached to the 327th Airborne Battle Group of the 101st Airborne Division flown into Little Rock from Fort Campbell, Kentucky. Armed with rifles and bayonets, those paratroopers enforced the integration of Central High School on the following day.

The "Declaration of Constitutional Principles" had helped set the stage for that tragic confrontation. Hubert Humphrey, among others, appealed at the time for reason, not rhetoric.

... This is a truly sad, bewildering, and difficult day in the Senate of the United States. This great body is sworn to uphold the Constitution of the United States. . . .

Once the Supreme Court of the United States has spoken, not merely upon statutory law, but upon constitutional law. . . , the presumption is, and should be, that the order of the court and the rule of the court is the law of the land—to be obeyed and upheld. . . .

[The] Fourteenth Amendment is a part of the Constitution of the United States. The fact that the Fourteenth Amendment has not been applied in some specific instances throughout the past decades does not in any way weaken or vitiate this power of law. . . .

[This] amendment is all-important in our constitutional structure. For years it has been interpreted and primarily applied to the economic interests of our country, under the doctrine of what we call reasonableness, "due process of law" being interpreted as a reasonable rule of law. It was applied that way to economic matters and to large corporate interests.

The Supreme Court, in the case involving school segregation, applied the principle to citizens of the United States, to human beings rather than corporate beings, to people rather than property. . . .

I must say with all due respect—and I certainly respect the knowledge and experience of my colleagues—that the Supreme Court did not write the law; it merely applied existing constitutional law. It applied the principle of human equality—equal treatment under the law—Mr. President, which, since July 4, 1776, has been declared as the fundamental tenet of our republic. . . .

[The] principle of federalism leaves no room for nullification; and. . . it leaves no room for interposition. Interposition fully developed becomes nullification, as the courts of our country have stated. Nullification is a violation of the Constitution. It cannot be condoned. . . .

If there is one plea that I make here today, it is that we continue to reason with one another, rather than be the victims of passion or emotion. . . .

[If] ever there was a time when senators and members of the House of Representatives should be calling upon the people of their states to work together, to build together, to reason together, it is now. Once the Supreme Court has ruled, arguments over law will yield little or no results, except to arouse passions and encourage delay and obstruction.

The task is to plead for persevering patience, to proceed to the fulfillment of human equality, to encourage compliance with the law. No man in his right mind wants violence or force. What we seek is orderly progress, systematic progress, in the spirit of friendship and helpfulness. . . .

I plead with my colleagues that if we persist in antagonism and bitterness, or if we persist in trying to hold back the rule of law, we shall only persist in leading future generations to terrible catastrophe and conflict. . . .

Therefore, let us hope and pray that out of this body will come voices and out of the statehouses will come voices that will call upon the people as I have heard our majority leader [Lyndon Johnson] do many times, in the words of Isaiah: "Come now, let us reason together."

Mr. President, I add: Come, let us plan for forward progress together; come let us build together and live together. That is the only choice we have, Mr. President.

We cannot live apart. We must be as one.

The Adlai Double-Cross

While the "Declaration of Constitutional Principles" did help set the stage for the confrontation at Little Rock, it did not dominate the political scene in 1956. The presidential election did.

This time around, Adlai Stevenson was not the reluctant candidate he had been in 1952. He had been bitten by the presidential bug in earnest during that first campaign and now he was determined to get another crack at the White House. He decided to challenge Kefauver, who had also announced that he was in the race, in the presidential primaries.

It was no contest. Even before the convention opened in Chicago on August 13, Kefauver conceded that Stevenson had the nomination and pledged his support.

But Kefauver had stayed in the race all the way through the June 5 California primary, and he had waged a bitter fight. When he withdrew on July 31, he still had 300 or so delegates committed to him, and it was obvious that he could convert those delegates into vice-presidential ballots if the opportunity arose.

In mid-July, Stevenson met with Humphrey in a Washington hotel room. Under no circumstances, he told the Minnesota senator, did he want Kefauver on the ticket with him. An acceptable running-mate had to be found to block a Kefauver bid for the second spot. Did Humphrey have any suggestions?

Of course, Humphrey had suggestions and he made them. Suddenly, Stevenson turned to the senator and suggested that he, rather than anyone else, be the vice-presidential candidate.

Humphrey was stunned for a moment but finally admitted that he was interested. Stevenson then told Humphrey that the nomination was his—provided he could demonstrate an ability to garner Southern support.

Humphrey and aide Max Kampelman immediately set out to find that support. It would not be an easy task, they reasoned; with Southern tensions mounting over the Supreme Court's desegregation decisions of 1954 and 1955, it would be very hard indeed to find prominent Southerners to support the Senate's most outspoken advocate of civil rights.

But they were wrong. By 1956, senators from both parties and from all national regions had come to respect Humphrey highly. They saw in him an honesty and frankness that was uncommon in most politicians. His stand on civil rights, they knew, was rooted in principle, not politics. He was a man with endless ability and boundless energy.

For those reasons, six prominent Southerners quickly rallied behind the Humphrey bandwagon. Four of them—Senators John J. Sparkman (the party's 1952 vice-presidential nominee), Lister Hill, Walter George, and Richard B. Russell (who had called Humphrey a "damn fool" for his stand on civil rights in 1949)—were important supporters, but the other two were even more significant: House Speaker Sam Rayburn and Senate Majority Leader Lyndon B. Johnson.

Humphrey went to the Chicago convention confident that, in a few short days, he would be the Democratic nominee for vice-president of the United States.

What Humphrey could not know (because Stevenson had neglected to tell him) was that the soon-to-be-nominee had changed his mind. He would let the convention choose its own nominee.

After Stevenson was nominated, he announced that the vice-presidential nominee was an open contest. He would abide by the convention's decision, he said.

Humphrey was taken by surprise and was, therefore, unprepared for the floor fight that followed. His cause was doomed from the start, but he decided to make the race anyway.

Two other candidates had come to the convention hoping that Stevenson would not name his running-mate, and they were ready: Kefauver and Senator John F. Kennedy.

The ensuing floor fight was a bitter one. The Kefauver and Kennedy forces battled tooth and nail for every delegate they could get. At the end of the first ballot, Kefauver had the lead: 483½ votes to Kennedy's 304. New York City Mayor Robert F. Wagner had 162½ votes. Humphrey wound up with 134½ votes. He was out of the running.

On the second ballot, the lead went to Kennedy. He received 618 votes, only 68½ votes fewer than he needed to win. Kefauver's total, meanwhile, had risen to 551½.

At that point, various states that had been committed to Humphrey and Senator Albert Gore, Kefauver's home-state colleague, began switching votes. In a few short minutes, Kennedy picked up 30 more votes and was within 38½ votes of the nomination. Suddenly, the senator from Massachusetts rose and addressed the convention. Inexplicably, with victory seemingly only minutes away, he asked the delegates to nominate Kefauver by acclamation.

Humphrey left the convention feeling very bitter, one of the few times in his life he did. He had been double-crossed, he felt. The following day, Stevenson called to apologize, but Humphrey would not accept it. He was polite, but cool, to his party's standard-bearer.

But Hubert Humphrey never carried a grudge for too long. He soon plunged full force into the Stevenson-Kefauver campaign.

Stevenson's second race was an even greater disaster than his first one. Instead of losing by 6 million votes, he lost by nearly 10 million.

With the election out of the way and the Senate back in session, Humphrey *set to work on a number of important pieces of legislation that had not been acted upon by the upper house in the 84th Congress. Among them was the administration's modest civil rights bill, which had passed the House in 1956 but never made it to the floor of the Senate.*

The senator also continued his travels across the country, speaking to as many groups as possible.

In one speech, delivered on February 13, 1957, Humphrey combined two pet themes. Although he was urging his audience—comprised of members of the Washington branch of the Society of American Foresters—to get involved, he also had the opportunity to put in a number of plugs for conservation.

It is a pleasure to have this opportunity to appear before your Washington section of the professional Society of American Foresters, founded here just over fifty years ago by Gifford Pinchot. His ideals still inspire and guide us today.

Our forest programs, which assure us of our present-day timber supplies, are in large measure due to the dedication of Pinchot and his fellow foresters to the philosophy that government has an active responsibility for the custodianship of our God-given resources.

All of us concerned with conservation need to keep that philosophy to the forefront, and make sure our government does not neglect its responsibilities.

Fortunately, ever since Pinchot's time, foresters have continued to give strong leadership to the conservation movement. They have earned a distinguished place among the American professional groups.

Foresters have stood four-square in the public interest against those pressures from seekers of privilege who would corrupt governmental processes for personal gain. Never in the history of the Forest Service, which employs large numbers of you and which is responsible for custodianship of billions of dollars of national assets, has the breath of scandal touched a professional forester. . . .

I sincerely hope the American people realize and appreciate your unselfish devotion to an ideal. And I hope that this great tradition among professional foresters in their devotion to the public interest will continue unchanged, despite mounting pressures from those seekers of special rights in the property belonging to all citizens. . . .

In recent years, some have come to think that the battles over control over our natural resources have no application today. Perhaps we have lulled ourselves into a sense of false security because we have made great achievements in the widespread application of soil conservation, reforestation and wildlife-management measures. These technical applications are vital to sound conservation. Nearly everyone today agrees that proper soil, water and forest conservation techniques should be applied extensively.

But that is only a part of the conservation battle.

Pinchot observed fifty years ago that control over natural resources gives control over the economic and political life of the nation.

Make no mistake, gentlemen, the conservation battles of the last four years have been over the control of our national forests, water-power sites, and oil-underlain wildlife refuges, rather than over the technical applications and practices to the resources.

This is a never-ending struggle.

It should certainly surprise no one that this struggle becomes reflected in American political life, for political action is a means of achieving our aspirations and objectives in a democracy.

The fact that conservationists want the cooperation and support of elected officials or administrative officers of both political parties in our country should certainly never become a bar to recognizing and approving what a political candidate stands for or does that is right, nor to recognizing and repudiating just as firmly whatever a political candidate or administration stands for that is not right. . . .

We need more, not less, emphasis on these vital resources issues in our political campaigns—and we need conservation leaders with courage enough to speak out boldly when they see the public's interest being ignored. . . .

Forest policy is a broad field to try and cover in a limited time, so primarily tonight I am going to outline what I feel should be some of the important objectives in forestry which we in our generation should reach—and to suggest some of the policies which I feel will work in the direction of assuring adequate timber supplies, watershed protection, wildlife and other recreational benefits from our forestland resources.

We are the posterity which Pinchot, Teddy Roosevelt, Franklin Roosevelt and other foresighted leaders prepared for when they set aside the national forests, extended fire-protection programs, put unemployed boys to work planting trees and improving timber stands.

Now, upon our shoulders rests the task of providing for the posterity of the year 2000. And, gentlemen, we have no vast forests of virgin timber to bequeath our grandchildren. We must grow timber—lots more of it than we are today—if they are to continue to enjoy the fruits of our high American standard of living. And a timber-cropping economy takes some real effort, as you foresters are only too well aware. . . .

Either we begin to grow this timber today, or our children will have to pay absurdly high prices for what little there is left by then. . . .

Our political economy is so complex today that in this field, as in most others, we need to have the advice of technical people in making our decisions. I hope that foresters will not shun this duty under some sort of mistaken assumption that it is improper to advise your congressmen and senators, or to take a position in favor of what you believe to be sound forest policy.

In making our plans for the next fifty years in forestry, we have to develop one set for use on the greater areas of public forests occupying one-fourth of our forest land, and another set for the large area of private forest land. The first calls for direct action by public agencies, while the second, for cooperative working relationships with private owners—large and small.

We in the Congress, and in the state legislatures, too, must continue to assure that sufficient funds become available for management of public lands, including the planting, protection from insects and diseases, and stand-improvement measures. We must make sure that the federal government's share of the cooperative programs with the states for fire protection, nurseries and extension work are properly met—and on a scale which will expand tree growth to meet our future needs.

But the job does not stop with federal appropriations, and the government is not in the business of dictating to private owners what they should do.

The proper role of government toward private forest lands seems to me, in our democratic political economy, to be one of providing a favorable economic and social climate for individual owners to do those things on their forests which are in the public interest.

Both the public forests and the larger industrial tracts are apparently being fairly well managed and such management will improve as your professional techniques improve. But I am told that lack of a solution of the small-owner forestry problem is one which is giving foresters much concern. And well it should, for such lands make up the majority of our commercial forest area. . . .

The plain facts are, . . . that none of us have clear-cut answers to the small-owner problem. The Congress is willing to do all it can to help, but the ideas must come from the forestry profession.

One thing seems clear: If we are to have a strong and vital forest economy, greater research effort must be given to the problems of the small owner and independent logging operator. . . .

I might be so bold as to suggest that one reason you are so far along in the solution of your public and industrial forestry problem is because you foresters have done an excellent job in those fields. But, conversely, your lack of success with extending to small ownership is because you are devoting comparatively little research to this problem.

Because it does embrace several millions of small owners and thousands of independent farmer-loggers, our forest economy is a vital part of rural America.

It represents one of the remaining parts of our economy which has not been swallowed up by huge combinations of corporate enterprise. I hope it will never be.

Our forest industries, even the large ones, are highly

decentralized and provide markets for the products of the self-employed logger. Our public forests and those under private ownership will continue, I hope, to assure that this great group of independent woodsmen will have free access to raw material which will not have to be cleared through a Washington bureau office or a New York corporation office.

If that ever happens, I think America will have lost more of her free and independent spirit than I care to contemplate.

The Real Enemies

Saving the nation's forests was a noble cause and one for which Humphrey diligently worked. But saving forests would be of little use if the world went to war again.

Humphrey was a passionate advocate of keeping the military strong by improving weapons technology. In no way, he believed, could the United States ever afford to let the Soviet Union maintain superiority in that area.

But better and more powerful weapons only delayed another world war; they did nothing to end the threat to world peace—and nuclear holocaust—once and for all. That, Humphrey maintained, could only be accomplished through acts of peace, brotherhood and friendship.

During his lifetime, the senator from Minnesota proposed many such people-to-people plans.

In a speech before a joint session of the American Pharmaceutical Advertising Clubs of New York, the Midwest and Montreal, Canada, delivered on June 5, 1957, he offered one such program.

On July 24, 1957, he offered yet another program—this time to the annual luncheon meeting of the national board of directors of CARE (Cooperative for American Remittances to Everywhere). That program was the beginning of Humphrey's Food for Peace program.

Excerpts from those two speeches follow.

It is indeed an honor to be speaking before this great assembly of representatives of many pharmaceutical firms and of the professions of pharmacy and medicine today, on the opening day of the American Medical Association annual convention.

I am even more pleased because there is a special personal element in my appearance before you. As many of you know, I am still a registered pharmacist and a part owner of our family drugstore in Huron, South Dakota.

My dad was a pharmacist and pharmacy was my first love. I studied it and worked behind the prescription counter. So this setting is warm to my heart. . . .

But while there is this personal element, I want to speak to you as a United States senator who is concerned with the problems of world health and how they influence our foreign relations. . . .

Living here in the United States—in this prosperous country of ours and in light of our technical accomplishments—it is difficult for us to believe that more than two-thirds of the world is sick. There are those who would say the figure is closer to four persons out of every five. This is serious food for thought.

Millions of suffering people are bound by the oppressive chains of disease. In large sections of the world, malnutrition, illiteracy and inadequate shelter are still part of the everyday life of many millions of our fellow men. . . .

Forward-looking groups such as yours can and should perform a service in advancing ideas and establishing a favorable climate for a new world health leadership. Science has given us the tools with which to wipe away disease from the face of the earth. What we need is the personnel and research to carry out the work and the funds with which to operate.

There is a need in the world today for a nonpublic, international, professional medical group or foundation whose aim would be to lift the burden of disease from the shoulder of mankind through research, study, assistance and information exchange.

This foundation could be composed of representatives of

medical and pharmaceutical professions and the pharmaceutical industry from all parts of the world. . . .

Sometimes any kind of intervention—whether to alleviate hunger or to alleviate ill health—may be misunderstood or resented. People who may be wary of accepting aid from the United States will more readily accept the assistance of an international organization to which they themselves belong. The world professional foundation, of which I have talked, could be one such organization through which professional and industrial members can work to help each other and to help themselves.

Permit me to summarize the aims of this plan. . . : They are to bring the great benefits of American advances in chemotherapy to more people everywhere; to encourage the development of pharmaceutical research and other facilities in countries less advanced than ours; to encourage the adaptation and application of our medical and pharmaceutical institutions in other countries; to encourage more person-to-person exchanges; to help alleviate shortages of trained personnel and to focus attention of all governments on aspects of the medical field as developed by the plan.

Through official and private channels, the foundation could offer help with public-health education, distributing visual and literal aids.

Meetings could be held in major cities of the world to discuss the pharmaceutical challenges in relation to world health problems. The group could encourage the dissemination of knowledge through publications and, as I have said, person-to-person contact.

Unless I have overlooked limitations of a highly resistant nature, I think the American pharmaceutical industry will not shirk its humanitarian obligations. Again and again it has demonstrated that it cares by shipping needed drugs abroad to help their fellows overcome emergency.

Yours is an industry that has thrived on the challenge and the excitement of creating new medicines. You sometimes even "live dangerously" as business goes, by making a maximum financial effort to find an elusive aid against a disease, with no assurance of success and return to your stockholders.

Such a plan as I have outlined cannot and should not be achieved solely by the efforts of governments working either independently or together. We need the coordination of private interests and private investments—we need the sharing of skill and experience—we need the helping of the weak by the strong. . . .

People can only start thinking of freedom and the rights of the individual when they are freed from the day-to-day concern of trying to eke out a bare survival and are in good enough health to turn their attention to matters other than sheer subsistence. In helping others to help themselves, we are achieving in a practical way a means for those people to live fuller lives. . . .

Clearly we cannot expect to live peacefully in a world slum overflowing with disease, tension and hate. Nor can we impose peace by bombs and tanks.

As former President Truman said: "The only kind of war we seek is the good old fight against men's ancient enemies . . . poverty, disease, hunger, and illiteracy."

We must join in this all-out attack. . . . All of us—through consistent, practical, concrete action—must demonstrate in unmistakable terms our genuine concern for the rank-and-file of humanity, and our willingness to help them build a better life.

Such a program will take time. The poverty and insecurity that beset the majority of the world's people were centuries in the making, and they will not be erased overnight.

But delay cannot be tolerated. We must march ahead with confidence, hope, imagination and boldness.

. . . I believe that our foreign policy has real importance and genuine constructive effect when we search for, find and use the key to what we call the American way of life.

What is it that really typifies our country. . . ?

No country on the face of the earth has the number of voluntary organizations that we have in the United States— voluntary organizations that are so generously supported and that have such a wide scale of activities. . . .

We are engaged today, fellow Americans, in a struggle with a totalitarian force. It is unfortunate that the American people are not being educated as to what is meant by totalitarianism. All too often they assume it is a political party in control of a country; they assume it is just another political force at work.

It is not; it is more than that. It is a political force, a military force, an economic force, a social force, a human force—put in one package, mobilized, directed and energized for the purpose of the leadership of a state.

Now, our government is only part of America. Therefore, when the government of the United States joins the issue with the Soviet Union, a totalitarian state, we have, so to speak, one arm strapped behind our back and one leg cut off. The government of the United States alone cannot successfully compete with a totalitarian power. But the government of the United States plus the voluntary organizations, plus every social and political institution that we have in America, cannot only compete but can win. . . .

So, my friends, there is a great role for organizations such as CARE to play. You are not engaged in something now that is just going good; you are engaged, as you and I know, in a life-and-death struggle.

This is a one-game world series. I don't know how many innings it is going to go, but you do not have four chances out of seven in this one. . . . This is a one-game world series against forces of evil, of imperialism, of totalitarianism—and we either win or lose. How long it goes on only we can tell, by what we do each day. This is where CARE is important.

What does CARE, then, represent?

It represents self-help. This is good.

What else does it represent?

It represents compassion and charity by living application. There is something noble in being charitable. . . .

I have no desire to be the richest man in the cemetery. I desire to use the good things that the good Lord gave me. I have never made a fetish to see how many dollars can be saved; I prefer to find out how many can be well invested, and for what purpose.

Many people have saved and saved only to destroy themselves and their families; countries have done exactly the same thing.

I grew up at a time when this country closed its doors to immigrants, when it closed its mind to new ideas, closed its heart to the crying suffering of other people. Finally we ended up closing our factories, our businesses and our banks, and almost destroying the whole temple of American democracy.

I remember because that was the impressionable period of my life. From 1920 to 1933, I listened attentively to those who were then the spokesmen of American ideals, and their sense of idealism was only to save, to amass money, to guard it, to protect it—don't let anybody touch it, don't let anybody use it, and don't be too good to anybody.

In the process, they were among the first to suffer and the first to be destroyed.

I remember when bankers were jumping out of hotel windows faster than pheasants were depleted in our South Dakota cornfields. I am not saying this to be unkind; I am saying it because it is true. I am the happiest man in the world to have since lived in a time when the government of the United States has been criticized for being overgenerous, rather than for being a tightwad.

I am happy to have lived in a time when the American people have been asked again and again through the Community Chest, through the CARE program, through the Crusade for Freedom, through all the many programs sponsored by generous-minded citizens, to contribute and contribute and contribute. And interestingly enough, my good friends, look and see what has happened. The record reveals that as contributions to voluntary agencies grow larger, the economic index indicates the prosperity of the country is that much better. Study it sometime and see if I am not right.

You will find that when people show a spirit of generosity,

of openness, of kindliness, for some peculiar reason the country itself is in a better economic, political and social state of health.

That is why I feel the way I do about politics and that is why I feel the way I do about these great programs. . . .

I have been told by three prominent officials that our food program did more to defeat communism in Italy than the government of the United States had been able to accomplish through any of its other agencies of aid. I happen to think the forces of religion helped immeasurably, too, but if you put those two together, that is what did it. Not our military assistance, not one bit. We need that, just as sometimes we may need to remove our appendix. It isn't something planned nor longed for; yet it sometimes is necessary. But constructive aid is preferable.

I was told in Greece, for example, that without our food program, and particularly without our CARE program, Greece would be fighting for her life, despite all the military assistance we poured in, despite the hundreds of millions of dollars in grants we gave to Greece. I was told by the prime minister, the foreign minister and the present American ambassador to Greece that our food program was the difference between success and failure in Greece.

I have gone home to Minnesota to tell a few of our farm people about this, because too often they have been criticized for producing food. I want to say to my friends of the metropolitan press, farmers have been abused daily because they produce an abundance of food. Any country or government that doesn't know what to do with food is intellectually sterile and hopelessly lost.

Can you imagine what Bulganin and Khrushchev would be doing if they had the surpluses of food and fiber that we have? Can you imagine what those "Gold Dust Twins of Disaster and Despair" would be doing? They would be tying to the Soviet one country after another economically. Yet we go around crying about our food surplus as if it was the worst thing that ever happened to a free country. . . .

When I think of what I have read in American newspapers

about waste of food, I say every American ought to be ashamed that such waste occurs. Any American who is willing to permit even as much as one bushel of our wheat to be wasted is committing a sin. Whenever I hear an official of government talk about how much it costs to store this grain, I say, "Why don't you give it away, then it won't cost so much." It doesn't cost too much to store it right inside the stomachs of hungry people.

It often costs more when we don't act. If we are interested only in saving money, shall we take our children out of school? Of course, it will be costly because they are going to remain ignorant. If we are interested only in saving money, shall we refrain from seeing the doctor? We may not live long, but we will save money.

I repeat, there is not a single thing that will not cost money. The amount that we spend on the total food program is insignificant compared to the total foreign policy and defense expenditures of our government. It's significant, I think, how much we are given free in service from CARE, for example, and other voluntary organizations. And what an impact this makes upon people. This is the best-spent money that we will ever spend. . . .

This is my crusade. I want you to know that. I am more interested in this subject right now than almost anything that has ever touched my life. I believe that in this food program, going beyond what you do in CARE alone, there is an opportunity for the redesigning of a foreign policy with great potentialities.

In the sale of our food, we provide economic means for other countries. We momentarily ease the tension and the suffering. We develop new markets and habits. We carry with it a message of American generosity, kindliness and democracy, particularly when you tie in donations through voluntary agencies.

We build new contacts. We touch the lives of many people and we reach the man in the street, so-called little people whose minds are still open, those whose spirits have yet to be fully roused. . . .

People all over the world today are demanding a place in the sun, are asking for recognition, and, unhappily, some of these people believe the only way they can gain status is through the totalitarian method.

Regrettably, in a free country governments are timid. Most of the time, unless under duress and emergency, they lack courage. Where is there no timidity? In the people.

Most members of Congress are more timid than the people. There are some of us that aren't timid; I guess I qualify on occasion. But timidity is a characteristic of free government; courage and zeal to meet any emergency is a characteristic of a voluntary agency.

We must have that or I am afraid we might lose that one-game world series I spoke about. . . .

The Will To Survive

Between his speeches to the Pharmaceutical Advertising Club in June and the CARE luncheon in late July, Hubert Humphrey visited the Middle East as chairman of the Foreign Relations Committee's subcommittee on the Near East and Africa.

He had always been drawn to the state of Israel; for him, it stood for what he stood for: people working together to create a better life for themselves, and for government working together with people to help further that goal.

But he was not fully prepared for what he found when he got there. He had heard much about the "miracle of the desert," but now he saw it first-hand. The remnant of European Jewry, literally snatched from the arms of the angel of death, had joined together with young coreligionists to rebuild a nation that had been dead for 2,000 years and to reclaim the soil that had been barren for almost as long.

They overcame disaster and disease; flowers bloomed where once there were swamps; trees brought forth fruit where only cactus used to grow; modern cities appeared where only ruins once stood.

It was indeed a miracle—done without sacrificing democratic principles and under the unrelenting guns of the Arab states surrounding it.

When he returned to the United States, Humphrey wanted to get the message of Israel across to as wide an audience as possible. He spoke about what he had seen at every opportunity, both on the Senate floor and off. And he wrote a series of four articles for general distribution.

The words Humphrey spoke and wrote in 1957 are as applicable today as they were then. Too many people in power today tend to forget the truth of those words, especially as they relate to the Palestinians.

What follows is a combined and edited version of a speech he made to the Senate on July 10 and his series of articles.

In one of the oldest areas of the world in terms of history, it is quite an experience to find perhaps the most youthful spirit of the twentieth century.

That is the paradox of Israel today. Israel is a country rich in tradition. Every mile of its land is like a chapter of ancient history. Yet, it is today a nation filled with dreams of tomorrow, motivated, strengthened and sustained by a centuries-old culture and faith.

Israel is a political and economic oasis in the Middle Eastern desert of feudalism, economic imbalance and grave social inequities.

Indeed, there is a most remarkable spirit of national unity in the state of Israel. There is a sense of pride in national accomplishments and confidence in the national ability to meet whatever the future may hold.

Among my many vivid impressions of Israel, etched deepest in my memory perhaps is the evident spirit of youth. Every place you see children, and in every walk of life young people are taking a decisive and important role. Coupled with the enthusiasm of youth, one notices the strength and steadiness of those who have found early maturity by the shouldering of responsibility.

In Israel the attention is upon people and water, rather than upon privilege and oil.

The Israelis have proven themselves skilled conservationists and excellent farmers. They have turned rock into soil, barren hills into forests.

Water is regarded as a precious resource. There is an overall, comprehensive nationwide plan to obtain maximum utilization of water resources. Pipeline construction, small dams and well-drilling operations are pressed forward, particularly in the southern part of the country. . . . The land is fertile and productive, when the life-giving water is made available.

I was tremendously impressed with what I saw—the terracing, the tree planting, the orchards and the fields of grain. Upper and lower Galilee are very productive areas, and particularly beautiful. The hills of Judea are again being made fertile and productive.

One gets the feeling in Israel that everything is possible. . . .

The people of Israel are convinced they have a great future. They already have a memorable history. What Israel needs now is the dedication and faith of her friends. . . .

The spirit and story of twentieth-century Israel is reminiscent in many ways of the old American West.

One finds the same easy informality, the same feeling of self-reliance, and the same kind of courage and daring by which a pioneer people lives. Yes, even the topography reminds an American of our own West. . . .

An American can feel very much at home in Israel—that is, an American who loves adventure, and who realizes that our own great country was once a little nation wedged between the sea and wilderness.

America and Israel have much in common. Both countries had to fight for independence. Both had powerful forces for many years aligned against them. The people of both countries had to conquer a wilderness. Each people learned to sacrifice and to share. In both nations, there is a spirit of equality which lends dignity to labor and strengthens the drive toward achievement and progress.

Is it any wonder, therefore, that Americans are sympathetic to the state of Israel? We Americans like people who dedicate their energies to building, creating, and developing the physical and human resources. We like people who can face adversity without fear.

To be frank about it, we like people who are willing to stand up and fight for their rights.

And, indeed, we have a high regard and respect for people who have learned and practiced the art of self-government— who believe in democratic institutions and principles. This is why there is a strong friendship between the United States and Israel. . . .

Israel is a friend of the United States. There can be no doubt about this. She is a natural ally.

Without any formal treaty of alliance, we have in the people and government of Israel a loyal and brave ally. This unwritten alliance is based upon mutual understanding and respect.

Our interests are closely aligned.

Israel is not only anticommunist, but she is profreedom. She is anticommunist because many of her people already know what it has meant to live under dictatorship in other lands. She is anticommunist because of her religious faith and cultural tradition. She is profreedom because the people of Israel are individualistic; the prophets of old taught them the meaning of human dignity.

The history of Israel is one of fighting against oppression, seeking liberation and emancipation. Besides that, the people of Israel know and have proven that freedom affords the best opportunity for a productive society and general happiness.

The Israelis are prepared to defend that freedom. They have developed the strength in both economic and military terms to defend themselves.

I am convinced that Israel now has the respect of her neighbors. But the people and leadership of Israel do not want to spend their resources and time on military matters; they seek to release themselves from the burden of patrolling the borders and paying the heavy costs of military equipment.

While Israel's army is the best in the Middle East, it should not be forgotten that their regular and standing army is, indeed, a very small one. The secret of Israel's military strength is in her reserves, and the quick and efficient mobilization of those trained reserves. The young men and women of Israel are all trained to defend their country. And defend it they have and will, because they believe in it. It is their country. It belongs to the people. It is their hope for today, and their promise for tomorrow. . . .

But the people of Israel are not militarists; they seek to live in peace with their neighbors. They seek to find the answers to Arab-Israeli difficulties. Those difficulties include the adjustment of boundaries and borders, the Arab refugees, the boycott by Egypt of use of the Suez Canal. There are other problems, but these are the main ones.

I talked to Prime Minister Ben-Gurion quite frankly about all these problems, and I found him understanding and longing for their solution.

He was not intransigent or obstinate on the refugee question. He is perfectly willing that Israel shall take back into its borders some of the refugees—and, indeed, already has—but he made it quite clear that it would be impossible to take them all back. To do so would threaten the very security of the state.

He further indicated the desire of Israel to compensate those who had lost their lands. But he made it quite clear that most of the Arab refugees left Israel not because they were driven out, but because their leaders asked them to leave with the promise that the Israelis would be driven into the sea—and then the Arabs could come back and not only have their old lands, but more that would be taken away from the Israelis.

Of course, those Arab plans did not work out. The Israelis won the war and the refugees were out of the country. This is not to say that there were no attacks upon Arabs, because there were by some of the extremist groups. However, the government of Israel had asked the Arabs to remain. Those that did stay live in peace within Israel today.

The question now, of course, is not just who was right or wrong. The point is that a solution must be found. . . .

The settlement of the Arab refugee problem must be given priority on the world's agenda.

The fact is that the Arab states have. . . used the Palestinian refugees as political hostages in their struggle with Israel. As a matter of concerted policy these people have been kept penned up in the camps in conditions of wretched hopelessness in order to embarrass Israel before the eyes of the world. While Arab delegates in the United Nations have condemned the plight of their brothers in the refugee camps, nothing has been done to assist them lest political leverage over Israel be lost.

Human lives cannot be left to remain as mere political pawns; world opinion must force dispersal and resettlement of these refugees one way or another.

But above all else, my tour has reaffirmed my own deep conviction that the only realistic basis for any effective American policy toward the Middle East must rest first of all on the firm assumption that Israel is an integral part of the region—and there to stay.

An Egghead Hunt

Hubert Humphrey was a happy man as summer gave way to fall in 1957. For the first time in eighty-two years, the Congress of the United States had passed a civil rights act.

Nine such bills had passed the House since 1933 but they invariably died in the Senate, usually because of Southern-led filibusters.

The same thing seemed to be happening again. The House had passed the administration's moderate civil rights bill—which established a Civil Rights Commission, provided for another assistant attorney general and gave certain new powers to federal courts—by a vote of 286 to 126.

But on the Senate side, the bill was being talked to death. South Carolina's Strom Thurmond broke the filibuster record that year by speaking for twenty-four hours and eighteen minutes, although rarely ever addressing himself to the issue.

This time, however, things were different. Arkansas Governor Faubus had defied court-ordered integration of Little Rock's Central High School by calling out the National Guard. The Constitution and the rule of law were seriously threatened.

Amid the building tension over Little Rock, the Senate uncharacteristically shut off debate on the Civil Rights Act of 1957.

On September 9, a small band of whites (about thirty in all) turned back six blacks who were about to enter North Little Rock's all-white high school.

The Eisenhower administration, clinging to its position that the law must be obeyed and would be at all cost, nevertheless failed to take immediate action. It would be another fifteen days before the president ordered 1,000 armed paratroopers into Little Rock to enforce the law.

The Senate, however, was quick to react. Within hours of the incident in North Little Rock, it passed the civil rights bill by a lopsided 78 to 18 vote.

Finally, Hubert Humphrey knew, the barrier of resistance had been broken in the Senate. Much more had to be done, but now he was confident that it would be done. It was only a matter of time.

It was also only a matter of time before Soviet technology would so far surpass the United States' as to make anything but capitulation impossible.

On October 4, the Soviets amply demonstrated their technological superiority in a most dramatic way: they launched man's first satellite into outer space. The 184-pound Sputnik I, circling the globe every one-and-a-half hours, was chilling testimony to the fact that the United States was sorely deficient in the development of its most vital natural resource: brain power.

As if to drive the point home more clearly, the Soviets on November 4, 1958, launched Sputnik II, which weighed in at an astonishing (to U.S. scientists, at least) 1,120 pounds. The United States was then preparing to launch its first Vanguard satellite, which weighed only 21 pounds.

But it wasn't just the weight that surprised everyone this time. For Sputnik II was carrying a living, breathing passenger: Laika, a female dog.

Nikita Khrushchev summed up the startling achievement this way:

"Artificial earth satellites will pave the way for space travel and it seems that the present generation will witness how the freed and conscious labor of the *people of the new socialist society turns even the most daring dreams into a reality."*

Dr. Edward H. Teller, developer of the hydrogen bomb, looked at it a little differently. The Soviet achievement "has great military significance," he said, "because, among other things, it shows that the Russians are far along, very far along, in rocketry development."

To Hubert Humphrey, this challenge had to be met quite literally head-on. Over 150,000 bright students a year were being forced to quit school without going to college because they could not afford it. Humphrey, therefore, proposed a massive student loan program to help deserving youngsters develop their full potential.

He explained this "egghead hunt" in a speech to the Minnesota State Association of Student Councils, meeting in Thief River Falls on November 8, four days after Laika took her journey into history.

. . . Anti-intellectualism—the fear and distrust of thinking people—is a disease we simply must stamp out. We cannot afford any more the luxury of laughing at eggheads as too often some have done, or of suggesting there is something treasonable about being an intellectual. . . .

Frankly, I am on an egghead search. I am looking for more scientists and engineers, more gifted young people in every field of American effort. . . .

Not all eggheads are geniuses. Not all eggheads are potential scientists and engineers. An egghead is simply a thinking, reflecting person, who may well have a strong streak of creativity in him—or her. The basic hallmarks of the egghead are concern primarily with ideas, a restless, inquiring mind; a dedication to something higher and outside himself.

Some are hard-boiled and some are soft-boiled—but we need them all, and it is high time that the American people and our United States government decided to make it possible for a far higher percentage of young potential scholars to move up into positions of leadership. . . .

Every time a gifted young man or woman fails to go on to

college, or has to drop out of college because of lack of financial support, we lose a battle in the cold war. In this total struggle between ways of life, we must engage the enemy in depth. We must have reserves. We must look far into the future. . . .

Just to show you the caliber of the opposition, and the degree to which a Russian high school graduate is being force-fed with scientific education—a recent estimate indicates that such a graduate will have had ten years of mathematics, four of chemistry, five of biology, five of physics, and one of astronomy. . . . This is all before they go on to college. . . .

Now, what can the federal government do to help in this gigantic national effort which our people must make to provide the yeast of opportunity for the gifted young people among us?

Many things can be done.

Let me touch on some of the high points embodied in. . . my youth-opportunity program, and if it was vitally important before the sputnik began sailing over our heads, it is doubly important now.

First of all, we need a really intensive program of federal scholarships, administered on the basis of merit and need. We need to make available at least three times as many scholarships as are now available through private and industrial sources. . . .

I have proposed a long-term, low-interest loan program for college students—loans to be made by the colleges themselves and insured by the federal government, much as we insure housing loans through the Federal Housing Administration. . . .

The bill provides that a college graduate who enters the teaching profession upon graduation may write off his loan, a certain percentage of the loan being forgiven for each year he or she remains in the teaching profession.

We need to encourage young men and women to dedicate their lives as grassroot ambassadors, both in international public service and international private service for churches, foundations, and private enterprise. . . .

I am convinced that we need a Foreign Service Academy to provide us with most of our professional diplomats, and I intend to introduce legislation to this effect. But we can also proceed right now, without constructing one building, to get an incentive program underway in our colleges and universities to provide a corps of young men and women to carry out a technical-assistance program and a foreign-economic policy which could also accomplish wonders in winning the understanding of the peoples of Asia and Africa.

These young people should be carefully selected for their personable qualities as well as for their intelligence, for their ability to get along under unusual conditions as well as for their technical skills.

They should be drawn from all levels of our population, from all parts of the country, especially from farm families and the families of workingmen, from our people who have themselves known difficulties, who have had to work hard with their minds and their hands.

These are the kind of young people who could make contact with the peoples of Asia, Africa, and South America, who can talk their language—both literally and philosophically—who have the common touch.

These are the kind of people we ought to have in India and Pakistan and Indonesia—good, solid American young men and women, tough-minded and practical and knowledgeable. . . .

There is a real challenge to student organization here. There is the challenge to develop systematic procedures to steer promising students into college. And there is the equal challenge to encourage promising students even at the freshman and sophomore levels to take courses which will help prepare them to go on to higher education. . . .

I said that I am on an egghead hunt. Let me invite you to join me. Let me urge you to make it your personal business as student leaders to look for the other eggheads in your high school.

Most of you are the fortunate kind of egghead—the kind who has drive and initiative, and rises quickly to leadership. Not all eggheads, you know, have that ability. Many are shy, retiring. Many are slow starters. They need a helping hand—and no one is better equipped to give it to them than you are.

Do your part to help find our potential leaders in science and industry, the professions, in government. And I shall try to do mine—to provide these young people with the opportunity they deserve, and which our nation's own vital self-interest demands, the opportunity to develop their talents and faculties through higher education.

Mobilization for Peace

The launching of the sputniks pointed up more than just the Soviet superiority in brain power. It also demonstrated just how far technology had come since World War II.

These were perilous times, and they called for decisive action. But not the kind of action that would start a new war. Rather, what was needed now was an all-out "mobilization for peace."

On November 10, 1957, the day after his speech in Thief River Falls, Minnesota, Humphrey spoke about his "mobilization for peace" plan in a speech delivered to the National Convention of Young Democrats, meeting in Reno, Nevada.

The world is teetering between threatened annihilation, and the greatest era of new discovery and new progress mankind has yet known.

All of us share the sobering responsibility of guiding our destiny on its precarious course—to avert the destructive disaster of war and to achieve, instead, a far greater fulfillment of man's aspirations than history has yet recorded.

Those twin objectives are inseparable, each dependent upon the other.

In an age when war could mean annihilation, the maintenance of peace is our most urgent business. It is everybody's business, yours as well as mine. . . .

The last ten years have seen almost incredible changes in our world.

Atomic energy, with all its shattering dangers and unlimited opportunities, is intruding into our lives more each month. We have a bear by the tail, a locomotive that threatens to run away downhill with us. We have to tame this great power, before it enslaves us—or destroys us.

The beep-beep of the first Russian satellite told us that we have crossed another threshold—into the age of space flight. No longer is it idle speculation that man may some day reach the moon and the planets.

The new speeds of today, of a revolutionary nature, are destroying all our old ideas of space and distance, revolutionizing military strategy, revealing new concepts of communication and travel.

But the vast political changes in the world, in the relationship between nations, the breakup of the old colonial empires, the creation of a new Soviet empire headed by ruthless and tenacious leaders, the birth of new nations and the rising tide of nationalism in Asia and Africa: these political social changes in the world pose an equal challenge to American leadership. . . .

Nikita Khrushchev has thrown down the gauntlet across the board. He boasts that the Soviets will be supreme in nuclear power, in consumer-goods production, in cultural activities, in agricultural production, in education.

It is time we realized that the Soviets are waging all-out war on us, without a shot being fired. It is economic warfare, political warfare, cultural warfare, educational warfare and scientific and technological warfare. . . .

We have not yet fully faced up to the implications of this competition. We have not really assayed the costs in energy, in money, in worry, in sacrifice, to compete effectively with the Soviet Union across the board.

If we are to compete effectively, there must be a fundamental change in America toward the intellectuals and the scholars in our midst.

What America needs is more eggheads, and fewer fat-heads. . . .

If we are really to mobilize for peace, the place to start is with our brainpower, our experience, our intellectuals.

Just as we are suddenly facing the necessity of mobilizing our scientists to compete with Russia, so too do we need immediately to mobilize our intellectuals in every field who have a contribution they can make toward meeting Russia's challenge in other fields. . . .

The image of America which has been projected abroad for four years is a distorted image. In its changing and misshapen character, it is like a shadow leaping on the wall thrown by the light of a flickering candle. This is an image which has never in four years become stabilized—which has expanded and shrunk, leaned this way and that, until the world does not really know what this nation is.

And it is vitally important that our enemies, as well as our friends, know what we are, what we intend, what we will do—we must make very clear our basic policies. . . .

It is time that we walk confidently, with the full stature and strength of our history—and our present capacities as a people, if we will but fully use them.

In a world that is desperately in need of capital, we have the greatest capital resources of all.

In a world where people are anxious for the blessings of science and technology, we are richly endowed with these blessings.

In a world where the majority of people are ill-housed, ill-fed, and ill-clad, we are privileged to have an abundance of food and fiber and the knowledge of scientific progress for health and shelter. . . .

We must make greater use, not less, of our economic strength to help other free nations develop themselves, and bring the blessings of freedom to their eager and impatient peoples.

This is a weapon of peace and plenty which the Soviet Union cannot match. . . .

Even as we go forward with programs of international good will, we must remember that we still confront a formidable and implacable adversary—we must keep our defenses strong. . . .

But all our military strength can buy is time—time to build in other ways toward the peace we seek.

While we maintain our armed strength, we must continue to explore all possibilities for agreements to control armaments. And we must manage to convey to the world the positive sincerity of our passion for peace, and for control of arms as a means of diminishing the danger of war.

Above all else, we must keep ever foremost in our minds and hearts the knowledge that our strength is far more than military—that it must be the strength that comes from the spirit of human equality, economic progress, political liberty and social justice.

Ours is a nation of compassion.

Our heritage befits us for the great challenges we face.

That challenge, to you and me and to all of us, is to show the world a way to eradicate the shame and scandal of poverty, of exploitation, of oppression or of greed—without resort to social revolution and class struggle and dictatorship. . . .

Negotiating from Strength

On February 4, 1958, Humphrey rose in the Senate to make a lengthy and impassioned plea for disarmament—not unilateral disarmament, but worldwide disarmament.

The United States had to regain the technological lead, he argued; but the United States also had an obligation to take the lead in ending the threat of nuclear holocaust once and for all.

The only way this could be achieved, Humphrey told fellow senators, was if the United States came to the bargaining table from a position of strength.

... In recent weeks the American people, members of Congress, and indeed our allies have given prolonged thought to the military and foreign policy implications of the launching of the two Soviet earth satellites.

The sputniks have caused us to realize that the Soviet Union is exerting tremendous effort to accomplish impressive feats in science and technology.These accomplishments have alerted us to reexamine and reevaluate our defense policies, our defense organization and the state of our military preparedness.

Sputniks I and II have made us realize that, if we hope to maintain our defense capabilities and if we do not want to be outdistanced in the vital area of outer space, vastly increased effort and expenditures of funds may well be required. . . .

We have the resources to match—yes, even to surpass—the Soviet Union in military might. We are prepared to speed up production of missiles, and to equip our Army, Navy, and Air Force with weapons which can, if necessary, meet any type of attack. We are able to devote whatever is required to defend our shores, our fields, our industries and our cities against the new weapons of mass destruction.

But even when all this is done, the world will still be dangerously divided into two highly armed camps.

The peace we seek must be more than the absence of armed conflict. It must be a peace that embraces the expansion of the areas of political freedom and the development of closer bonds of international cooperation among all nations and peoples.

We who have the responsibility for appropriating funds for the new weapons of defense must keep reminding ourselves it is essential that we search perserveringly for the ways and means of securing a just and enduring peace so that the terrible reality of the use of these weapons will never happen.

We need the same courage and patriotism in our search for peace that would be required of us in the defense of our nation from hostile attack. . . .

Modern science and technology forewarn us of the appalling destruction that threatens us in the nuclear age. 'That same science and technology, however, beckons us to beat our swords into plowshares and our spears into pruning hooks, and that man shall study war no more.

The nuclear age can be an inferno of death and destruction or a garden of peace and plenty. This decision is the difference between good and evil—man and beast.

Our immediate task, therefore, is to prevent the two great power systems of the communist bloc and the free nations from colliding head-on either by design or accident, and thereby touching off World War III.

The world needs time—time to think, time to negotiate, time to find answers, time to realize the utter futility of armed conflict. . . , and the wondrous opportunities to be found in peaceful living.

The world needs leadership—inspired and humanitarian leadership—to point the way patiently, yet firmly, to peace.

This peace we so zealously desire will not come easily. Peace, like war, requires sacrifice. It requires also the mobilization and planned use of our material and human resources.

It is within this frame of reference that I venture to discuss the difficult and perplexing problem of the control and reduction of armaments. The discussion of disarmament policies and proposals must be undertaken within the context of our entire foreign and military policies.

Nor should we be restrained by inhibitions and preconceptions which so often bind us to the policies and attitudes of the past. This generation has witnessed two amazing and sensational scientific developments: the harnessing of nuclear energy and the breakthrough into outer space.

The diplomatic and political formulas of yesterday are not adequate for this era of power. . . .

There is reason to believe that those who conduct and design foreign policy make two false assumptions regarding the Soviet Union.

The first is that the United States has such political, military, and economic superiority that it can force the U.S.S.R. to accept our terms in any series of negotiations.

The other assumption is that the internal domestic difficulties of the Soviet regime are so great that all we need to do is continue to apply pressure and the collapse of the system will automatically follow. Both of these assumptions have been stated or implied many times.

Recent developments have shattered the validity of these assumptions:

—The Soviet sputniks indicate that the U.S.S.R. is, or will be in the near future, capable of launching intercontinental and intermediate-range ballistic missiles.

—Reports from Sweden seem to indicate that the Soviets have, or are in the process of building, atomic-powered submarines among their gigantic fleet of some 500 underwater vessels.

—May Day parades and public celebrations of the October Revolution reveal highly mechanized and mobile tank units and artillery.

—We now have disturbing evidence of the sizable expansion of Soviet economic aid, political infiltration, propaganda and cultural offensives.

There is evidence that the Soviet system has many weaknesses. Soviet industry is suffering from manpower shortages. Efforts to open up and cultivate new land have not been too successful to date. Soviet citizens are still relegated to a standard of living considerably below that of the countries of Western Europe, and some of Eastern Europe, as well.

But there is little sign that these problems are about to force any sudden fundamental changes in the regime.

Too often, United States proposals regarding the settlement of political problems and arms control appear to stem from the assumption that Western military and economic pressure will produce unwilling compliance on the part of Soviet leaders.

In point of fact, the United States itself weakened its own strength during the course of disarmament negotiations in London last year with the Soviet Union.

While the U.S.S.R. was making naval sallies into Middle East waters, funneling arms into that area, hurling threats of nuclear annihilation at our allies, and announcing boastfully its achievement of an intercontinental ballistic missile, we were lowering the ceiling on our defense expenditures, cutting back or pulling back our armed forces, and curtailing or slowing down our military aircraft and missiles programs.

It is difficult to see how we could have presented a strong negotiating front to the Soviet Union when we were so busily engaged in unilateral disarmament. . . .

A foreign policy designed to meet the realities of international life requires that we face up the true power and political relationships between the U.S.S.R. and the United States.

On the one hand, we cannot act as though we have the strength to force the Soviet Union to accept our terms without offering reasonable compromises and concessions. On the other hand, our capacity to defend ourselves and our allies must be sufficient to discourage the Soviet Union or any of the Sovietized states from embarking on misguided and miscalculated military aggressions.

While we have allowed ourselves to fall behind in three crucial areas—missiles, outer space, and capacity to deal with limited arms conflicts—it would be wrong to assume that we are so weak that we are inviting Soviet aggression or that the Soviets could force us to accept their terms in any series of negotiations.

Fellow Americans, we need not tremble at the thought of sitting face to face with Soviets at the conference table.

Negotiating from strength means not only the appearance of strength, but the fact and reality of strength. By strength we must include military preparedness with modern weapons, alliances that are strong and secure both militarily and politically, and a vigorous and expanding economy.

The friendship, goodwill, and understanding of other nations is another source of strength that we should seek and merit. Favorable world opinion is one of those immeasurable and intangible factors, while not decisive in matters of world politics, is at least worthy of our concern and attention.

The Soviet Union too must come to accept the reality of the balance of power existing between it and the Free World. It may be under an illusion that its achievements in missiles and rockets have so elevated its power position that negotiations with the United States can only be on Soviet terms. Perhaps this is why the Soviets abruptly broke off the London disarmament talks of last summer and why it is boycotting the newly expanded United Nations Disarmament Commission.

Soviet leaders must be persuaded through our increased defensive strength, through a broad program to pursue works of peace and a willingness to conduct negotiations at any time, that neither side can force terms on the other.

Any agreement reached, to be effective, must serve the national interests of both countries as well as the many countries allied and associated with us in our search for peace. . . .

In discussing United States disarmament policies it is necessary to evaluate them in light of the changing definition of disarmament. Today, "disarmament" has meaning only if it is defined in terms of five key words: strength, understanding, limitation, inspection and control.

Strength is the continuing prerequisite for effective bargaining, the one persuasive catalytic agent without which negotiations are futile. . . .

Understanding signifies broader and better public conception of the difficulties and complexities involved in disarmament in a nuclear age.

Limitation, inspection and control are the essential features of an effective system, without which disarmament is a mirage. . . .

No government, least of all the government of the United States, should ever be casual and negative about limiting the arms race. We must never devise proposals that obviously have no chance of being accepted. Every proposal of ours, and every rejection of proposals from the Soviet, should be given only after the most thoughtful and scrutinizing study. . . .

Let us be the people of progress, the people of performance, and the people of peace. . . . The key to obtaining peace is to bring the people of the world together in cooperation. . . .

The Role of the People

"Bring the people of the world together," Humphrey said that day in February. After all was said and done, it was still up to the people.

If the politicians were to take the bold steps that needed to be taken, if they were to make the innovative initiatives that needed to be made, they would need the support and the prodding of the people.

And that was what he planned to tell the Climax Drive Workshop of the Citizen's Committee for the Hoover Report on March 31, 1958. Legislative business, however, prevented the senator from attending.

But it did not prevent his speech from being delivered nonetheless. He sent Miles Scull, a staff member of Humphrey's subcommittee on reorganization, to read the speech for him.

. . . At no time since the Founding Fathers forged the Constitution upon which this great republic rests has government been of greater importance to us. Not only America, but the free peoples of the world, look to our government for leadership as the universe crosses the momentous horizons of the space age, where man holds in one hand the lighted torch of miraculous human progress and in the other the awesome power to destroy himself with the hydrogen bomb.

Whether mankind holds high the lighted torch of progress as he crosses the threshold of space or whether he smashes everything for which civilization stands in a maddening maelstrom of nuclear warfare, hinges greatly on government's leadership in these fateful days of danger, decision and crisis. And—nowhere does the responsibility for government's leadership lie more heavily than on the individual citizen.

For in a democracy, the course government takes, the power good government wields, the strength with which it arms itself and the principles of liberty, justice and freedom for which it stands all depend upon the will, the strength, the courage and the willingness to sacrifice, if need be, of its individual citizens.

In the final analysis, the citizens of America are the government—the invisible power, strength and force for good that is behind the portals of the White House, the marble columns of the Capitol dome and of which the American flag is the shining symbol. No responsibility they bear is greater than that—to their country.

I suppose it could be said the citizen's responsibility to his government begins with that precious privilege—the right of franchise. It is at the ballot box in the country schoolhouse that the caliber of government is initially determined when the citizen votes for his elected representative to carry out his wishes—at the town hall, at the state capitol, or in Washington.

If the citizen makes a conscientious choice, if he persuades good, public-spirited candidates to stand for office, and if he himself knows what the issues are, he discharges his responsibility properly. If he does not—or if he lets John do it—as many do, he not only fails to exercise a precious right, he fails to perform a duty he owes to himself, to his family and to his country. He cheats himself and them.

Along with the right of franchise goes the responsibility of knowledge—knowledge of government, knowledge of candidates, knowledge of issues.

No longer is the day when the citizen at the crossroads can look upon the federal government as a distant authority at Washington City which, in some vague way, looks after his national interests, as was the case fifty years or so ago.

Today, the federal government's influence is everywhere, in the states, in the cities, in the towns, on the highways, in the airways, in the Main Street bank, in the country store, affecting his life in a hundred different ways every hour of the day, every day of the year.

Thus, the responsibility of knowledge in today's era of expanding government activity and influence is imperative, for without knowledge, judicious exercise of the ballot is futile. . . .

[The] more that the governed are aware of their government, the more knowledge they possess of its operations, the more alert they are to its inescapable frailties, the greater their voice is going to be and the better their government is going to be. . . .

Oh, I know today's government has its shortcomings, its weaknesses and, at times, its failures. But, my friends, so does any human enterprise of its magnitude, fraught with the crises that today's world presents, besiged by a foreign ideology which seeks to conquer it, at times torn apart by political dissension, yet, still standing like the Rock of Gibraltar, shining like a beacon to free men the world over—strong, vigorous, ready to face whatever uncertainties a troubled future might bring—in truth, the greatest government the world ever has known. I ask you, would you trade it for any other?

The weaknesses we seek to shore up. The shortcomings to correct. The failures not to repeat. But, let us go about this with reality. Let us not endanger the house because grease is burning in the kitchen oven. Let us not condemn all government because grievous mistakes have been made or a part here or there has failed us.

To be sure, let us correct that which has failed, but let us look upon the whole, not the part, and to the future, not the past. And let us march foward solidly, together to build the whole ever greater and stronger.

My friends, only by doing this can we hope—as the leaders of the Free World—to succeed, or to survive.

Turning on the Switch

In early 1958, the United States made its first attempt to compete with the Soviet Union in the space race. But the Vanguard rocket—"that graphic symbol of frustration and enchained intelligence," as Humphrey described it—sputtered, fluttered and failed.

*Shortly thereafter, that humiliation was erased somewhat by the success-
ful launching of an Explorer rocket. But it was not enough; someone, Humphrey
told the National Education Association's Department of Audio-Visual
Instruction on April 23, 1958, had to turn on the switch to set the American
dynamo of ideas humming.*

It is always stimulating to meet with men and women for whom
ideas are fresh, vivid and living things. It is my good fortune to
have the opportunity to discuss with such a group as this the
problems and the importance of getting good ideas into effective
motion.

This is the reason for existence and the motivation, after all,
of all teachers. Getting ideas translated into action is also the goal
of us who are in public life. And each of us takes tremendous
pride in achieving that goal, in our own way.

For anyone who works with ideas, these have been particularly challenging times. Somehow, our great nation has given
the impression of a giant in chains, our tremendous strength
somehow impotent.

Yet seldom has there been more of a ferment of ideas, nor a
more restless, seeking spirit among our people. But our ideas
seem to sputter, flare up and fade away before they can be
translated into affirmative action. As a nation, we just don't
seem to be able to get off the ground. . . .

A rocket on a launching pad has a lot of potential. An idea on
the launching pad of an intellectual's mind has a lot of potential.
But it is the push, the thrust, that we can get behind the rocket,
and the idea, that is so very critically important.

Putting ideas—good ideas—into motion takes a great deal
of energy, decision, and skill.

We are not short on ideas in this country. Far from it. This is
one of the blessings of this democracy; that everyone feels free
to think up new ideas, and we have a bubbling of opinion and
thought that is very healthy and useful.

But to translate the best of these ideas into motion and

action there must be a matching decision and a full use of the wealth of techniques of communication. . . .

We are looking, then, for that thrust that gets us off the ground. All the rich and diverse talents and resources of this democracy await the vital forward impulse that can be released only by the topmost political leadership of the nation, and particularly by the man who holds the vast powers of the American presidency.

Someone must turn on the switch to set the American dynamo humming. Khrushchev challenges us to compete. Our first decision must be to accept the challenge in the realm of ideas, as we accepted the military challenge of the Soviet Union first made over ten years ago.

You can't run a footrace, you know, if you are forever bending down to tie your shoelaces. . . .

Now let us assume—and let us devoutly hope—that someone will at least turn on the switch. Let us assume that we are determined to do something.

Now comes the second great task of political leadership: putting the massive power of the United States behind the right ideas.

A democratic leader has sometimes been compared with an orchestra leader, to get some idea of the diversity which he must weld into unity. Surrounded as I am with men and women steeped in the audio-visual production tradition, I am tempted to compare the democratic leader with a producer.

In a sense, the leader in a democracy is like the producer of a motion picture, a television program, a radio broadcast, a sound-slide series. He is trying to persuade people to do something. And to help him in his task, he is truly fortunate in our country to be able to call upon the skills of many people, many specialists, many talents.

Like the producer, his job is too big to do by himself. He must however, select the basic idea, furnish the motive power, and then prepare to follow through, to supervise, encourage and stimulate his team of specialists.

The producer must find the right idea—the right story, or

concept. He knows that the finest of technicians and the most superb talent will give him nothing more than a mediocre production unless he has an important idea to work from.

Similarly, the democratic leader must spend much time and energy in selection of his program and policy. That is basic. From all the deluge of advice and entreaty, he must select the most promising, judge it against his own intelligence and experience and training, and make that primary decision: This is the program behind which I will throw all my resources and energy. . . .

How difficult it is to pick that right idea, amidst the bombardment from all sides. But how important. For the producer, it is the opportunity for a smash production, fame, possibly fortune. For the democratic leader, it can be the opportunity for greatness. . . .

Of all the powerful ideas at work in the world, none has more strength than the world's yearning for peace—and not simply the absence of war, but peace with progress.

We must identify ourselves vigorously, simply and directly, with this great idea in terms of positive progress toward better housing, more jobs, more food, and for dignity and freedom for the men and women who have had nothing for so long.

Ideas, you see, are in motion—powerful ideas that are sweeping away old political institutions, breaking through the encrusted traditions of five centuries.

Nationalism, and fierce nationalism at that, is an idea and a movement among the Asian and African peoples that must be recognized and taken into the most serious consideration by American policy planners.

The idea of equal opportunity and nondiscrimination on the grounds of religion or color is another powerful idea that is upsetting the old order. The peoples of colored skin in this world are in the majority, and it has long since become evident that they will no longer tolerate the inferior status we of the West have assigned them for these five centuries of Caucasian domination.

The magnificent conception of international organization

for peaceful purposes is still another tenacious and vigorous idea important in our world—and very much in motion. Steadily, in the face of the huge buildup of weapons of mass destruction, men and women of vision and purpose are working to strengthen the economic, social and cultural organizations that are some of the brightest hopes in an often bleak international picture.

The idea that all peoples should be free of the age-old scourge of disease is being magnificently carried forward—in malaria-control programs, in the attack of trachoma, tuberculosis and scores of other plagues.

Still another idea powerfully at work in the world, but one which our government regretfully has not yet adopted, is that food and fiber are great national treasures, and can be vital instruments of foreign policy. Mr. Khruschev is the first of the Soviet leaders to recognize this fact, and in the face of our leadership's indifference to the opportunity to use food intelligently and wisely, the Soviet leaders are surging forward in an effort to overtake us in food and fiber production. American food and fiber abundance is not something we should be ashamed of, but an asset of incalculable value.

Finally, the idea of providing the kind of education that will permit individuals to realize their full intellectual potential, the idea of ensuring that gifted young people will not be denied higher education opportunities simply because of a lack of family finances, is gathering real momentum.

In our history, we have steadily widened the opportunity for education for everyone. But it is only recently that we have come to realize the great gaps in our educational structure. It is nothing short of tragic—for the individuals and for our nation—that we have not devised a system that would provide the 150,000 or so young high school graduates with very superior ability who do not now go on to college each year for lack of funds, the opportunity to develop their potential through higher education. . . .

The task of encouraging and training the young people of our nation to assume political, economic and technical leadership is of noble and intense importance. You teachers, and you specialists in the visualization of the idea, deserve the warmest support and encouragement of the nation. I can only assure you that there are many in the Congress of the United States who share my conviction that the profession of teaching must somehow receive the social and financial rewards that have for so long been denied to educators.

This is just another idea that I hope to get into motion. . . .

The Rule of Law

On May 1, 1958, Humphrey spoke at a Law Day dinner at Georgetown University. He used the occasion to call on lawyers everywhere to help educate the people in the meaning of law.

Tensions were still high in the South as court-ordered integration continued along, albeit at a snail's pace. The voices of defiance were getting louder; violence often replaced reason.

Lawyers, Humphrey said that evening, must play an important role in helping to stem the tide of civil disobedience.

. . . As I look at the torrent of mail, including hate literature, which comes into my office, as I travel in various parts of this country, as I read the newspapers about current racial conflict in the South, and some Northern communities as well, it seems to me that we are increasingly clouding all of the real issues at stake under competing smokescreens of conspiracy.

The White Citizens' Councils in the South who are shouting most loudly and most extravagantly are always crying conspiracy and are waving documents to show that the unanimous decision of the Supreme Court in the school case was a part of an international communist conspiracy.

But there is an equal danger on the other side. In the midst of their understandable grievances and frustrations, some spokesmen have at times, it seems to me, blanketed all Southern opposition to desegregation as a conspiracy against the Constitution and against fundamental human rights—equally ignoring on their side the varying degrees of opposition, of understanding, and of possible cooperation which may still exist.

At times, this almost seems to be a mutual determination to solidify differences, to freeze antagonisms, and to set up barricades against those compromises upon which progress usually depends.

The result is that in this domestic cold war of ours in the human relations field, we are increasingly getting little more than propaganda and counterpropaganda.

Somewhere in the process, law, respect for law, and above all, respect for the process of persuasion on which our law fundamentally depends—these are forgotten. The opportunity for persuasion, indeed, the necessity for persuasion, is lost in the meantime.

The role of the law as a catalytic agent in resolving human differences is forgotten. The role of the law as a teacher through the process of reason and choice is lost.

It is almost as though we had picked up some of those inoperable aspects of our foreign policy—massive retaliation—and let it permeate our thinking so that in the civil rights field we are faced with demands for massive resistance against demands for massive enforcement of the law.

The people who talk this way, my friends, are simply reducing the whole argument to a battle fundamentally hostile to the legal process. They are in fact turning the debate into a competition between conspiracies—conspiracies against the spirit of our laws. . . .

But it is not the civil rights field alone that is endangered by our current competing doctrines of conspiracy. . . , it is the whole fabric of American law and respect for the processes of reason and choice on which our law must rest.

To restore and revitalize these processes, it seems to me

that lawyers have the first responsibility, or at least that lawyers and educators share it jointly. They, by their profession, are dedicated to the process of persuasion, to the idea of a republic of learning.

By their conduct and example, by their fearlessness in the face of intimidation and their respect for the resolution of issues through peaceful reasoning, by their refusal to treat their adversaries as conspirators, by their insistence upon entertaining the ideas of their adversaries no matter how much their adversaries try to act like conspirators, perhaps they can create a new climate.

If this spirit is radiated from the courtrooms and the schoolrooms of the country, the subversion of our republic caused by the doctrine of conspiracy may be checked. . . .

Lawyers and educators cannot just cry law, when in part of the country there is no law that is accepted.

A law—or court decision—is a teacher in that it asks of each of us a question: Is this a good, proper, just law? But the answer must come from us. In a republic, the answer comes from "we the people."

And on a fundamental question of law like this, it seems to me that the American bar has a responsibility that it cannot escape. In this regard, so far, it seems to me that it is we who have not been good to the law, it is we who are failing the law.

"The law will never make men free," Thoreau said, "it is men who have got to make the law free." I would add that it is lawyers and teachers of law who have got to persuade their fellow citizens to keep the law free.

Israel Must Live

On August 6, 1958, the Senate began a lengthy debate on the administration's Middle East policy. The debate was prompted in part by President Eisenhower's decision earlier in the year to send U.S. Marines into Lebanon. It was also prompted by attempts by some senators to make it more difficult for American Jews to donate money to help develop the ten-year-old reborn Jewish state.

Among the issues raised during the debate was what to do with the Palestinian refugees.

To Senator Humphrey, it should never have been an issue. The refugees should have been resettled long ago.

... Our foreign policy has as a purpose to try to create—through the use of diplomacy, economic aid, and all we have to offer—a world in which people can express themselves, a world in which people can have self-government, a world in which political institutions based upon democratic principles can live and grow, with an application of modern science and an improvement in industry and agriculture.

We seek a world in which there are governments which dedicate themselves to human welfare.

We seek a world in which there are nation states which are politically responsible and mature members of the international community.

We seek a world in which there are nation states which can take on their share of the burden of helping others.

I happen to believe those are the real, legitimate aspirations and aims of our government. I find all of those things being fulfilled in the state of Israel. Therefore, I have an interest in Israel's survival.

Every time a free country is destroyed, I think it weakens us. It does not weaken us, necessarily, in terms of military strength or in terms of economic strength, but it weakens us morally and it weakens us spiritually. Therefore, when we find countries which are trying to practice liberal principles of government, which are trying to adapt themselves to the twentieth century, which are trying to rebuild great physical and human resources, I feel we have a special obligation to those countries and we have a privilege and an opportunity to work with them.

One of the issues which has been raised again and again in the Congress and outside the Congress is the issue of the Arab refugees. I, too, have visited the refugee camps. I want to say it has been very difficult for Mr. Labousse, who was the United Nations director of the refugee program, to get even a scintilla of cooperation from the Arab states.

I spent time with the workers in the camps, with the directors and with the program planners. I was told that a couple of years ago in Israel when an attempt was made at one of the refugee camps to build a community outpatient clinic to take care of the health needs of the refugees, the refugees themselves and outsiders from the country of Syria tore down the building. They were not going to have any care, the theory being, "If you take care of our health, it means that you are going to try to keep us in the camps. We want to be miserable."

It seems incredible, but it is the kind of emotional irrational-ism with which we have had to deal, and with which the United Nations has been faced.

I feel that we can make a real contribution in this area by being a little more firm and definite in our policies. For example, take the Arab refugee question. The sooner we tell people that the answer to the Arab refugee question is resettlement rather than repatriation, the better off we shall be.

It is true that some refugees may well go back into Israel; but it would be foolish to expect that the nation state of Israel would accept refugees who might turn into a fifth column.

They will take back some, of course. I believe that the state of Israel ought to compensate for lands and properties taken over. As I understand, the state of Israel is willing to do that. But resettlement is the answer and we ought to make it unequivo-cally plain that that is what we believe in.

Some people say, "What do you mean by telling the Palestinian Arab refugees that they must be resettled?" I ask, where are all the tears about the refugees in India. . . ? What about the refugees in Pakistan? What about the refugees in Hong Kong? There are a million of them. I do not hear anyone making speeches about them, shedding tears and indulging in wails of anguish about those refugees.

The reason is that some efforts are being made by the other governments to resettle refugees. Refugees are not all going back to the countries from which they came. They are being resettled. I believe that should be done in the case of the Arab refugees, and we ought to be very firm about it.

To date we have not been firm. Resettlement is the answer. . . . [There] is plenty of room in Iraq. There is plenty of room in Egypt and in many other countries. Particularly in Iraq, there could be resettlement of hundreds of thousands. It is the obligation of the Israeli government to help in this work and it is also the obligation of the other nations of the world.

Let us not forget that the state of Israel was established by the United Nations. The state of Israel sought peace with its neighbors, but it was attacked. It drove off the attackers and beat them to the ground. Outnumbered, it still won its struggle. . . . The state of Israel has sought peace with its neighbors, and its neighbors have refused to talk peace.

I have not said a thing here that I have not said to representatives of the Arab countries. I know many of them personally. . . . I do not believe that one has to be accused of being anti-Arab if he is friendly to Israel.

Also, I say to my friends in Israel that one does not have to be accused of being anti-Israel if he believes that the Arabs ought to have some opportunities. They are deserving of every opportunity. I am for the development of both the Arabs and the Israelis. I believe we should make it unmistakably clear that we consider Israel to be an integral part of the Middle East region.

I invite attention to the fact that when I wrote my report last year, after my trip to the Middle East, one of the points was that there must be the following assumptions in our Middle East policy:

First: That Israel is an integral part of the region and is there to stay.

Second: That the 1949 armistice boundaries constitute inviolable political boundaries subject to change only by the joint agreement of the states concerned.

Third: That resettlement in Arab lands, with compensation for property left in Israel, is in fact the only effective and realistic way of solving the Arab refugee problem.

Fourth: That the stability and security of the region demand an early settlement of the Arab-Israel conflict.

It is because I hold these views that I suggested. . . that if there was to be a summit meeting, Ben Gurion, the head of the state of Israel, and President Nasser, of Egypt, should be invited. Why? Because those two heads of state ought to talk face to face.

Secondly, I do not want to see pressure brought to bear on our government which would compel us to yield in a compromise solution at the expense of Israel.

Furthermore, I am of the opinion that in open negotiation there is hope for some limited agreements between Egypt and Israel, because the heads of both of those countries are intelligent. They are political leaders. They are working politicians, and they understand that there are some things which must be agreed upon. . . .

I leave this final thought. . . : I hope the Congress will realize the good work which is being done by the many Jewish philanthropic organizations which are helping in some of the activities in Israel. I have spoken at dozens of meetings, in my state and elsewhere, in behalf of philanthropic organizations and philanthropic activities. Some of those speeches have been made in behalf of the United Jewish Appeal or the Joint Defense Appeal, as it is called in some areas, or the United Jewish Fund.

Some of that money goes to help the immigrants and refugees coming into Israel. The money is being used to build new lives, to construct hospitals and schools, to provide out-patient clinics, and to provide vocational instruction.

This is wonderful work. Would that more of it were done.

I believe that, rather than trying to curb what the Jewish philanthropic organizations are doing, we should encourage others to do the same thing. We should be encouraging the people of other national extractions or faiths to do the same thing—and some of them are. . . .

I believe frank discussion of these problems is long overdue. I sincerely believe that Israel is one of our best allies. She is the only really dependable ally we have in the Middle East. She is an ally without a treaty. She is an ally without an alliance. She is a political ally. She is a spiritual ally. She is an economic ally; and she is the best military power in the Middle East, save none.

So far as Israel having expansionist ideas is concerned, I would speak just as vigorously against any type of territorial expansion on her part as I am speaking now in her defense. She should be told unequivocally that we would be unalterably opposed to such expansion.

There are population-growth problems, but. . . the population-growth problem is taken care of by economic productivity. . . .

There are far fewer population pressures in Jordan, or even in Egypt, but the standard of living in those countries is not half so high as that in Israel. In Israel, the people work. They apply modern science to the problems of the day. They have a government which is interested in the problems of the people. They stress education. They are able to increase the productive output of their farms, industries and shops, and thereby build a better standard living for a growing population.

I am sure that much of it has been because of help and economic assistance. I want to make sure that that help and economic assistance continue. I want to make sure that there is no diminution of it either by private interests or by public interests.

Crisis in Berlin

On December 7, 1958, voters in West Berlin inflicted a serious propaganda blow upon the Soviet Union. The Socialist Unity Party, comprised of Moscow-aligned communists, had campaigned in the city's municipal elections on a platform of a unified Berlin free of Allied domination. But when all the votes were in, the communists had received less than two percent of the vote.

Khrushchev was furious. He saw the vote as much a slap in his face as it was a defeat for his West German allies. He then issued an ultimatum to Britain, France and the United States: Get out of West Berlin!

Khrushchev insisted through the early months of 1959 that the three Western allies must leave West Berlin and the four-power occupation of the entire city be brought to an end. Berlin, he said, should be turned into a "free" city pending an eventual peace treaty and unification of the two Germanies.

He called for a foreign ministers' conference to be held in May to resolve the issue. Soviet and East German troops, meanwhile, began making threatening moves.

It seemed as though the long-dreaded East-West confrontation was near at hand. There were those in the United States and elsewhere who argued that the Berlin issue was not worth risking a new world war. Others cried "appeasement" and "Munich" and urged the Allied powers to refuse the invitation to negotiate.

Hubert Humphrey, however, disagreed with both sides. Appearing on April 11, 1959, at a dinner of the Westchester County Democratic Committee in New Rochelle, New York, he outlined his position. Simply stated, Humphrey told his listeners at the Glen Island Casino that Saturday evening that we must negotiate—but only from a position of strength. Anything less would indeed be appeasement.

The Soviets once more are threatening freedom in Berlin. They are probing to see whether that unique and indispensable community which is NATO can indeed endure. . . .

We will not surrender. We will not be pushed out.

But firmness before the Soviet threat, though indispensable, is not enough. Firmness alone will not preserve NATO, nor assure the survival of free Berlin.

Our firmness must be matched by our imagination and our willingness to negotiate.

Standing firm and a willingness to negotiate are not, as some suggest, contradictory policies. They are the two elements in any viable policy in the Berlin crisis. We can negotiate success-fully only if we are prepared to stand firm. And we can command the political support necessary to a posture of firmness only if our negotiating position is clear, consistent and realistic. . . .

There is no alternative. We must negotiate on Berlin, on Germany and on the general question of European security. We must go to the summit, and more than once if that is necessary. . . .

There has been much loose talk about Munich—about the dangers of being taken in by the Russians at the negotiating table.

I do not need to tell the audience that Berlin is not Munich.

To negotiate is to appease. But we must understand very clearly what makes the difference between legitimate negotiation and inexcusable appeasement. Three requirements must be fulfilled if we are to come to the negotiating table prepared to seek reasonable adjustments without fear of succumbing to unreasonable demands. First, there must be unity of policy within the Western community. Second, we must be militarily prepared. Third, our people must understand the full gravity of the situation we confront. . . .

We must meet the demand for firmness on the part of nations most exposed to the Soviets—principally the Germans.

We must reconcile this demand for firmness with the opposing demand for flexibility on the part of other nations less exposed—principally the British.

We must understand the French desire for national prestige.

We must remain sensitive to German resistance to policies that appear to demand greater sacrifice of German interests than they do of the interests of the other partners.

We must never forget that all these points of view are legitimate....

[We] must be open-minded and imaginative. We must understand that negotiated agreements designed to reduce the hazards of war are not appeasement unless they alter the status quo to our disadvantage....

[We] must be patient. We must understand that nothing will be solved overnight, that settlements will in fact take years and that we face a long road of uncertainty and insecurity....

[We] must be resolute and willing to sacrifice. We must be willing to spend money—hard-earned money—to do what is necessary to maintain the strength of the Western community of nations.

The requirements of the present crisis are high. I came here tonight to speak about Berlin and the prerequisites of effective negotiation. I cannot leave without reminding you that the imagination, patience and resoluteness, which as a people we must now demonstrate, is necessary at every level in our contest with the Soviets—in aid, in trade and in appeals to the minds and souls of men and at every point in our contest with the communist bloc—in Asia, in the Middle East, in Africa, at the UN.

I think I understand well the communist threat. I have talked to Khrushchev. I have seen at first-hand his vigor, his determination, his ruthlessness. I know the power of totalitarian might. We must never underestimate this massive threat.

More to be feared than Soviet hardness is our own softness.

More to be feared than ruthless Soviet purpose is our own aimlessness.

More to be feared than the pernicious appeal of communist slogans to the disinherited of this earth is our own inability to develop a clear sense of purpose and to give mankind a vision of a noble destiny.

I do not believe the pessimists who say that as a people we Americans cannot or will not meet the demands of the present trial of Western civilization.

I do not propose that we chastise the American people; I propose that we challenge them.

The measure of our responsibility is such that we must act with greatness. No people have ever risen to greatness without being called to greatness.

The tragedy of these years is that the voice that should summon us is silent.

Works for Peace

Peace was very much on Hubert Humphrey's mind in 1959 because of the continuing crisis in Berlin. It would be even more so in 1960. In speech after speech, Humphrey talked about peace.

But the senator was not content with merely mouthing nice-sounding words that audiences wanted to hear in those tension-filled days. Peace, as he had said so often in the past, could not be achieved on a battlefield. It could only be won in the hearts of people.

On April 16, 1959, Humphrey introduced to the Senate a bold new program. He called it "Food for Peace." Nine days later, on April 25, in a speech delivered at a Jefferson-Jackson Day dinner in Salt Lake City, Humphrey called for all manner of "Works for Peace."

Following are portions of Humphrey's "Food for Peace" speech to the Senate and his "Works for Peace" speech in Salt Lake City.

. . . I speak today concerning one of the most pressing of the long-range challenges confronting the American people; the challenge posed by our unprecedented wealth in a world three-fourths needy and no longer willing to remain so.

This contest is most dramatic and immediate in the paradox

of leapfrogging food overabundance at home in the United States and leapfrogging hungry populations abroad.

How absurd if surpluses of vitally needed commodities become minuses in America's ledger, for to have too much and not share is surely far worse, in conscience and in practice, than to have too little to begin with.

Thus, common sense and common decency combine to tell us to use our famed know-how and our vast natural energies to devise ways in which our good fortunes can become the blessing of all people, and not a symbol of selfishness to God's children elsewhere.

The whole ethical sweep of our traditions and the imaginative resourcefulness of our ancestors cry out the senselessness of any posture which makes food seem a curse in the midst of want.

It is, then, in this spirit that we propose today a program which I have called "Food for Peace," and which should help to make clear the concern of Americans for all human beings, and the eagerness of Americans to share their good fortunes as a contribution toward the removal of privation and inequity from our midst and in our time. . . .

It is not a hastily designed program. It is the outgrowth of long study and careful research. . . .

"Food for Peace" is not merely a slogan. For the last four years, I have been devoting much time to studying this concept of using our abundance more wisely as a tool of international policy and international friendship. . . .

Here is. . . a program which truly makes sense, a program to convert the abundance of our farms and the abundance and the productivity of our soil into economic power for our nation and into uses based on neighborly compassion and humanitarianism on the part of our nation, and to convert the production of our farms into strategic minerals which are needed by our country, or to convert the production of our farms into currency for the use of our country. . . .

Sometimes I wonder what has come over this nation, that some persons should complain of a God-given gift. . . to alleviate hunger and suffering and sickness, or that there should be any hesitation to use this food in ways which will be of help not only to the foreign policy of our country—a use which in itself is most commendable—not only for the economic development of our nation and other nations, but also to feed the sick and the hungry and to help the unfortunate.

If the purpose of what we seek is thoroughly understood, I believe that every person in the United States will support this endeavor. . . .

Agricultural surpluses in the hands of the Commodity Credit Corporation have mounted to very large proportions, and have exercised a depressing effect on domestic farm prices, and have resulted in heavy cash outlays for storage—in fact, about one billion dollars a year for storage. What I am suggesting is that we no longer spend the one billion dollars a year for storage, but that we spend it to make the food available for use for the benefit of humanity and for the benefit of progress, peace and justice.

I venture to say that not one member of Congress could justify before his constituents choosing to store food, at an annual cost of one billion dollars, and complaining about that, instead of using the food—at the same cost in money—to feed the sick and the hungry and to build a more just society.

We in this country had, therefore, and we still have, a definite, practical dollar-and-cent interest in protecting our own farm prices and in reducing the amounts of surplus agricultural commodities we hold in storage. . . .

Nearly eight years ago—on May 24, 1951—President Truman said, "The only kind of war we seek is the good old fight against man's ancient enemies—poverty, disease, hunger and illiteracy."

His words were drawn from the heart and the wisdom and the history of the American people. But he knew, as we know, that words, however eloquent, are not enough; nor do good intentions, however generous, suffice.

They must result in works for peace.

It is ten years since President Truman enunciated what

became known as the Point Four idea—the idea of aiding the peoples of the underdeveloped areas of the world.

That idea did not spring out of empty air. It was firmly grounded in the lifeblood and life experience of the missionaries our great churches have for generations sent out to all corners of the world.

The strength of our best missionaries is that they not only preached the faith to all peoples, but they also fed the hungry and healed the sick. . . .

In a day when we hear much of the ugly American, it is well to remember these dedicated Americans. For they were the real progenitors of the Point Four idea. . . .

Those who are suddenly concerned about the competition with communism in Asia, Africa and the Middle East do not realize that we had a very long head start upon them. While the early Bolsheviks were wrangling over the café tables of Europe, our missionaries were at work helping people grow two blades of wheat where only one grew before, helping them to resist disease, helping them to lift the burden of illiteracy.

But despite this head start, we have dissipated much of our lead. In too many underdeveloped areas of the world, the communists are making far more headway than we.

Why? Not because of the righteousness of their ultimate cause, for it is an oppressive and godless cause.

It is because of the communists' total dedication to their goals—a total dedication which today the West is not equaling.

Too many Americans have lost the zeal and dedication that motivated the missionaries of the past.

Perhaps this is because we have lost the spirit that guided the missionaries: the desire to help people for no other reason than that they are our brothers; that they are God's children; that they are hungry and need food, or sick and need healing.

Today, our aid to poor nations springs not so much from love as from fear—fear that if we do not help others, they will be lost to the communists. . . .

It does us no good to complain that the communists are busy everywhere, preaching their own secular heresy.

It does just as little good to complain that, as "Ivans-come-lately" in the field of overseas aid, they are peddling their loans and their technicians in many crucial areas of the world. . . .

Today, in Congress, we are debating the details of a meager and unimaginative program.

While we debate, a new world is coming into existence around us. Most of Asia has achieved freedom since the war. New nations are being born every year out of Africa. Latin America is only now achieving the full fruits of freedom.

This new independence and liberty carried with it strong desires for self-help—desires we should strive to foster. . . .

The overriding fact is that mankind is on the move—and at least half of it in a hurry. We can seize the opportunity to move with them—or run the grave risk that they will move without us, or even against us.

I hope that there is enough of the missionary spirit in all of us that we will play our full part in this great chapter of the world's unfolding history. I hope that we will do this because it is the right thing to do and not solely out of fear of our adversaries.

All Americans need is to be themselves. Why is it that so many feel embarrassed by the prospects of doing something noble and disinterested?

The mistakes made out of greatness of heart are forgiven —the mistakes of meanness, never.

I would much rather stand in the Senate and defend my government against the charge of having spent generously to help India achieve the goals of her five-year plan than to join in some future inquest, as to why we gave too little and too late. . . .

What the world needs today is not massive retaliation, but massive doses of health, education and food.

We must move on the offensive and declare war against mankind's most ancient and terrible enemies of hunger, disease, poverty and ignorance.

We need a bold new "Food for Peace" program, dedicating our God-given abundance to serving the need of humanity— rather than complaining about it.

We need a dramatic, worldwide "Health for Peace" program,

with vastly expanded international medical research—and perhaps a white fleet of mercy ships carrying our medical know-how and wonder drugs to the disease-ridden and suffering in the far corners of the earth.

We need to launch a broad program of world educational development—a plan for education for peace.

These are truly the works of peace. . . .

The Call for Leadership

As April 1959 drew to a close, Hubert Humphrey began seriously to consider running for the Democratic presidential nomination in 1960.

He thus began to test the political waters, traveling around the country giving hard-hitting, often moving campaign-type addresses. The speech he delivered to a Democratic Party brunch in Casper, Wyoming, on Sunday, April 26 (the day after his Salt Lake City appearance) was typical.

Sunday is a day for sober thought about the things that are lost sight of in the clatter of the working week—a busy week for all of you as it has been for me, traveling throughout this great West of ours.

It is in this respectful spirit of sober thought that I am here to talk about politics—the same kind of politics that sounded this morning from pulpits in Casper, Wyoming, and from thousands of others across the land.

Here this morning, and everywhere else, congregations of Americans were called upon to rededicate themselves to two tasks:

The first task was to know the difference between justice

and injustice, between freedom and oppression, between order and disorder.

The second, and related task, was to act in the right as God gives us the power to know where the right resides.

I feel deeply this summons from the pulpit to unite the mind and the will in social effort.

To play a part in the art of government, to play a part in the mainstream of our political life, is to respond to that great summons.

Politics is a creative social act that must be engaged in by anyone who takes seriously the call to thought and action he hears from the pulpit.

Through the art of politics we define, advance, test and decide whether this or that proposal can best serve the common interest.

Through the art of politics, public opinion makes its presence felt as a controlling, disciplining and guiding force in the operations of government.

In this complex world of politics, as well as life itself, not all is sharply black or white, good or evil. People of differing views can have equal depth of conviction.

Neither political party in America is perfect; neither political party is all bad.

But having said that much, I proclaim my pride in being a Democrat.

We are the only national party there is in America—the only party with a representation in the national government rising from the South as well as the North, from the West as well as the East. . . .

[A] national party has special communications problems. It must talk across great spaces, amid the roar of great rivers of humanity, and must overcome great barriers to sight and sound.

When a Democrat in Alabama speaks his heart and mind to a Democrat in Wyoming, he has to raise his voice in order to be heard. For a Democrat here in Wyoming to be heard by one in New York, he, too, has to raise his voice.

There may at times appear to be differences within our family, as there are on occasion in any family—but it would be a fatal mistake for our political opponents to ever think for a moment that we do not stand shoulder to shoulder together as Democrats for common goals of progress and development.

We have room for and want people of conviction who will speak up for those convictions within our party's framework. We are not a party of thought control or rigid intellectual discipline. We want to be a blend of the best that is in all of us— and all of us have something to contribute. . . .

The fact that we Democrats argue among ourselves on occasion says something good and fine about the size and health of our family.

It says that we are the only party with interests that are as varied as the nation itself. We are the only party that embraces the laborer and the businessman, the farmer and the miner, the rancher and the office worker, the field hand and the white-collar professional, the young and the old, the consumer and the producer—and a lot more besides. . . .

In an otherwise uncertain world, there is at least one certainty. It is that any single interest in the Democratic Party, which tried to make every other interest act like all were a pack of identical twins, soon would find itself standing all alone in not so splendid isolation. A party in which so many strong national interests are included will not tolerate dictation by any one or any combination of them. Instead, we are going to keep up a running debate about how best to adjust and resolve conflicts between equally legitimate claims for support by the party as a whole. . . .

Yes, we Democrats are restless as well as argumentative. Yes, we are never content to let well enough alone, but are always restless to get on with the business of exploring new horizons.

We are restless because we know that America cannot stand still and continue to live. It can live only if it grows. We are restless because we do not want to crop our size to the monuments of the national past. We want to honor the monuments of the past by building beyond them to an ever-expanding future.

We are restless because we do not want to be embalmed in the case of a mummy. In pharaoh's Egypt, the whole of the national energy went into the worship of death—but America is not such a nation. We affirm the goodness of life and we want to spend our national energy in liberating and purifying life from the corrosive presence of fear, disease, want, ignorance and intolerance.

We are restless, because we are eager to redefine America as being something more than just a giant plot to make money. We affirm that our economic system can provide a living wage, a proper education and a decent home for every American.

We are eager to redefine our national purpose in terms of something more than an IBM machine punching holes in a soulless stack of cards. We affirm the vitality of our constitutional principle of equality and the right of every man, woman and child to human dignity without regard to race, religion or ancestry.

We are restless because we reject the view that good government is fulfilled merely by good administration or good bookkeeping. If that was all there was to good government, then nobody should be allowed to stand for public office except certified public accountants.

But to us, as Democrats, with our roots deep in the people, good administration is not a substitute for good policies.

We are restless for the same reason that Democrats were restless in the years immediately preceding the election of Franklin D. Roosevelt in 1932. Both times, the Republicans had held the control of the executive for a long stretch. Both times in that long stretch, we had a government dedicated to the postponement and evasion of solutions to urgent domestic and international problems. Both times, the weight of executive energy was bent to the end that things should stand still. . . .

We want this nation of ours to breathe again. We are eager to be once more a people on the move, a people who voluntarily assume the yoke—and the glory that goes with it—of advancing mankind's best hopes for justice and peace.

We were in times past, and in a very literal sense, the giver and the protector of light in a sorely troubled world. There is no reason why that should not be the case right now. America still has tremendous, unsurpassed resources in material, strength, in energy and in creative talents.

Why then have we come to live with a bad taste in our mouth—with a sense that despite our material comforts, we have no inner joy?

Why then do we live with fear in our eyes—with the sense that tomorrow may be the day of the apocalypse?

Why then do we live with shame in our hearts—with the sense that because of some self-inflicted wound, we have fallen from the heights we once occupied?

This bad taste, this fear, this shame, all have a common cause. The cause, dating from 1953, is the infectious disease of slothfulness and indifference caught from a breakdown in leadership at the very summit of the nation.

There may have been a time when the presidency could serve as a place of dignified retirement in one's old age.

There may have been a time when it could be awarded to a man as a sort of good-conduct medal for performance in a lesser station.

There may have been a time when it was enough for a president to do nothing in particular but to do it very well—like some ceremonial figure in an empty pageant of state.

There may have been a time when a president could put himself so far above politics as to become politically invisible or unapproachable.

There may have been a time when the presidency could resolve itself into a long and tedious exercise in attitudes, platitudes and beatitudes—to the exclusion of concrete action.

But if ever there was such a time, that time is not now.

Now, the presidency is the vital place of action—the only staff and command post that can unite and give direction and purpose to three worlds: One is the divided world of our government proper; the second is the larger world of the whole nation which encompasses the world of our governmental machinery; and the third is the still larger world beyond our shores—a world whose very survival may depend upon leadership from our own White House.

The Congress cannot do the president's work for him. Under modern conditions, the Congress can lay down general policy lines. It can revise policies it receives in draft form from the executive. It can veto those policies. Or it can oversee the way they are executed by the president.

But Congress cannot fill the presidential vacuum. If the president defaults on his role as a national world leader, there is no force to fill that vacuum. . . .

What we have had of late is a caretaker government, a mark-time government, a do-as-little-as-you-can sort of government, an artificial sunlamp government—a government spouting aphorisms from *Poor Richard's Almanac*, while the communists are everywhere on the march with their perverse zeal to remake the world in their own image.

What we have had is a government whose first and last line of defense always is that it means well.

Well, simply to mean well never was and is not now good enough in the affairs of great nations. The graveyard of history is crowded with the bones of peoples who had good intentions but lacked the imagination, the exact knowledge and the driving energy that could translate those good intentions into specific realities in a formidable world.

Nor is it good enough these days for a great nation merely to wait for events to happen and then to react to them. A great nation must march at the head of events and, by measures born of foresight, produce the events it wants.

The Democratic Party has absorbed this lesson of history. That is why it is the oldest political party, with the longest unbroken history of any political party in the world today. For the same reason, that is why it is an eternally young party, supercharged with eagerness to release the giant powers of America for greatness in building here at home and abroad.

And again for the same reason, that is why our party at critical moments in American history has raised from its midst the presidential leadership that has sounded the call to action stations the nation was waiting to hear.

It is waiting to hear that call right now. And our party is ready.

5

The Presidential Road

Blueprint for the '60s

On December 30, 1959, Hubert Humphrey made official what everyone had known for the past six months: He was a candidate for president of the United States.

He was, he told the nation's press, the candidate of "the plain people of the country."

Six days later, on January 5, 1960, Humphrey appeared before the National Press Club in Washington to outline his blueprint for the '60s.

. . . As we enter the 1960s, I see America adrift, with much of her enormous reservoir of energy, power and good will un-tapped—unused.

There are powerful currents in the world today, but they are not currents of our making or liking. They are currents that sweep us along. We are the victim, not the shaper of events.

Just four decades ago, at the dawn of the 1920s, America entered upon the "age of normalcy."

Thirty-three years later, in 1953, America entered a new era: The "age of complacency."

A profound change came over the American government. The decision was made to confine the solutions to the problems of the 1950s within rigid, artificial, budgetary walls.

That change did much to shape the remainder of the '50s. It set in motion a unilateral cutback of America's defense forces—with the result that we embark on the summit talks of the 1960s not militarily supreme, but second best in a variety of fields.

"A bigger bang for a buck" was the slogan designed to justify the stripping of our conventional military strength. "Massive retaliation" was used to comfort Americans who sensed, but were never told, that the power of the Soviet Union was growing ever more complex and subtle. . . .

[Programs] and solutions were not measured against the

size of the problems to be solved, but were tailored to fit the economic strait jacket we had designed for ourselves.

The foreign-aid program fell victim to the fixed-budget philosophy as the secretary of the treasury became a controlling voice in the fashioning of our foreign policy. We appeared to the world to become a nation that cared more for dollars than for human welfare. . . .

Here at home during the '50s, the number of schoolchildren grew faster than the classrooms, but there was no money for schoolrooms or teachers in the budgetary strait jacket.

Streams grew more polluted, cities more crowded, slums more squalid, but America, in her fiscal strait jacket, could at best attack these problems only halfheartedly.

The problems of automation, of urban living, and the technological revolution in agriculture were neglected and shunted aside. . . .

Slogans were substituted for programs.

Public relations replaced public service.

And these policies of slogan and slowdown have cost us dearly.

The next president of the United States is going to inherit a series of problems that have been swept under the rug—where they have been festering and intensifying. Someone—the American people, ultimately—must pay the price of this ostrichlike attitude. And it will be a price that had been accumulating compound interest.

We will hear much talk about peace and prosperity in the months ahead.

We all want prosperity. But the prosperity we want must not be lopsided. It should be a prosperity that springs from an expanding economy with full shares for all—businessmen, farmers, working people, the young and the elderly. We seek a prosperity for America that insures social justice.

We all want peace; peace is no partisan issue. But the peace we want must be enduring. It must have deep roots.

Peace is not passive; it is active. Nor can peace be won by slogans.

There can be no peace in a world plagued by poverty, hunger, disease and illiteracy. There can be no genuine and lasting peace in a world plunged headlong in a reckless and unrestrained arms race. . . .

In America's so-called surplus food and fiber production, we possess wealth of a uniquely useful character—not a curse, but a blessing.

We can and we must use this enormous wealth for the benefit of all men—not only because it is the right and just thing to do, but also because it is fundamentally in our own interest.

We can and we must give leadership to a worldwide cooperative attack upon poverty and ignorance—the eternal enemies of peace and freedom.

At the same time, we must explore every opportunity— relentlessly, tenaciously, patiently—to find agreement on a safeguard system of arms control.

The job of the next president of the United States is to take off the wraps—to liberate America's energies and resources— and to tell the American people the plain truth. For the critical dilemma of American leadership will be how to preserve the spirit and the luster of freedom in America, while organizing our society to compete with the monolithic, disciplined and onrushing communist system. . . .

The next president of the United States must be more than an executive. He must in a very real sense be an educator.

He . . . must tell the people that if the age of complacency continues, America will soon become a second-class power.

He must tell them that we have already been surpassed in a number of military and scientific fields, and that a vast effort will be needed to regain the posture of strength necessary to negotiate with the Soviets in any field, including disarmament.

He must understand that science has given politics new dimensions in which to work—not just for war, but for peace.

He must tell them that America needs strengthening inside, that she has been starved for the public and social services, the research and discovery, that must undergird a growing nation and an expanding economy.

Yes, he must tell them that these programs will cost money and will have to be paid for.

I myself am convinced that they can be paid for if we can stimulate our economy to the growth rate America achieved before the 1950s and that it can and must have in the 1960s. They can also be met, in part, by closing tax loopholes.

But if the needs should prove larger, then the American people should be asked to face up to that prospect and pay the bill. They should in any event be disabused of the notion that the Internal Revenue Code of 1954 is as immutable and heaven-sent as the Scriptures.

We can afford to do what needs to be done.

But there are some things America cannot afford, and the next president must make this abundantly clear.

He must tell our people that we cannot afford a second-best defense, or inadequate schools, or underpaid teachers, or second-class citizenship for anyone. We cannot afford cities clogged with traffic, cloaked in smog and riddled with slums. We cannot afford prolonged recessions and unemployment.

Above all, the next president must remind the people of a vital lesson of history: that America can do anything she wills to do. . . .

America has shown that when summoned to the heights, she can rise to the heights.

But she will not be summoned by men who everywhere see obstacles rather than opportunities.

She will not be summoned by men for whom good intentions are a substitute for action.

The world cries out for leaders who seek and enjoy endeavor, who will achievement and point the way to it. . . .

Defending the Over-Fortys

In February, 1960, Senator Humphrey addressed himself to the plight of the nation's citizens who had reached age forty and beyond.

It was becoming increasingly difficult for them to find good jobs, he wrote in an article released by his office. This was a terrible waste of manpower.

To see the widespread discrimination against older workers, you don't have to look any further than the "help wanted" section of most large daily newspapers.

"Prefer men under 35." "21 to 40." "Age 25 to 45." These are the barriers which too often face older men and women who must find a job.

But the age limits in these advertisements tell only part of the story. The age barrier appears again in a less blatant form when the older job applicant turns up in an employer's personnel office.

"Sorry, the job has been filled." "Sorry, we are looking for someone a little younger." "Sorry, we only hire temporary workers over forty."

Is it any wonder that discouragement, frustration and hopelessness overcome the older jobseeker? It is bad enough to be out of work, worrying about food, rent, children and health expenses. But even worse is the feeling, "No one wants me; I am too old to get a job and too young to get a pension."

This is a terrible blow to any person's self-respect. Without a job, a man feels loss of his status as a breadwinner in his family and in his community, plus a terrible loss of his dignity as a human being. . . .

We cannot afford to waste any of our manpower. Our manpower—young and old—is our greatest resource in achieving prosperity at home and in meeting the challenge of Soviet competition abroad. The age barriers not only are wasteful, but have profound human and social consequences. Age discrimination may turn an able unemployed worker into a bitter, hopeless idler, a ripe victim for any demagogue's propaganda.

What is behind the reluctance to hire older workers?

Some employers claim that older people are less productive, too often sick or absent, unwilling to learn, prone to accidents, quick to "job hop," or hard to get along with. Like most prejudices, these ideas simply cannot be substantiated.

The facts show that older workers are as good as, or even better than, younger workers. This has been determined in studies by government agencies, by universities, by labor unions and by management groups. It is clear to me that age discrimination in employment stems from a few hasty generalizations—not from a serious study of the facts.

Employers often follow quick "rule-of-thumb" restrictions on hiring older workers. One frequently expressed concern is the added pension and welfare costs in hiring older workers. Because of this cost, younger workers—even those with a minimum of experience or training—are often hired instead of older men.

Obviously, employers must take account of any added costs in hiring older workers. I believe we must remove such roadblocks which often cause employers to discriminate against older people. It is not fair that we should ask an individual employer to bear alone the additional expense of pensions, welfare funds or special training when hiring older workers. These are costs which our whole society should bear—and should be willing to assume. . . .

Therefore, I have introduced legislation to allow employers a tax credit to cover the added costs of hiring older workers. . . .

I am convinced that this tax-credit bill would encourage many more employers to hire middle-aged and older workers and would in the long run be of benefit not only to the workers and employers but to the entire economy of our country.

Of course, the employment problems of our older citizens will not be solved by any one approach. Age discrimination has many faces—and we must act on many levels. . . .

We must face the fact that it is not easy for older people to find a job. We must give them extra guidance and placement services. And we should make sure that our systems of unemployment compensation do not leave them high and dry just when they need help most.

In many states, unemployment compensation is grossly inadequate and far too short in duration. We must set up minimum federal standards of unemployment compensation and provide special employment services to make sure that these people get the help they need and get it as soon as they need it.

It is heartening to see growing activity by public and private organizations to help older workers find jobs. More and more, both labor unions and management are becoming aware of the problems, the needs and the abilities of older workers.

But we must set forth a national policy against discrimination because of age. I have joined in sponsoring legislation to prohibit age discrimination by private firms working on contracts with the federal government. This is a first step toward a sound national policy to break down the tragic, wasteful and needless barriers of prejudice and discrimination.

This policy will reflect the wisdom and compassion of the American people in bringing new hope to those who now are unable to find employment—not because of lack of ability, but simply because of their age.

Lost: Money for Main Street

Agricultural policy was always one of Hubert Humphrey's major concerns. He was, after all, a senator from an agricultural state.

He had introduced many pieces of legislation relating to agriculture during the eleven years he had thus far spent in the Senate. One bill, introduced late in 1959, dealt with development of family farms, a subject dear to his heart.

On March 3, 1960, in a speech to the twenty-ninth annual banquet of the Farmer's Union Central Exchange, he attacked the Eisenhower administration's agricultural policies, and specifically the stewardship of the Agriculture Department by Secretary Ezra Taft Benson.

Although he had addressed groups of Minnesota farmers before and said similar things, the speech he delivered that night in St. Paul was different in one respect: This time, he was not merely their senator; he was a candidate for president.

Republican farm policies are turning this great agricultural region—America's great dairy land and bread basket—into a vast economically depressed area.

There is no longer much argument about the objectives —nor the effects—of the Benson-Eisenhower-Nixon farm program. When the academic euphemisms about "adjustment" and "freedom in the marketplace" are stripped away, the plain truth is clear enough for anyone to see.

Mr. Benson's aim is to drive what he considers "surplus" farmers off their land with low prices, economic ruin and despair.

From time to time, Republican farm planners get impatient with the stubborn persistence of farm people to stick on their farms even in the face of sliding incomes and discouraging prices. In their impatience, the Republicans even become a little generous. If farmers don't move out fast enough because they're going broke, the Republican administration will speed up the exodus by paying farmers to shut down their whole farms and put them in the soil bank.

The Republican administration has paid farmers more money to plow under their growing crops or simply to leave their land idle than the Democratic administrations of Presidents Roosevelt and Truman spent to support farm prices during the entire twenty years from 1933 through 1952.

The Republican administration has managed, however, to

see to it that none of their big-spending generosity stays with the farmers.

Mr. Benson took office in January 1953. Since that time, the annual total farm net income has declined by 23 percent.

This drop in farm income represents $3.5 billion a year that was taken away from the cash registers on the Main Streets of the farming region of the nation since 1952.

In the past seven years, the economy of our farming areas had lost a cumulative total of $24.5 billion out of what they would have received if farm income had been maintained at the 1952 level—when farm prices averaged 100 percent of parity. . . .

If farm income had increased as much during the past seven years as our overall national income increased, total net farm income would have been $20 billion—which is almost double what it actually was last year. . . .

The hardship and worry that farmers have been going through is not necessary. Worse than unnecessary—it is senseless and inexcusable.

Our agricultural economy can be managed so that it will provide equality of opportunity for farm people to enjoy their fair share of the good things of life—if we will just apply a little common sense and a lot of sincere determination to the job.

Last fall I introduced a bill entitled the "Farm Family Program Development Act."

This bill would give the major responsibility for designing the details of farm programs right to the people who can handle it best—to the farmers themselves. . . .

This approach to the farm problem is one that can work. It is sound from the standpoint of developing realistic, practical farm programs that will do the job of restoring farmers' incomes. It is sound from the standpoint of administration, with a broad scope of powers and influence and detailed administrative responsibility placed directly in the hands of working farmers. . . .

There is no longer any excuse for anyone to pretend that the farm problem will simply evaporate and go away if we continue to drift along with Ezra Taft Benson's assurances of "parity in the marketplace." The Department of Agriculture finally got around to doing the job of economic analysis it was hired for—a job it should have started just as soon as the president and the secretary of agriculture started to think about turning our farm programs around toward the so-called free-market direction.

Better late than never—and maybe just in the nick of time—the Senate Agriculture Committee has prodded the department into taking a look at what would happen to farm prices and farmers' incomes if free-market conditions were put into effect. The conclusions of this study give the lie to the "parity in the marketplace" myth.

If price supports were eliminated, says the Senate report, net farm income would plunge 47 percent below 1958 levels by 1965.

Make no mistake about it, this is the best-informed estimate it is possible to obtain of the probable consequences of the farm policies recommended by Benson and developed, according to Mr. Benson himself, with the aid and advice of Richard Nixon.

The administration has gone on record time after time in favor of the objective of reducing price supports to the point that they will not "accumulate surpluses," accompanied by the elimination of controls on production. If you don't "accumulate" the surplus and take it off the market, or if you don't give farmers the opportunity to keep their production in line with demand, then you do not have a workable farm program.

It doesn't take much imagination to foresee the economic calamity that would overtake the communities of this great farming region if the Eisenhower-Benson-Nixon farm philosophy is given another four years' extension. The handwriting is there on the wall, written in the sorrow and discouragement of living experience during the past seven years, for all to see.

For farmers and their families it spells out deepening

hardship, widening inequality and spreading defeat of the hope for security, dignity and a fair share of life's comforts.

For the businessmen on the Main Streets which serve agriculture and depend upon farm income for their own prosperity, it spells declining sales, dying opportunity, closed doors and empty stores.

For the rural communities, it spells social decay, inadequate schools and other public services, and the drifting away of young people to seek their fortunes in more promising places.

There is something terribly wrong about this prophetic picture. . . .

We still need food in America. We still need our farmers. We still need busy, bustling, prosperous Main Streets.

The so-called surplus is really very small, when it is considered in relation to total farm output. It is ridiculous to allow the tail not only to wag the dog, but to make us almost lose sight of the dog altogether.

But more important is the fact that there is no surplus of food at all in a troubled and fearful world in which one-half of the human race lives and dies on the raw edge of hunger. . . .

In the human upheavals of our time, food is both a dynamic engine of economic change and a crucial lever of political power. Soviet rockets have beaten ours to the moon, but Soviet farmers cannot match the abundance of our fields. No one in America has outdistanced the performance of communism by a greater margin than our farmers have.

Our American agriculture gives us one of the most significant advantages we possess over our communistic competitors. Yet we hide our light under ten billion bushels—piled up uselessly, unimaginatively, resentfully, in government storage. . . .

Progress creates hope and faith—faith in the ability of the democratic system to provide the necessities and comfort of life, with freedom, that the communist propagandists promise as the price of freedom.

Too Many Gaps

With the Wisconsin primary a month away, Humphrey began in March concentrating on beating the Kennedy machine, which was outspending and outmaneuvering the poorly financed Humphrey effort.

One of the major topics in that primary campaign was the upcoming East-West summit conference, to be held in Geneva in May. On March 6, Humphrey talked about the summit and the ineffective Eisenhower adminis-tration foreign policy in a Milwaukee campaign appearance.

. . . It is sixteen months since Khrushchev launched his ultima-tum against the freedom-loving city of free Berlin, and he is losing no opportunity to show his impatience—his toughness.

He very badly wants to push the West—and freedom—out of Berlin. . . .

"West Berlin," he said, "is on the territory of East Ger-many."

The 1958 ultimatum has already yielded big dividends to Khrushchev—two foreign ministers' conferences, his visit to America and an invitation to a series of summit meetings. But the appetite grows with eating and he wants more and more and more.

At his press conference last month, our secretary of state, (Christian) Herter, acknowledged that the tough Soviet talk on Berlin has him worried. He attributed this tough communist talk to the lead the Soviet Union now holds over the United States in intercontinental missiles—the so-called missile gap.

This raises a very grave question—what have we done with the sixteen months since Khrushchev launched his warn-ing?

One thing we certainly cannot complain of—the attitude of the free people of West Berlin. Under the leadership of their gallant mayor, Willy Brandt—a man whom I am proud to number among my close friends—they have remained stead-fast in the face of a long series of threats.

I was in Europe in 1958 when the Khrushchev ultimatum was delivered, and I went direct to Berlin to assure its mayor and people that the American people backed them to the hilt.

I remember, as if it were yesterday, how warmly Mayor Brandt welcomed me and with what pride he showed me his half of the city—from its bustling shops and factories to its modern housing for workers.

In long and frank talks as we drove about the city, he shared with me the grave problems in maintaining this little island of freedom in a totalitarian sea.

At the heart of the city, by the famous Brandenburg Gate, we stood together on the very frontier between freedom and slavery. . . .

I spoke to many Berliners and asked them how their nerves were standing up under the strain. They told me: "Don't worry about our nerves, and we won't worry about yours."

I don't worry about our nerves—but I do worry about the yawning gaps in our readiness to meet a crisis which may burst upon us in ten weeks time—or even sooner.

I am concerned, as many well-informed observers are, about the space gap and the missile gap.

Soviet sputniks and luniks are blazing out into space with a magnitude of thrust which, even now—two years after the first sputnik—we are unable to match.

I am alarmed by the prospect that, within the next two or three years, the Russians may have a 3-to-1 advantage over us in missiles—but I am even more alarmed that the administration reacts to this appalling prospect as if it were nothing more than the Russian victory in the winter Olympics.

It is the "complacency gap" which troubles me even more than the missile gap.

We have been warned—again and again and again. But all the administration does is to administer us another tranquilizing pill.

There is another huge gap that bothers me—what I call

the "testimony gap," the gap between what we are told and what we uncomfortably suspect to be the painful truth. . . .

Then there is a third threatening gap—the "moral gap," the gap between what we preach and what we practice.

Almost six years have passed since the Supreme Court's decision outlawing segregated schools. Yet the administration and Congress still shirk their share of responsibility for enforcing that decision.

We haven't even heard from the White House what we have every right to expect—a clear and unequivocal affirmation of the moral rightness of that historic decision.

We talk of our prosperous society—and yet we leave over 20 million of our people languishing in poverty: the aged, the sick and those marooned in the depressed areas which pockmark our country.

Khrushchev doesn't need a "seeing-eye" satellite to spy out our weaknesses. As he sees it, ours is a dying system—and his hands are itching for the spade so that he can "bury" us— to quote his own blunt word.

There isn't any quizmaster who can slip us, under the table, the answers to the grave questions which hang over us. There isn't any "payola" that will ensure our prestige in the world, unless we earn it by deeds as well as words.

I have made a careful study of Soviet strategy.

There is no day-to-day fumbling in their policy, as there too often is in ours. They think in terms of years and of decades. They weigh future trends as well as present facts.

They will have one kind of policy if they think America is rising in the world—a policy of respect and carefulness. They will have another, a much more unpleasant one, if they see we are sinking.

They will be watching what we do, listening to what we say, in the coming weeks. They will form their own shrewd judgment about whether we will continue sleepwalking into the limbo of second-class powers—or whether we will, at long last, wake up and rally our great energies and capabilities for the crisis that lies ahead.

It is good that we—Democrats and Republicans alike—have said in one united voice that we will stand firm on Berlin. But we must do more than say the right words—much more. We must move to close the gaps that cloud with doubt the firmness of our purpose.

I have just heard that Mayor Brandt of free Berlin has canceled plans to visit America and put the case of his beleaguered city before us—because of the renewed gravity of the situation there.

He wants to be on the job twenty-four hours a day, to meet and to cope with whatever may come. Oh, how I wish that our own government had been on the job twenty-four hours a day for all these recent seven years.

For myself, I shall continue to blow the bugle, sound the warning, seek to awaken the American people to the peril in which they stand. Given the full facts and alert, on-the-job leadership, we shall—I am utterly confident—surmount this coming crisis.

A National Disgrace

On the day after his Milwaukee speech on the impending summit conference, Humphrey gave a radio address on the subject of the nation's senior citizens. Once again, he was pushing his Medicare proposal, just as he had been doing since first introducing a Medicare bill in 1949.

We often hear the word *crisis* thrown about these days. It is a word which is used all too often to describe problems of all types.

Today, I want to talk with you about a problem which is

truly critical. It is a problem which cannot wait for more talk and more study. It is the crisis faced by our nation's senior citizens.

Let me first give you an idea of the immensity and growth of this crisis. In the year 1900, there were only 3 million Americans over the age of 65. Today, there are nearly 16 million. In ten years, there will be more than 20 million.

But these are just figures. They do not tell the pathetic story of the needs of our senior citizens in terms which all of us can understand.

They do not tell the story of the elderly widow whose income is so low her day begins and ends with a sense of hunger.

They do not tell the story of the elderly man who needs, but cannot afford, hospital or nursing-home care for illness or disease.

They do not tell the story of the elderly couple who live each day in fear of losing the roof over their heads.

We hear noble talk about "the golden years." But more and more people are finding that these are years of despair and anxiety.

This is a disgrace for a nation with our wealth and luxury.

I'm not just talking about a few isolated cases. Millions of Americans, through no fault of their own, are existing without adequate incomes, health care, or housing, and without a recognized role in the community.

The Department of Health, Education and Welfare tells us that it costs at least $2,300 a year for a couple to live by themselves in modest fashion. But the average retired couple on social security receives only about $1,440 a year.

And 60 percent of the individuals retired on social security have less than $1,000 a year in money income.

Even more desperate is the crisis facing the 1,300,000 aging widows who now receive an annual social security benefit of $56 a month.

I ask you: Is this what our mothers and fathers deserve?

Do these fine citizens deserve a shabby rented room and a diet of bread and soup in their final years?

There are selfish and narrow-thinking persons who say the problem is not theirs. They say: "It's every individual for himself." They say every individual has total responsibility to plan for retirement.

I agree that we should all plan on an individual basis to provide for our future needs. But the best plans and preparations of all men can be crushed by forces beyond their control. Disease, economic fluctuations and just plain bad luck can make a mockery of even the wisest investments and preparations.

What we need is a new dedication to end the crisis facing our senior citizens. What we need is a government with heart and understanding. And what we need right now is action on a program to allow our senior citizens to live with dignity, security and a sense of usefulness. . . .

Moratorium

As chairman of the Senate subcommittee on disarmament, Humphrey had been able to influence—to some degree, at least—Eisenhower administration policy.

But more needed to be done, Humphrey told audiences in 1960. In Pontiac, Michigan, in October 1959, he had outlined a disarmament program. On March 26, 1960, just ten days before the Wisconsin primary, Humphrey talked about his plan to a campaign crowd in Wausau, Wisconsin. (Despite syndicated columnist Joseph Alsop's prediction that Humphrey would be lucky if he came out of Wausau with as much as a hundred votes, the senator defeated John Kennedy in the city.)

Today has been a colorful, exciting day—full of caravans and bands and the stuff of American politics that stirs the blood and makes the heart glad. It has been a thrilling day for me—and, I hope, for you, too.

But when the bands have gone, when the banners have been furled and the crowds have disappeared, you and I are still left to face the problems of the day, to contemplate their complexities, and to search for their solutions.

Of problems there are many; but the greatest of them all, I think you will agree, is the winning of a true and lasting peace.

The world has so long been at war or on the verge of war that the winning of the peace has become a sort of liturgy—a phrase we all say and believe in, but whose meaning we no longer question or fully understand as we say it.

Of course, mankind has always yearned for peace. But in the 1960s, peace takes on a new meaning. It means the preservation of civilization from its own destruction.

We live in a unique age. Man has gone on, through the years, perfecting more and more deadly and destructive weapons. Now, we appear to have achieved the ultimate in destructiveness: The power to destroy civilization itself.

Fifteen years ago, man exploded the first atomic bomb. Try to think back twenty years—or even sixteen—to the times before the bomb was a reality. Would any of us ever have dreamed that we would today, such a short time later, consider a weapon with the explosive power of 19,000 tons of TNT a small weapon? Yet that is the degree of destructiveness man has achieved: 38 million pounds of TNT is a small weapon.

You may now begin to see why the winning of a true peace takes on a special meaning—and a special urgency. It means the capacity to save ourselves from total obliteration.

In the winning of peace, therefore, the problem of disarmament takes the central place upon the world stage.

As chairman of the Senate subcommittee on disarmament, I have had the duty of concerning myself with this awesome problem, of struggling with its technicalities, of groping for new avenues of approach that might offer the hope of an agreement between nations that they will not blow each other into oblivion.

Today, the world stands as close to such an agreement as it has stood since nuclear weapons first emerged. Today, for the first time, agreement is within sight, if we and the Russians can grasp the opportunity and have the capacity to bridge the remaining gaps that divide us.

Last October, in Pontiac, Michigan, I presented the outlines of a possible solution to the disarmament impasse. It was a four-point program:

—First, a treaty permanently banning all nuclear tests except small underground tests, with adequate inspections to enforce the treaty.

—Second, a temporary moratorium on the underground testing of the smaller weapons that are difficult to detect.

—Third, a joint research program with the Russians to improve the techniques of detecting small underground explosions.

—Fourth, if the research should bear fruit, the expansion of the treaty . . . to include a prohibition against the smaller weapons tests. If it failed, the moratorium would be ended and the small testing would resume.

Today I renew my proposal of last October. I call upon our government to agree to a moratorium of specified duration on the underground testing of smaller weapons—but only on condition that the Soviets agree to an adequate number of inspections to make a major test-ban treaty safe and enforceable.

There are those who will say there is risk in agreeing to a moratorium that cannot be enforced. There is danger, they point out, that the Russians will cheat and will secretly go on testing smaller weapons in underground explosions that cannot be distinguished from earthquakes.

Yes, there is risk, but I say it is a small risk. We would have some means of detecting the smaller explosions if the Russians went ahead with their tests. We would have control stations inside Russia under the permanent test-ban treaty that would precede the moratorium. We would continue to have the listening stations in our own country and in the countries of our allies. And we would have our regular intelligence sources. . . .

Yes, there is risk in moratorium, but the risk is small—and it must be weighed against the risk of a continued stalemate and a continued buildup of the power of annihilation on both sides.

Remember, my friends, the nuclear club is no longer as exclusive as it once was. France has broken down the door and it is only a matter of time before other nations force entrance as well. And, as the club grows larger, the dangers of nuclear war by accident grow, too, and the difficulties of reaching and policing a disarmament treaty multiply.

Time is against us, my friends. We must make every effort to seize the opportunity now offered to us, before it is too late. . . .

Peace is not passive; it is active. It will not come to those who wait for it, who are afraid to reach out for it, who are too timid to risk little to win much. Nor can peace be won by slogans. . . .

The world cries out for leadership that will reach out for peace, that will undertake willingly the long, tedious, and costly—but richly rewarding—task of creating a decent world in which peace can take root and flourish.

Humphrey on Cancer

When Hubert Humphrey entered the 1960 presidential campaign, he was filled with hope and exuberance. He was confident that the United States of the 1960s was ready to listen to issues; he was certain that his liberal, progressive record would impress the voters.

He had counted on these things to carry him through to the convention that summer in Los Angeles and give him a good shot at the nomination. What he had not counted on, however, was John F. Kennedy; his money, his organization or his anything-to-win campaign style.

Humphrey had long been a leader of liberal causes, a spokesman for the underprivileged, for the worker and for the common man. He fully expected the men who had been his allies over the years to rally behind his banner. It never occurred to him that they would rally around Kennedy, whose entire career was spent to the right of everything the liberals had stood for. But many of them, like Arthur Goldberg and United Auto Workers president Walter Reuther, did rally around Kennedy nonetheless, and Humphrey felt betrayed.

In the Wisconsin primary, especially, Humphrey was deserted by people he had thought were sure supporters. Most notable of the defections was the state's junior senator, William Proxmire. When Joe McCarthy died in 1957, Proxmire ran for his seat. Humphrey and his aides raised money for Proxmire and helped him in other ways. Humphrey even interceded with Senate Majority Leader Lyndon Johnson to get Proxmire some choice committee assignments. But when the chips were down in Wisconsin, Proxmire was on the other side.

The reason, in retrospect, is obvious. Everyone likes to be with a winner, and John F. Kennedy did indeed look like a winner, despite the fact that he was a Roman Catholic and a rich man's son. He was young and charismatic. His brother-in-law Peter Lawford was a movie star. And his father was a multimillionaire who was determined to use his fortune to put his son in the White House.

Kennedy had the press on his side while his father had the politicians in his pocket.

In theory, Humphrey had everything going for him when he entered the Wisconsin primary. Wisconsin is an agricultural state. Humphrey had an excellent record in agricultural matters; Kennedy's record was poor to downright awful. Humphrey came from the same kind of background as the people of Wisconsin and spoke their language; Kennedy was one of Boston's elite and his accent was pronounced.

But the Kennedy organization was determined to win in Wisconsin and they were not willing to rely on money and media alone. They decided to turn Kennedy's Catholicism into a plus on Primary Day.

Wisconsin is a crossover state—that is, Democrats and Republicans can vote in each other's primaries. A great many of Wisconsin's Roman Catholics were Republicans. A way had to be found to get them to cross over and vote for Kennedy.

A way was found, although the Kennedy organization denied having anything to do with it. Virulently anti-Catholic, profundamentalist Protestant literature was sent to the state's Catholic voters of both parties. The inference they drew was obvious: "Humphrey" was trying to "scare the Protestants" with visions of the White House being controlled by the Vatican.

On Primary Day, April 5, many of the Roman Catholic Republicans did indeed cross over and vote for Kennedy, who went on to win six of the state's ten congressional districts (although the friendly media had been predicting all along that Kennedy would sweep the state). He outpolled Humphrey by nearly 107,000 votes, capturing 20½ of the state's 31 convention votes.

Disappointed and defeated, Humphrey and his advisers met to plot their next move.

A few advocated withdrawal from the race. Kennedy, they argued, had too much money and was too well organized. And besides, people actually believed he was the liberal he claimed to be—especially people in the media, some of whom had not forgiven Humphrey for his anticommunist bill in 1954.

Other advisers suggested that Humphrey face Kennedy next in Nebraska. Agriculture would again be the chief issue there, and even more important, only Democrats would be allowed to vote in the Democratic primary.

Humphrey, however, opted for the West Virginia primary, to be held on May 10. He stood a better chance there, he reasoned.

Five days before the primary, on May 5, Humphrey spoke to an audience at Wheeling College. His topic that day was "The War That Could Be Won." The war of which he spoke was the war against cancer.

I take my theme for today's talk from one of the youngest of living Americans—former President Harry S. Truman.

He said on May 24, 1951: "The only kind of war we seek is the good old fight against man's ancient enemies—poverty, disease, hunger and illiteracy."

Poverty, disease, hunger, illiteracy.

Each of these ancient enemies could be the topic of many volumes, let alone a single speech.

Today I shall talk mainly about the worldwide fight against one disease—cancer. . . .

Because cancer has reached epidemic proportions in this country, we must mobilize every resource to conquer it.

I, therefore, pledge to the American people that, if I am elected president, I will call a White House conference early in 1961 to bring together the best medical and scientific brains in this country to plan an accelerated attack upon this disease.

I earnestly hope that all other candidates for the presidency will take the same position.

Cancer strikes without regard to political party. . . . It pays no heed to the Iron Curtain, either.

Almost a year ago, a Senate government operations subcommittee, of which I am chairman, issued a report entitled: "Cancer: A Worldwide Menace."

That document pointed out that cancer kills two million people a year in all parts of the world, that its incidence is rising in thirty-three countries and that it is the second leading cause of death in the Soviet Union, as well as in the United States and most of Europe.

In transmitting this report to the Senate, I pointed out that this disease is one "whose ultimate conquest will undoubtedly involve an unparalleled effort of worldwide biomedical research."

American doctors who have visited the Soviet Union recently report that Russia has embarked upon a massive fifteen-year plan for medical research on cancer.

We keep secret—and the Soviet Union keeps secret—the

research that goes into the development of ever more devastating weapons. But we have no reason to keep secret—and every reason to share—the research aimed at this deadly enemy, which spares neither American senators nor communist commissars.

That is why, when I had my eight-hour talk with Mr. Khrushchev a year ago, I spent much of it urging upon him a worldwide attack upon the killers and cripplers of mankind—cancer, heart disease, tuberculosis, malaria and many others.

It made sense to him—even to this hard, cunning and dedicated communist. He liked the idea of what I call "Health for Peace."

Indeed, I have long advocated a "Works of Peace" program aimed at poverty, hunger and illiteracy as well as disease.

I have voted again and again for programs of overseas technical and economic aid. And I have always maintained that the Americans of Cabin Creek are as fully entitled to help—the kind that helps people to help themselves—as the people of Afghanistan or Africa.

I have talked, too, about "Food for Peace"—putting a coordinated, worldwide attack upon illiteracy which would make use of the soft currencies we receive in repayment for development loans and for sales of surplus food.

These ideas—these "Works for Peace"—are not original with me. They draw upon a rich American tradition—and, may I say, a Jesuit tradition as well.

The great Jesuit missionaries preached the word of God—but they also healed the sick, fed the hungry and taught the illiterate.

Indeed, in many places they gave the people among whom they worked the very gift of literacy—putting into writing languages that hitherto had been only spoken.

There are some people who say that wars among men will only end when we face the attack of a common enemy. Half cynically, half humorously, they have suggested that the world will unite only to repel invaders from Mars.

We don't need to wait for the little green men to launch

their science fiction attack. Our common enemies—poverty, disease, hunger and illiteracy—have always been with us.

Until the day before yesterday, we lacked the knowledge and the resources to attack them effectively. Now what we principally lack is the intelligence and the will.

I pray that, within my lifetime and certainly within yours, this will be the only war that anyone in this world will seek.

The Peace Corps

Hubert Humphrey was right: his best chance against Kennedy was in West Virginia.

—There were no great cities in the state and it was thus more adaptable to Humphrey's press-the-flesh campaign style. That fact would also minimize the advantage of heavy radio and television advertising, which the Kennedys could afford and which Humphrey could not.

—Its per capita income was $1,635 (Minnesota's was only about $300 higher; Massachusetts's per capita income was nearly $1,000 higher).

—It was a heavy labor state and Humphrey has always derived his biggest support from labor.

—It was also an almost exclusively Protestant state, meaning that the Kennedy forces could not play on religious emotions.

But the Kennedy machine knew all this—and they were ready. They would "buy" the election, if necessary.

According to Humphrey, Boston's Richard Cardinal Cushing admitted several years later that, in good part, the West Virginia election was decided in his study. As Humphrey related it in his autobiography, the cardinal and Joseph P. Kennedy sat in the study one evening before the primary and decided which Protestant churches would receive "donations" and how much. They particularly concentrated on black churches, Humphrey recalled the cardinal saying.

Until that day, Humphrey never knew about the Kennedy contributions to the state's Protestant churches. But he did know of the other kind of "contribution" Kennedy's aides had made around West Virginia.

County Democratic chairmen in the state were permitted to issue candidate slates to voters. Candidates "won" the right to be on those slates based on the amount of money they could "contribute" to the county organization. Humphrey did not stand a chance of outbidding Kennedy for a spot on the various slates.

On May 10, it was all over. Hubert Humphrey's presidential dream was shot down in a fusillade of Kennedy votes. The young senator from Massachusetts, sounding more liberal than he was, had even managed to win big in the black communities that owed so much to Hubert Humphrey. Kennedy wound up with 61 percent of the vote.

Humphrey was bitter but he was not about to let it destroy him. His Senate term was up in 1960 and he decided it was time to drop out of the presidential race and run for reelection to a third term.

Winning reelection was not going to be a problem for Humphrey and he knew it. So, after dropping out of the presidential race and announcing again for the Senate, he returned to Washington and settled back down to the work the people paid him to do.

In one of his first acts once back in Washington, Humphrey introduced a bill on June 15 to create a "Peace Corps of young Americans," an idea he had developed during his presidential campaign. On that same day, he explained the idea to his fellow senators.

. . . The purpose of this bill is to develop a genuine people-to-people program in which talented and dedicated young American men will teach basic agricultural and industrial techniques, literacy, the English language and other school subjects, and sanitation and health procedures in Asia, Africa and Latin America.

A respected American diplomat said recently before the Senate subcommittee on national policy machinery that the Soviet Union does not understand words at diplomatic conferences quite so easily as it understands situations.

In other words, the specific situation of the United States enjoying good relations with noncommunist countries and helping them along to economic self-sufficiency is much more persuasive to the Soviet Union than the most articulate statement prepared for a foreign ministers' or summit conference.

One of the most explosive situations today is that the rich nations are getting richer and the poor nations are getting poorer. Communism is nurtured not so much by poverty as it is by frustration.

The peoples of the underdeveloped countries have seen our magazines and our movies, and they say, "Why cannot we live like that?" They see the gap growing greater rather than less, and they desperately desire to break through the sound barrier of modernization. In this type of a situation, communism can often look attractive. It is for this reason that we must offer them a suitable alternative.

And yet. . . , I wish to make it very clear that the bill I am introducing is not meant primarily as an anticommunist measure. If Marx and Engels had never lived, there still would be just as much need for action to develop the potential of the underdeveloped nations. We in the West must not only think about negative policies to stop communism—but also about creative efforts which reflect our own elevating visions of the kind of world in which we would like to see mankind live.

We are living in the most revolutionary epoch in the history of mankind. Events which used to take centuries to develop are now taking place in a few years. The imagination and boldness of our plans must be consonant with the greatly accelerated pace of our age. It is with this in mind that I have introduced this bill.

Before discussing the bill's provisions, let me say that a Peace Corps is something that I have discussed publicly for two years. Whenever I have mentioned the proposal, it has received an overwhelmingly favorable response. I have received a steady flow of letters on this subject and I have yet to receive one letter in opposition to this proposal. . . .

As to the provisions of the bill, the Peace Corps will be a

separate agency, but will work in the closest cooperation with the Department of State, the U.S. Information Agency and especially the International Cooperation Administration.

Discretionary provisions are included so that the president could place the agency within an existing department or agency for administrative purposes. This would allow the president flexibility in the administration of our overall foreign aid program.

However it is administered, I wish to emphasize the fact that the whole orientation of the corps and director must be toward the people-to-people approach. The basic people-to-people orientation is sometimes missing in the way our foreign aid program is carried out. . . .

One of the critical projects the [Peace Corps] members would undertake would be to teach literacy. Surely, there is no greater need in the world today than that of teaching people to read. Over two-thirds of the people of Asia, Africa and Latin America are illiterate. There is no nation on the face of the earth which can compete in today's world without a literate population. One cannot read the simplest instructions on a seed packet or directions on how to run an uncomplicated machine without being literate. The half of the world today which is in poverty and hunger and disease also happens to be the illiterate half.

Further, democracy itself rests upon the premise that there is a literate, well-informed electorate. . . .

Another great need is for English-speaking teachers. School systems in, for example, former British colonies in Africa need qualified American college graduates to teach until such a time as those countries educate enough of their own people to be teachers. Especially, there is a burning need for teachers to instruct in the English language. . . .

Besides the necessity of supplying teachers and literacy instructors, there is also, of course, the compelling need for training in basic agricultural and industrial techniques. This is so manifestly obvious that I do not think the point needs elaboration. I should only point out that our helping the people to help themselves can have dramatic effects on their increase in industrial productivity and agricultural yield.

There are other programs on which the Peace Corps could embark, including community development, youth organizations, social welfare, vocational education, and sanitation and health programs. Members of the corps who had obtained degrees in public health or who had graduated from medical schools could suggest ways in which even simple improvements might drastically reduce the disease rate of particular areas. . . .

There is a great body of idealistic and talented young men in this country who are longing to have their energies harnessed. The Peace Corps would tap those vital resources. There is nothing which will build greater people-to-people and government-to-government relationships than to have fine young American men helping the people of the emerging countries to help themselves. They will not only act as instructors but also will show that they are not afraid to dirty their hands in their common endeavor.

There is also the fact that the graduates from the Peace Corps will form a large pool of experienced young men, trained in some of the more remote languages and knowledge of the emerging areas from which [we] . . . can draw. . . .

[In] this turbulent decade of the 1960s, we need imaginative and constructive plans for action which are consonant with the greatness and humanitarian ideals of this nation.

It is for this reason that I have proposed the Peace Corps. . . .

Another Term

After his defeat at the hands of John Kennedy, Humphrey was bitter. But, as with his bitterness over Stevenson's duplicity in 1956, it did not last very long.

Soon, he was on friendly terms with his Massachusetts colleague. He introduced him to such Minnesota political allies as Governor Orville Freeman and economist Walter Heller. He even passed along advice and various position papers submitted by Heller.

Freeman, Heller and a few others were taken by Kennedy and he with them (Freeman would become Kennedy's agriculture secretary; Heller would be chairman of the president's Council of Economic Advisers). Other Minnesotans, however, did not look too kindly on Kennedy. Some did not like him for what he had done to Humphrey; others did not trust him; still others remained loyal to Stevenson, who wanted to try for the presidency one more time.

Humphrey, too, was loyal to Stevenson, but political pragmatism required that, as a senator, he support Kennedy, who was virtually assured the nomination and stood an excellent chance of being the man who would have to sign or veto any Humphrey bills Congress would pass. In late June, therefore, Humphrey indicated to Governor Freeman, who was now part of the Kennedy team, that he would support Kennedy at the convention.

But Humphrey's heart was with Stevenson; nor was he willing in the final analysis to betray the majority of Minnesotans who had no faith in Kennedy. Thus, when the July 11 convention came, he put pragmatism aside and announced that he would cast his vote for Adlai one more time.

With 761 votes required for the nomination, Kennedy on July 13 received 806 votes on the first ballot; Stevenson's total was a sorry 79½.

The next day, Kennedy surprised everyone by his choice for vice-president: Lyndon B. Johnson of Texas.

Immediately after the convention, Humphrey divided his time between running for reelection and campaigning for the Kennedy-Johnson ticket. If there was any bitterness between the two men over Humphrey's defection to Stevenson, it was nowhere in evidence. Humphrey would become one of Kennedy's most ardent supporters.

(Humphrey's decision to support Stevenson apparently was vindicated on Election Day, November 8. While Humphrey beat his Republican opponent, P. Kenneth Peterson, by over 240,000 votes, Kennedy's margin of victory over Nixon in Minnesota was a mere 22,000 votes; Kennedy clearly won Minnesota's eleven electoral votes on Humphrey's coattails. With only

Above left: Humphrey kisses
his mother, Christine Humphrey,
after a presidential campaign
appearance before the National
Press Club in Washington,
in January 1960.

Above right: On the eve of the
Wisconsin primary, sixteen-year-
old Robert Humphrey (left) and
twelve-year-old Douglas indicate
their choice. John Kennedy
beat Humphrey in Wisconsin.

Left: Humphrey jokes with
John Kennedy at a Democratic
dinner in January 1960,
kicking off the presidential
primary campaign season.

United Press International

Above: Almost sixteen years to the day after Humphrey called upon the Democratic Party to push for strong civil rights legislation, President Lyndon Johnson signs the historic Civil Rights Act into law before a nationwide television audience. Seated in the front row (from left to right): Attorney General Robert F. Kennedy; Senate Minority Leader Everett Dirksen; Senator Humphrey, who led the fight for passage in the Senate; George Meany, president A.F. of L.-C.I.O. (partially obscured); House Judiciary Committee Chairman Representative Emanuel Celler; and House Speaker John McCormack. Mrs. Humphrey is seated in the third row, directly behind Martin Luther King Jr.

Right: Humphrey and two of his grandchildren, Vicki (left) and Jill Solomonson.

United Press International

Above: The Humphrey family pose for this Christmas
1965 photo. Front (left to right):
Jill Solomonson; Humphrey; son Douglas;
Mrs. Humphrey; Vicki Solomonson.
Back (left to right): Son-in-law Bruce Solomonson;
daughter Nancy Solomonson; Amy Solomonson;
Mr. and Mrs. Hubert H. Humphrey III and daughter
Lori; and Robert Humphrey.

Left: Humphrey relaxes on the dock of his Waverly,
Minnesota home after winning the 1968 presidential
nomination amid the chaos in Chicago, before jumping
into the bitter election campaign that awaited him.

Below: Humphrey reports to President Johnson on
his trip to Southeast Asia, February 1966.

Senator Muriel Humphrey

In 1970 the Humphreys visited
Israel. (Above) at a kibbutz;
(right) with Arab workers in
Jerusalem; (below right) at the
University of Jerusalem's
Harry S. Truman Center for
Advancement of Peace;
(below left) greeting Hadassah
Hospital staff members.

Senator Muriel Humphrey

Senator Muriel Humphrey   Senator Muriel Humphrey

Official White House photograph

Senator Muriel Humphrey

Above: Senator Humphrey talks to
First Lady Betty Ford, (left), as
President Ford and Mrs. Humphrey, (right),
listen. The Humphreys had arrived at the
White House expecting to be part of a
large dinner party. But President and
Mrs. Ford had a surprise for them:
a private dinner in the family quarters.
Humphrey was very moved by the
singular honor.

Left: The Humphreys and their
grandchildren, Waverly, 1976.

Below: The Humphreys are flanked by their
children at their fortieth wedding
anniversary party in 1976.

Senator Muriel Humphrey

Senator Muriel Humphrey

Above: Humphrey and his wife
Muriel relax outside their
home in Waverly, Minnesota
in the summer of 1976.

Right: Senator Humphrey
shakes hands with Israeli Prime
Minister Menachem Begin.
Minnesota's junior senator,
Wendell Anderson, looks on.

Senator Muriel Humphrey

Senator Muriel Humphrey

United Press International

Above: Humphrey and former
Israeli Prime Minister
Golda Meir listen attentively in
the senator's office as son Skip
makes a point, November 1977.

Left: Humphrey greets a crowd
of well-wishers at Andrews
Air Force Base as he returns to
Washington for the last time.
President Carter, who diverted
Air Force One to give the
senator his long-awaited ride
on the presidential plane, looks
on with Vice-President Mondale.

The memorial service for Senator Humphrey at the Capitol Rotunda.

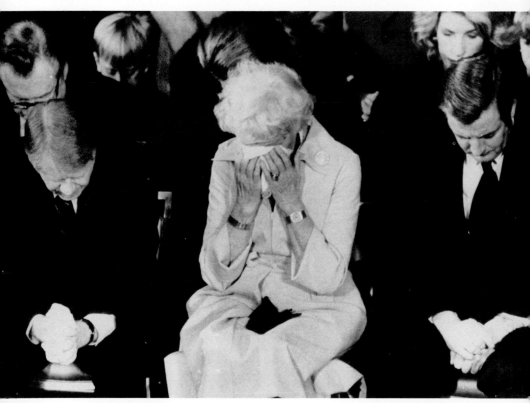

President Jimmy Carter and Vice-President Walter Mondale bow their heads in prayer and Muriel Humphrey weeps during memorial service for the late senator held in the Capitol Rotunda.

200,000 popular votes separating Kennedy and Nixon in the national tally, it is not too difficult to imagine what could have happened if Humphrey's name had not been on the ballot in 1960.)

On August 27, in one of his first speeches to the Senate after the nominating conventions, Humphrey tore into the Republican administration's labor policies.

[The] 1960 Democratic platform adopted in Los Angeles makes the direct and unequivocal pledge: "We will repeal the authorization for right-to-work laws."

This is a promise that Democrats do not mean to forget. For the purpose of the platform erected at our national convention was to present the American people with a crystal clear declaration of the Democratic Party's beliefs and guiding principles on the major issues confronting our nation, and to state the manner in which they will be carried out during the next four years.

The intent of the Democratic Party regarding the federal authorization in the Taft-Hartley Labor-Management Relations Act of 1947 that has made possible state enactment of the unpopular so-called right-to-work laws is unequivocal. We intend to repeal this anti-collective-bargaining provision. . .

[There] are . . . compelling reasons for the Democratic platform pledge—reasons that were accorded full consideration by the convention in approving this plank.

One important consideration is economic. It involves the necessity for the American economy to function equally under law on a nationwide basis rather than under a complicated melange of conflicting statutes. Not only do so-called right-to-work laws condone the Balkanization of our national economy, they actually invite it.

The effect of the authorization for right-to-work laws in the Taft-Hartley Act is the reverse of long-established federal labor-management policy. Law should not pit state against state for economic advantage, but instead should bring about national unity.

All America is progressing rapidly toward industrialization and no longer can this country permit piecemeal exploitation. We must become an economic entity and the same rules should apply to all industry and to all employees. This is the only fair approach to the problem.

As to the so-called right-to-work laws, there is no question but that they are part of a general antiunion package in the states where they have been adopted.

In almost every instance where right-to-work laws have been passed, the legislatures which passed them have included numerous other restrictive laws in their actions. In one state, for instance, a state senator was firmly for right-to-work because a union was then asking for a "guaranteed annual wage" and the legislator saw right-to-work as the only manner in which to punish the union for its daring.

Laws passed in conjunction with right-to-work laws have included restrictions against picketing, curtailment of the right to strike, harassing laws interfering with the internal operations of unions and even restrictions on the amount of land a union may lease or purchase no matter what the need.

Passage of right-to-work laws has also been linked to the refusal to consider legislation deemed necessary for the betterment of labor, such as an increase in payment under workmen's compensation laws. . . , the enactment of laws providing for the protection of women workers and child labor, and for laws establishing minimum wage and maximum hours for work.

In other words, right-to-work laws are passed generally not solely for reasons of opposition to the union shop but for reasons of opposition to unions as such.

This is in itself ample reason for repeal of the authorization of right-to-work laws in the Taft-Hartley Act. Such laws are aimed at a single group in our economy and such instances of discrimination against one segment of our population is foreign to our philosophy as a nation.

There are other arguments of great importance.

There is the fact that the slogan of "Right to Work" is in

itself a fraud. The courts of several states have made such a judgment.

The Supreme Court of Idaho so ruled in 1954 when it refused to sanction the submission to Idaho voters of an initiative measure mislabeled "right to work," which was, in fact, simply the usual anti-union-shop bill.

The attorney general of Kansas in 1958 ruled that the "right-to-work" label on the ballot was not a true description of the proposed amendment. The Supreme Court of Kansas concurred and ordered the full text of the proposal to be printed on the ballot.

In 1956, the fraudulent nature of the term "right to work" was demonstrated when the secretary of state of Washington and the attorney general refused to allow backers of the proposal to use that title on the ballot and also banned the use of a proposed substitute which used the equally fraudulent phrase "guaranteeing freedom of employment."

These anti-collective-bargaining laws abrogate a fundamental freedom. They outlaw the right of labor and management to arrive at a mutually agreed contract calling for union-security provisions.

Actually, laws or proposals which attack and prohibit union-security provisions in labor-management contracts have as their purpose the weakening and ultimate destruction of trade unions. This is the record of past experience.

This was true at the turn of the century when the archreactionary fringe of management threatened the very existence of labor organizations. They used the same phrase, the same arguments—and guns and clubs, too—to make the point of a compulsory open shop.

As a result, many weak and young unions were wiped out and only the determination of the rank-and-file union members to stand by the principle of union organizations saved labor.

The so-called American Plan drive of the National Association of Manufacturers in the 1920s resulted in the destruction of some of the unions organized during the days of

World War I and even the older, better-established unions lost membership and were handicapped in bargaining for improved working conditions and higher wages.

I have discussed the injustices which these repressive and discriminatory laws do to the nation's working people, to organized labor, to the nation's economy and to federal labor-management policies that have safeguarded our prosperity for a quarter-century.

I should also point out that the so-called right-to-work laws are equally harmful to the best interests of our management structures; and many of our leading industrialists are outspoken in their opposition to such legislation.

Responsible business—or management—wants strong, responsible unions, for only thus can working contacts be drawn that will be effective. . . .

Employers in many, many instances have strongly indicated their preference for union security arrangements to help build responsible unions. For example, the National Industrial Conference Board, a research agency wholly supported by employers, conducted a survey of management viewpoints. They found that union-security arrangements eliminated friction in the labor force, brought better discipline and more responsibility generally to the plant manager from a secure union. . . .

This unpopular and unjust legislation has also aroused the deep concern of our churches and religious leaders. Our leading faiths and many of our religious spokesmen have condemned the right-to-work laws as being immoral, unwise and harmful to the common good. . . .

There are at present some 17 million members of our working force who are members of unions. One of the popular myths constantly repeated by the proponents of the right-to-work laws is the palpably fraudulent claim that the individual freedom of workers is shackled by the union shop and that these laws are needed to protect workers from being exploited by a character known as the union boss, which exists largely in the imagination of editorial cartoonists.

Another claim by right-to-work advocates is that labor leaders exploit their membership for greed, power and political advantage.

Are such claims valid? Are our 17 million union members pitiful creatures, chained to the rack by their union-boss masters? Or are they instead a great and valued cross-section of our nation, working for fair wages and reasonable hours, who lead a happy family life, send their children to good schools, and are a major factor in keeping our nation prosperous by consuming the goods produced by our industries?

We have good reason to know that the rank-and-file of union members do support their leadership. On the question of the union shop, for instance, this has been shown conclusively by secret ballot. . . .

From August 1947 to October 1951, the National Labor Relations Board conducted 46,119 union-shop authorization polls among employees. . . . The union shop was authorized in 44,795, or 97.1 percent, of these polls.

Put another way, more than 5.5 million votes were cast for the union shop in these elections, or 91 percent of all ballots cast.

This is certainly a virtually unanimous endorsement of the union-shop arrangement by the working people who are directly affected.

Another major fact that reveals the covert intent of these right-to-work laws is that this legislation has been embraced by states whose wage scales are far below the national average. The facts show that the right-to-work states generally lag behind other states in hourly and weekly wage scales as well as in annual per capita income. This is borne out by every report of the Bureau of Labor Statistics of the U.S. Department of Labor. . . .

I remind my colleagues that the Democratic Party has historically defended the working men and women of this nation. I ask senators: Should we withdraw from this stand now?

The answer, of course, is "No". . . .

The Four Enemies of Freedom

With the opening of the 87th Congress in January 1961, Hubert Humphrey embarked on his third term as a senator of the United States—and the United States embarked on the era of Hubert Humphrey.

For the New Frontier of which John F. Kennedy spoke was the New Frontier for which Hubert Humphrey had long striven; and the Great Society which followed was the Great Society for which Hubert Humphrey—and Lyndon Johnson—had fought so hard.

On May 5, 1963, Robert C. Albright, writing in the Washington Post, *summed this up by calling Humphrey the "idea factory for Kennedy administration bills. The Peace Corps, the Arms Control and Disarmament Agency and the . . . youth opportunities and wilderness bills had their inception in Humphrey proposals."*

It was Hubert Humphrey who for so long had urged that the United States should "never negotiate out of fear; but let us never fear to negotiate."

It was Hubert Humphrey who for so long had called upon the United States "to bear the burden of a long, twilight struggle . . . against the common enemies of man: tyranny, poverty, disease and war itself."

It was Hubert Humphrey who for so long had called upon the nations of the world to explore with the United States "what together we can do" for all of mankind.

The words were the words of John F. Kennedy, but the thoughts were the thoughts of Hubert H. Humphrey.

Nowhere is this better exemplified than in a speech Humphrey delivered on June 11, 1961, at Brandeis University, Boston, Massachusetts.

. . . The goal of leaders in the social welfare movement has been to assure every American the basic security, dignity and opportunity that is his birthright. We have moved far away from that long, sad epoch of indifference to basic human needs, of exploitation of women and children, of the abrogation to a privileged few of the fruits of industry.

In housing, in health, in education—in all the branches of social welfare—we move ever closer to the goal of a nation with a just, compassionate and practical program for the welfare of every citizen.

In one very real sense, the United States is and has always been a welfare society, and we should be proud of it. Our Constitution specifies but two mandates to our government —to provide for the common defense and to promote the general welfare.

And for Americans, welfare must signify not simply aid to the suffering, the poor and the needy.

It means all of this and more. It means adjustment of social inequities. It means the elimination of bigotry, intolerance and discrimination. It means, not only charity, but also the privilege for every citizen for education and health. It means not merely economic security, but social and economic opportunity.

The welfare state is not a restrictive state. It is a humanitarian state.

We must demonstrate that a democracy can mobilize its energies for the welfare of its citizens. This is the message we should take to the world. This is the true voice of America, the spirit of our continuing revolution.

The terse statistics of human need—83 percent of the world's people underfed; 62 percent illiterate; 70 percent sick or poorly housed—these ugly facts must challenge us to be the democratic revolutionaries and reformers of the twentieth century.

Old tyrannies continue to suppress and to exploit people. And new tyrannies—masquerading as liberation—plunge people from one misery to another. The old and the new tyrants think not of human welfare but of their own arrogant power. To tyrants, old and new, man is flesh, not spirit and soul.

In vast regions of the world we see the results of the failure to promote human welfare and protect human rights. It is this failure that is the ally of dictatorship and the enemy of freedom.

If freedom is to survive, then we must concentrate our resources and our energies in the direction of reform, social progress, the general welfare of the people at home and abroad. . . .

The real, the basic, the vital challenge in the world today is not the dogmatic militancy of a Mao, nor the design and plan of a Khrushchev.

The real challenge is to defeat the ancient adversaries of mankind, the loyal allies of tyranny, the four enemies of freedom—poverty, hunger, disease and ignorance.

These are the conditions which have darkened the lives of untold millions, and still grip vast regions of the earth. On this broad base of misery and despair, tyranny has strutted, marched, conquered and destroyed.

But this need not be. It must not be.

The great zone of misery which circles the earth—including Latin America, Africa, the Middle East and Asia—is being transformed by the knowledge that there can be a better life.

Decision is replacing despair. Passion for change is replacing passive acceptance of the status quo. Action is replacing submissiveness to the old conditions and the old injustices.

It is time for Americans to abandon the travelog approach to Latin America, Asia and Africa. We must think of Africa as a land of vital people demanding freedom and not as the setting for Hollywood jungle dramas. We must realize that the quaint charm of the Orient is a fragile veil covering squalor and starvation.

We should know that Latin America is no longer the land of *manana* characterized by sleepy villages, but rather a region of ferment in which a vibrant people expect and demand change and improvement today.

The conditions of poverty, hunger, disease and ignorance are not new. The challenge to release mankind from their grip is not new.

But the pressing need for a sense of urgency is new. The restless millions of the world are awake and rising. They are not willing to wait for slow, evolutionary changes which might, perhaps—sometime in the distant future—bring security, dignity and justice to their children or grandchildren.

A revolutionary wave is sweeping across the world's underdeveloped areas.

This is not a revolution for communism; it is a revolution against the intolerable conditions of the past. . . .

We must turn away from the tolerance and support of dictators, and identify ourselves with the new forces of liberation, emancipation and human welfare.

We must be more than mere anticommunists.

We must prove that we are pro people—pro freedom.

If we are content to hide in the storm cellars of anticommunism, we may indeed survive for a time. But we will emerge to find a world that has fallen away from us, left us alone and friendless in a waste of totalitarianism.

A policy based only on anticommunism is a castle built of sand. The cathedrals of freedom are built by positive, creative and affirmative dedication to the welfare of human beings everywhere.

The cornerstone of world freedom will be laid when we have joined those who revolt against the tyranny of poverty, the slavery of disease, the corruption of ignorance. . . .

We must internationalize the concept and practice of social welfare, seeking for others throughout the world the same goals we seek for our own citizens.

We live in an era of potential catastrophe or potential glory. The same technology which produces weapons of destruction and death can—in our time—open the mysteries and wonders of outer space, cleanse the earth of disease, bring forth from the earth the food and fiber to feed the hungry and to clothe the naked.

This is a wonderful time in which to help. This time challenges the best in us. It calls for doing the impossible—performing miracles. Mediocrity must give way to excellence; timidity to daring; fear to courage. . . .

Another Minnesotan

Not everything that goes on in the Senate is of a serious nature. Sometimes, our national legislators find lighter subject matter to debate.

In the following colloquy (one never has a discussion on the Senate floor; it is always a colloquy), the great issue at hand is whether Roger Maris—who on September 15, 1961, was on his way to overtaking Babe Ruth's record of sixty home runs in one season—was to be considered a North Dakotan or a Minnesotan.

Republican Senator Milton R. Young of North Dakota, with the concurrence of his Democratic junior senator, Quentin N. Burdick, claimed Maris as a proud product of North Dakota.

For some days, Humphrey waited patiently for Senator Young to apologize for having so grievously misled the Senate. Finally, he could contain himself no longer. Having forewarned Senator Young (who could not be present), he rose to set the record straight.

Mr. Humphrey. Mr. President, will the senator yield?

Mr. Keating. I am happy to yield.

Mr. Humphrey. I am very happy to have the senator from New Hampshire give us the historical dissertation on the life of Samuel Wilson. I appreciate the objectivity with which they approach this historical subject, because not long ago in the Senate I was much disturbed by an inaccuracy with respect to a certain matter of a more current nature.

I say this in all good nature, because I have already spoken to the colleague to whom I am about to refer in regard to the question.

The senior senator from North Dakota some time ago, when Roger Maris had "belted" a couple of balls out of the ballpark, either in New York at the Yankee Stadium or at some other place, stood upon the floor of the Senate to indicate that Roger Maris was the product of North Dakota.

I observe that my good friend, the able and distinguished and competent junior senator from North Dakota, under the present circumstances, is the presiding officer and cannot reply. For this I am deeply grateful. . . .

I wish to make the record clear, since we are establishing from where these illustrious characters of American life come, that Roger Maris is a product of Minnesota.

[At this point Mr. Holland took the chair as presiding officer.]

Mr. Humphrey. Oh, oh. [Laughter.] In case Mr. Maris does not break the home run record, we shall be willing to share some of that sad moment with North Dakota. In case he should hit sixty-one home runs, we wish to have the record manifestly clear that his family still lives in Hibbing, Minnesota.

He is really a Minnesotan. He got his start in Minnesota. He may have wandered a bit in North Dakota, but his great prowess as an athlete and as a great player on the invincible New York Yankees surely must be attributed to his days in the great North Star state of Minnesota.

Mr. Burdick. Mr. President, will the senator yield?

Mr. Humphrey. I gathered someone might have a word of response.

Mr. Burdick. Mr. President, will the senator yield?

Mr. Humphrey. I do not have control of the floor.

The presiding officer (Mr. Holland in the chair). Does the senator from New York yield?

Mr. Keating. I am happy to yield to my friend from North Dakota.

Mr. Burdick. I say to my good friend from the state of Minnesota that we acknowledge that Roger was born in the state of Minnesota.

Mr. Humphrey. I thank the senator.

Mr. Burdick. In his formative years, Roger lived in Grand Forks and in Fargo. He attended the public and parochial schools in Fargo. He engaged in the American Legion baseball program with my son. So in the years which really count, he was in North Dakota.

Mr. Humphrey. Mr. President, will the senator yield?

Mr. Keating. I am happy to yield.

Mr. Humphrey. Of course, the senator from North Dakota is accurate in terms of the years Mr. Maris spent in North Dakota, but for my friends who are not acquainted so intimately with the North Dakota-Minnesota geography, I wish to say that Grand Forks, North Dakota, has a real claim to greatness because it is next to East Grand Forks, Minnesota. [Laughter.] That is just across the river.

Fargo, North Dakota, has its claim to greatness because it is just across the river from Moorhead, Minnesota. [Laughter.]

The real fact of the matter is that Roger Maris never could have been in Grand Forks or Fargo if he had not been born in Hibbing.

The most important years of his life are the ones right now. I understand the pay is good and that as a ballplayer he is superb. . . .

Mr. Keating. Before we forget, let us say a word for Mickey Mantle. [Laughter]

Mr. Humphrey. Mr. President, will the senator yield?

Mr. Keating. I should like to get some action on the resolution for "Uncle Sam." Then we can take up baseball.

Mr. Butler. Mr. President, will the senator yield?

Mr. Keating. I yield to the senator.

Mr. Butler. I have listened to the discussion with a great deal of interest. It seems to me that Minnesota once had Roger Maris, and North Dakota once had Roger Maris, but now New York very firmly has him.

Mr. Keating. The senator is correct. We appreciate having him, too. We are glad to have him.

Mr. Humphrey. We are glad to do any little thing we can for the senator. [Laughter.]

Mr. Keating. It is not the first thing that my distinguished friend has done for New York. I want him to know that we are always friendly.

Mr. Humphrey. We presented New York with Skowron from Minnesota, Blanchard from North High, Minnesota, and Elston Howard, who once lived in Duluth, Minnesota. I do not know how the New York Yankees would win without players from the state of Minnesota.

    Mr. Keating. Or without the Twin Cities team. We are glad to have them in the league.

    Mr. Case [*of South Dakota*]. Mr. President, will the senator yield?

    Mr. Keating. I yield.

    Mr. Case. The question that enters my mind is, what would Minnesota do for someone to speak so eloquently of her position and her athletes today if the senator from Minnesota had not been born in South Dakota? [Laughter.]

    Mr. Humphrey. I thank my colleague.

The Unfinished Task

The defiance that had begun in Little Rock, that had exploded in Virginia and that would culminate in Alabama and Georgia was very much on Hubert Humphrey's mind on September 24, 1962. For two days earlier, on Saturday, September 22, the United States celebrated the one-hundredth anniversary of "a milestone along the road of freedom that all mankind will hopefully travel"—the Emancipation Proclamation.

. . . On the one-hundredth anniversary of the Emancipation Proclamation, I believe we must resolve to complete the task begun by Abraham Lincoln.

    But I also believe this should be a day on which to pledge ourselves to a new revolutionary concept of emancipation— emancipation from the constant burdens of mankind, the burdens of poverty, hunger and disease.

Why should we consider emancipation in these revolutionary terms?

The answer I see is a simple one: Only by conceiving of emancipation as the dual challenge of freeing mankind from personal servitude, prejudice and injustice, and simultaneously attacking the physical burdens that encroach upon man's well-being, will this nation fully exercise the responsibility for human progress that is its destiny.

The century that has elapsed since the signing of the original Emancipation Proclamation is only a moment in the long history of mankind. But this represents a long time in the life of the United States—a period of time spanning well over half our life as an independent nation.

In this period of time there have occurred changes unseen in 1862, changes that eluded the imagination of the most visionary prophet of the mid-nineteenth century.

While we take almost for granted the continuity of our government and our fundamental democratic institutions, it is difficult to realize how rare this continuity is in a turbulent and rapidly changing world.

By 1862 the European nations had firmly established their domination over most of Asia. Today that domination has all but vanished.

In 1862 the European dissection of Africa had hardly begun. Now most of Africa is again free of colonial domination.

In 1862 communism was little more than a theory propounded by a handful of frustrated intellectuals. Today we witness veritable towers of tyranny built on this theory. And, to proceed one step further, we have also seen the first cracks appearing and spreading through . . . [that] once monolithic structure of international communism.

Against the background of these dramatic changes in the world about us, we must admit that the emancipation of our Negro citizens in terms of full participation in our national life has been painfully slow.

In 1862 certainly no reasonable man expected that the lot

of the slaves would be transformed overnight upon the stroke of Abraham Lincoln's pen.

In that first dawn of freedom the Negro Americans lacked almost everything: land and the tools to till it, skills, education and means of support. In fact, they lacked everything but liberty itself and the courage to face the future.

Yet it was reasonable to hope—and reasonable men, both white and Negro, did hope—that the newly freed men would overcome these handicaps within a generation or so. Indeed, just such an assimilation was being achieved by many destitute immigrants who had journeyed to our shores.

The key to achieve such full participation in the life of the nation seemed to lie in education. The father of a Negro family might be an unskilled laborer, the mother might work as a domestic servant; yet these people would have the capacity to raise fine children.

And if these people were fortunate, their children might graduate from high school, and some even attend college. Do we truly realize how many times the father's sledgehammer rose and fell, or how many times the mother scrubbed on her knees, that their children might stand erect?

But where were these educated Negroes to go? So many doors were simply closed to them because of the color of their skin.

They stood and knocked at these doors for many years in vain. Today the knocking grows louder. Today it is much more difficult to ignore. And today some of the doors are finally opening; but we know how much more remains to be done.

Five generations have passed since the Emancipation Proclamation, and there is still a long distance to travel down the road to human freedom and equality. . . .

Yes, there has been heartening progress in recent years, but—in all frankness—it seems to me the work of making this progress has been unequally shared.

The Supreme Court has spoken forthrightly on the matter of equal opportunities for our Negro citizens; but I cannot say that the other branches of government have always matched that forthrightness.

Many white Americans have joined their Negro fellow citizens in this struggle—and notably with many courageous young Negro students. But many other Americans have remained on the sidelines as if the struggle and its outcome did not concern them.

The progress of human rights can also be measured by the march of freedom beyond our shores.

In the same years, hundreds of millions of Asians and Africans have achieved national freedom and self-respect. Some have accepted the responsibilities that accompany this freedom more readily than others, but the total picture is most encouraging.

Already many of the new African and Asian nations have made impressive contributions toward world peace and international understanding. I look for increasing contributions in the future.

I cannot think of a more fitting memorial to the efforts of these pioneers of human rights found throughout the world than that historians should come to see this era as the "century of human freedom."

But if one can attempt to peer into the history books of tomorrow, it is within our grasp that this civilization will also be described as the "century of abundance." As I noted earlier, I believe the concept of emancipation serves as a bridge that gives full meaning to both these human potentialities.

Yes, emancipation in the social and political sense—the right to vote, fully protected; equal opportunity for employment without discrimination—these are all important rights.

But emancipation also in the sense of personal emancipation from disease, endless toil, poverty and hunger are vital. Today, for the first time in recorded history, humanity has the power—if we have the will and wit to use our resources of science and technology—to drive these ancient scourges from the earth. . . .

The Role of Congress

Hubert Humphrey was not above lecturing his fellow members of Congress on their proper role. Most often, he did his lecturing on the Senate floor. Sometimes, however, he would use other forums to deliver his message.

Thus, on September 6, 1963, Humphrey addressed the American Political Science Association, meeting in New York City, on "The Role of Congress in the American Political System."

. . . Democratic government has never been easy. This is why so few nations have been successful at it for any sustained period of time. It is, so to speak, "a glorious misery."

I believe it was Winston Churchill who said, "Democracy is the worst possible form of government except all others." It is the system which is always there with too little, too late. The same is said of Congress. And yet, at least in this nation, the "glorious misery" is still with us. So is Congress. . . .

In a democracy such as ours the elected representative, "the politician," has the heavy responsibility of making the decisions which determine how this country will function from day to day and from year to year.

To the ancient Greeks, *politics* meant "the science and art of government." A politician was, therefore, a scientist, an artist, in government, in the affairs of the state, in meeting human needs, in providing order and continuity for his people.

The state, of course, is not self-operating. No matter how advanced our computers become, human beings are and will be required to practice the art of government.

Heaven knows some of the practitioners leave something to be desired; but most of them I know spend their time honestly and faithfully trying to make right decisions in a world whose complexity seems more profound every morning.

This is a difficult and demanding task. The character of the persons selected to make these decisions reflect, in large measure, the character of the people they represent.

Is *politician* such a nasty word in our vocabulary? Thomas Jefferson was a politician. So was Andrew Jackson, Abraham Lincoln, Grover Cleveland, Teddy Roosevelt, Woodrow Wilson, Calvin Coolidge, Herbert Hoover, Franklin Roosevelt, Harry Truman, Dwight Eisenhower and John Kennedy.

Must we always reserve the appellation of *statesman* for the politicians of whom we approve, never to admit the simple truth that most statesmen are also politicians. . . ?

As the crises of our time accelerate the tendency toward decision making solely by the executive branch of the government, it becomes increasingly important, in my opinion, for Congress to participate more actively in these decisions. The Congress is the public forum. It is the voice of the people.

Like it or not, there are 190 million persons represented on Capitol Hill. Who is so brash and foolish to claim the total omnipotence of one group or section of these people over another?

For our democratic system to remain healthy and vital in the demanding years ahead, we must reach decisions that reflect the entire nation. Congress must provide itself with the institutional tools to become more of a participant and less of an observer in the formulation of long-term foreign and domestic policy.

I have proposed the creation of joint committees in the area of national security policy and international trade which would permit precisely such congressional participation. There are other areas, such as appropriations, which should be reexamined for possible procedural reform.

In the final analysis, the fundamental criterion by which to judge the operations of Congress is, in my opinion, whether or not Congress is seeking to resolve the truly critical issues of the day. . . .

What are these critical issues? I would list three.

First, do we possess the courage and determination to preserve our nation and the rest of mankind from nuclear annihilation while simultaneously defending freedom and democracy?

Second, are we sufficiently committed to the ideals of American democracy that we will banish racial prejudice and discrimination from these shores forever?

Third, do we possess the wisdom and common sense to capitalize fully on our free enterprise system, to achieve its full measure of economic growth and to eliminate unemployment?

These are the critical issues before the United States. And it is no accident that the top priority items on the agenda of the 1st session of the 88th Congress are the test ban treaty, the civil rights bills and the tax cut. Congress must learn and act on a new "three Rs"—ratification, racial equality and revenues. . . .

Let the word go out—test ban treaty, civil rights and tax cuts; these will guarantee the 88th Congress a proud place in the history of America.

While decisions of this magnitude cannot be taken easily, quickly or superficially, they will be done in 1963. They will testify that Congress still is a principal contributor to the "glorious misery" of our democratic system. . . .

The President Is Dead

Dallas. November 22, 1963. Black Friday.

Ever since John F. Kennedy's election, Hubert Humphrey had been a loyal, zealous proponent of the New Frontier. The bitterness he briefly felt in the 1960 primaries had been swept away by his realization that the "rich man with a richer father" had been transformed in the hills of West Virginia.

The stark reality of Appalachia had been indelibly inprinted on his conscience. The New Frontier of which he spoke had truly become the New Frontier to which he wanted to lead the nation.

And now, he was dead.

On December 11, 1963, Humphrey delivered this tribute to the fallen president.

Today, we cannot judge John Fitzgerald Kennedy. The fact of this assassination still stuns our minds; the loss of this man still sorrows our hearts.

If we seek to judge his life and work now, we must fail. Our thoughts will be like rough pebbles, unpolished by the tides of time and wisdom. Our words will be like hollow, gaudy ornaments attached to a man's soul.

Let us leave judgment to history, and to God.

If we remember his own words which expressed his own highest cause, we perhaps do best. This does not risk trying to gild what is already gold. For to me, at least, John Kennedy wrote his own epitaph: a man dedicated to "the strategy for peace."

He sounded this keynote in his first words after taking the oath of office as president of the United States. He reminded his countrymen and the world that one talon of the American eagle held the arrows of war, but the other clutched the olive branches of peace.

"We shall not negotiate from fear, but we shall not fear to negotiate." These words were a fresh and memorable assertion to the world that the power of the United States was not to be feared. Peace was its purpose.

John Kennedy met supreme crisis at the very brink of disaster when nuclear aggression threatened this hemisphere. The courage of peace was tested and not found wanting. Could courage and peace be combined? Could peace save its life by risking to lose it? Men must hope so, but can they believe it?

They can; and they did when they witnessed John Kennedy's devotion to peace matched by determined action.

That breathless moment a little over a year ago (the Cuban missile crisis) could have brought the exhaustion of hope, or the fears of hostility. It did neither. . . .

The theme of peace had become his hallmark. We came to expect it. His eloquence of phrase served to keep the passionate sincerity of purpose and goal from being redundant. If any scripture is ever sifted out of the torrents of the words of these years, surely his words in this high cause will survive.

He understood well the meaning of the mordant words of the Prince of Peace: "Be ye wise as serpents in order to be as harmless as doves." When John Kennedy spoke in such a vein, however, it was of a peace strong, not strident. He communicated a sense of power in the service of gentility.

In his address to the nation on the nuclear test ban treaty, he said:

"Let us, if we can, step back from the shadows of war and seek out the way of peace. And if that journey is a thousand miles or even more, let history record that we, in this land, at this time, took the first step."

Each of us lost a bit of ourselves at the death of the man who spoke these words, but our steps did not falter. . . .

Nineteen days ago, the worst of America struck down the best of America. For a few moments of time, violence shattered peace—fear cracked confidence—hate stood above reason.

But the worst of America did not prevail after those ugly moments. The tragedy of that day in November will not endure.

Because of the life of John Fitzgerald Kennedy, we are today a nation more fully committed to peace. Because of the death of John Fitzgerald Kennedy, we are a people more deeply determined to turn from hate and to embrace understanding and reason.

One simple line, from the book of Isaiah in the Bible, best expresses the message and mission of John Fitzgerald Kennedy:

"Come now, and let us reason together."

Our fulfillment of that plea will be John Fitzgerald Kennedy's triumph.

One simple paragraph, from his book *Profiles in Courage*, best describes the goodness and nobility of John Fitzgerald Kennedy:

"The courage of life is often a less dramatic spectacle than the courage of a final moment; but it is no less than a magnificent mixture of triumph and tragedy. A man does what he must—in spite of personal consequences, in spite of obstacles and dangers and pressures—and that is the basis of all human morality."

Yes . . . John Fitzgerald Kennedy is gone.

He gave us strength, and the strength remains with us.

But we are a stronger nation, and a better people today because of him. . . .

His "Greatest Achievement"

To Hubert Humphrey, passage of the mammoth Civil Rights Act of 1964 was his "greatest achievement." It had been the culmination of his life's work.

It was not that it meant the end of civil rights as an issue of concern, that there was nothing left to be done; on the contrary, much was left undone. But the Civil Rights Act of 1964 was what made all that had to be done possible.

If Lyndon Johnson had been alive on January 14, 1978, he undoubtedly would have credited Hubert Humphrey (as he so often did while president) with passage of that historic act. Characteristically, Humphrey ascribed most of the credit to Johnson.

The truth lies in between. For both men passed the great testament to democracy; it is to both men that history must give equal credit.

Johnson decided in early 1964 that the time was right to push a comprehensive, tooth-filled civil rights bill through Congress. The House, of course, would be no problem. The Senate, however, would be. Rule XXII would permit Southern senators to talk forever, if necessary, in an effort to kill the bill. It would require sixty-seven senators to impose cloture—i.e., to limit debate to a specified period of time. But Johnson was determined to use the full powers of the presidency to pass that bill, despite the inevitable filibuster.

Humphrey, as assistant Senate Majority Leader and as the man who had made civil rights a crusade, was chosen to guide the bill through the Senate. The strategy the two men, together with Majority Leader Mike Mansfield, decided upon was simple: Let the filibuster go on for as long as the Southerners wanted; let every issue involved be discussed to the point of exhaustion, then begin trying to vote cloture. No matter how long it would take, keep at it. No matter how many times cloture is voted down, keep at it; sooner or later, the cloture votes will be there.

After several days of preliminary efforts by the Southerners to delay bringing the bill to the floor, Humphrey rose on March 30 to open the historic debate.

. . . The Senate has wisely voted that H.R. 7152 should be its pending business. In doing so we have recognized the historic mission and obligation that confronts us.

Our Founding Fathers were faced with another historic task when they assembled in Philadelphia more than 175 years ago to save the weak and divided Confederation of States that had emerged from our War of Independence.

This sense of history was captured by our founders in the moving words of the preamble to our Constitution. I believe these words are appropriate today; and I should like to repeat them:

"We, the people of the United States, in order to form a more perfect Union, establish justice, insure domestic tranquility, provide for the common defense, promote the general welfare, and secure the blessings of liberty to ourselves and our posterity, do ordain and establish this Constitution for the United States of America."

I cannot help but marvel at the impact, the directness, and the sense of destiny captured in these fifty-two words. I cannot help but marvel at their relevance to the responsibility which now confronts the Senate of the United States. The preamble to the Constitution might very well have been written as a preamble to the Civil Rights Act of 1964.

"We, the people of the United States," not white people, colored people, short people, or tall people, but simply, "We the people. In order to form a more perfect Union. . . ."

We know that until racial justice and freedom is a reality in this land, our union will remain profoundly imperfect. That is why we are debating this bill. That is why the bill must become law. . . .

Surely these are the objectives that we seek in this legislation. Justice, domestic tranquility, the general welfare, and the blessings of liberty—these are what our founders sought 177 years ago—these are the objectives we seek today. . . .

I cannot overemphasize the historic importance of the debate we are beginning. We are participants in one of the most crucial eras in the long and proud history of the United States and, yes, in mankind's struggle for justice and freedom which has gone forward since the dawn of history.

If freedom becomes a full reality in America, we can dare to believe that it will become a reality everywhere. If freedom fails here—in America, the land of the free—what hope can we have for it surviving elsewhere?

That is why we must debate this legislation with courage, determination, frankness, honesty and—above all—with the sense of the obligation and destiny that has come to us at this time and in this place.

It is in this spirit, and expressing the same determination that captured the faith and imagination of our Founding Fathers, that I am privileged to present, at least in part, the affirmative case for the Civil Rights Act of 1964. . . .

The United States is founded on the principle of government by the people. Our War of Independence was fought on the slogan of "no taxation without representation." The basic documents of American history—the Declaration of Independence, the Constitution and the Bill of Rights—are all dedicated to the principle of popular sovereignty through majority rule.

The Fifteenth Amendment to the Constitution . . . specifically states:

"The right of citizens of the United States to vote shall not be denied or abridged by the United States or by any State on account of race, color, or previous condition of servitude."

Yet this basic right to vote is denied to millions of Americans on account of race. Millions of Negro citizens are taxed without representation, because they are not allowed to vote. Less than 7 percent of the eligible Negroes in the state of Mississippi are registered, compared to 70 percent of the white adult population. There are dozens of counties in Mississippi where less than 3 percent of the Negroes of voting age are permitted to register.

The same disgraceful pattern is found in all too many other states. . . .

It is difficult for most of us to fully comprehend the monstrous humiliations and inconveniences that racial discrimination imposes on our Negro fellow citizens. If a white man is thirsty on a hot day, he goes to the nearest soda fountain. If he is hungry, he goes to the nearest restaurant. If he needs a restroom, he can go to the nearest gas station. If it is night and he is tired, he takes his pick of the available motels and hotels.

But for a Negro the picture is different. Trying to get a glass of iced tea at a lunch counter may result in insult and abuse, unless he is willing to go out of his way, perhaps to walk across town. He can never count on using a restroom, on getting a decent place to stay, on buying a good meal.

These are trivial matters in the life of a white person, but for some 20 million American Negroes, they are important considerations that must be planned for in detail. They must draw up travel plans much as a general advancing across hostile territory would establish his logistical support.

If a white family is planning an automobile trip of some distance, it is a commonplace thing to write to a touring service for a guide book that will list the places where a family with a dog can stay the night. . . .

But now consider the problems facing a Negro family looking forward to a vacation. How can they plan their trip so as to be sure of finding a place to stay at night? If they write away, they too can obtain a guide book that lists places of public accommodation where a Negro can go with confidence. . . .

It is heartbreaking to compare these two guide books, the one for families with dogs and the other for Negroes. In Augusta, Georgia, for example, there are five hotels and motels that will take dogs, and only one where a Negro can go with confidence. In Columbus, Georgia, there are six places for dogs, and none for Negroes. In Charleston, South Carolina, there are ten places where a dog can stay, and none for a Negro. . . .

[At this point, Senator Humphrey detailed the eleven titles of the historic legislation. He spoke carefully and methodically, title by title, section by section, subsection by subsection.]

[This] is a fair, moderate and comprehensive bill. It deals with all the major areas of life in which Negroes and other minorities have been discriminated against: voting, education, access to public accommodations and facilities, equal protection of the law and employment. . . .

[All] these areas are interrelated; each is bound with the others. A man who would be free must have the opportunity to develop his mind and talents through education, to earn a living with those talents and to apply his education to public life through participation in the political process. Without opportunities for education, the Negro cannot get a job.

I would not want my remarks in support of this bill to be interpreted as indicating there was nothing left to be done in the fields of education, or health, or retraining or many other areas of life. The bill merely provides a legal framework through which men of good will can work out some difficult, long-term problems. We need to expand educational opportunities. We need to expand housing in America. We need to expand health services. We need to expand employment opportunities. We need a growing and expanding economy. We need to eliminate areas of discrimination and prejudice in order to have the full participation of the American people in their society and in their community life.

All this needs to be done. When I hear the opponents of the legislation remind us again and again that what is needed is more education, I agree. But more education for a person who has been denied equal rights and full participation in community life is no answer to that man's problems. What is needed is an opportunity to participate fully in all aspects of American life, including opportunities for education, health, job opportunity and political participation.

Without a job, one cannot afford public convenience and accommodations. Income from employment may be necessary to further a man's education, or that of his children. If his children have no hope of getting a good job, what will motivate them to take advantage of educational opportunities?

In short, the primary ingredients for a full and free life are inseparable from each other. Education cannot wait upon employment or political freedom. Employment opportunity cannot be postponed until the vote is won. The only way to break the vicious circle of minority oppression is to break it at every point where injustice, inequality and denial of opportunity exist. It is for this reason that we propose enactment of comprehensive legislation that will touch on every major obstacle to civil rights.

This bill is long overdue. Moderate as it is, it insures a great departure from the misery and bitterness that is the lot of so many Americans. This misery has found remarkably quiet methods of expression up to the present. . . .

I marvel at the patience and self-control of Negroes who have been excluded from the American dream for so long. But the passive stage is ending in the history of the American Negro. Within the past few years, a new spirit has arisen in those people who have been so long denied. How will we respond to this challenge? The snarling police dogs of Birmingham are one answer. The force of equality and justice is another. That second choice is embodied in the bill that we are starting to consider.

The same Negroes who win our Olympic games, the

same Negroes who are the stars on the baseball fields, the same Negroes who in many areas of our country have been permitted to practice in hospitals without discrimination, are rising as one man and asking that their brethren be given the same opportunity.

Freedom requires full freedom. There cannot be half freedom. There cannot be full freedom for whites and little freedom for Negroes.

I say with regret that all over America prejudice exists. It is not confined to one section of the country. It is more visible in some sections of the country than it is in others; but it exists everywhere.

I do not proclaim that the proposed statute will eliminate all the evils which plague us in the area of racial prejudice. I merely say that it sets a standard around which decent men can rally. It lays down the legal framework within which men of good will, of reason, and judgment, can work together. It provides the means for a constructive social policy that is long overdue. . . .

We would be foolish to deny ourselves the opportunity of enlisting in the common cause of freedom the millions of people who cry out to be a part of the great American dream. They are not asking to be left out. They are not asking to be put aside. They wish to be part of our national life. That is what this fight is all about.

It is my earnest hope that senators will recognize that the bill represents an investment of knowledge, energy and dedication by the executive branch and the Congress, by Democrats and Republicans alike. Its moderation and careful language represent almost a year of patient deliberation, study and discussion. . . .

It is my earnest hope that senators will respect and appreciate this precious investment, that they will realize what a great achievement it is to have brought this bill to its present place on the legislative schedule, and that they will honor the importance of the issue and the good faith of the bill's architects by passing H.R. 7152 as it now stands.

The goals of this bill are simple ones: To extend to Negro

citizens the same rights and the same opportunities that white Americans take for granted. These goals are so obviously desirable that the opponents of this bill have not dared to dispute them. No one has claimed that Negroes should not be allowed to vote. No one has said that they should be denied equal protection of the laws. No one has said that Negroes are inherently unacceptable in places of public accommodation. No one has said that they should be refused equal opportunity in employment.

This bill cannot be attacked on its merits. Instead, bogeymen and hobgoblins have been raised to frighten well-meaning Americans.

A bill endorsed by hundreds of prominent attorneys and professors of law is called by the opponents unconstitutional.

A bill endorsed by every major religious denomination in America is called communist inspired.

A bill passed by an overwhelming majority of 290 members of the House of Representatives to 130 for the opposition —Democrats and Republicans alike—is called socialistic.

Good Americans . . . formulated the bill and carried it through in the other body. I know that 290 members of the other body are not socialists. I know they are not communists. I reject that kind of smokescreen attack upon a sensible piece of legislation. . . .

It is called a force bill, when in fact it places first reliance on conciliation and voluntary action, and authorizes legal action only as a last resort.

It is called an attack on state government, when in fact the bill specifically directs that state and local officials and agencies will be used whenever feasible, and appeals to the states to perform states' rights rather than states' wrongs.

It is claimed that the bill would produce a gigantic federal bureaucracy, when in fact it will result in creating about 400 permanent new federal jobs.

It is claimed that it would impair a property owner's ability to sell or rent his home, when in fact there is nothing in the bill pertaining to housing.

It is claimed that the bill would require racial quotas for

all hiring, when in fact it provides that race shall not be a basis for making personnel decisions.

As I have said, the bill has a simple purpose. That purpose is to give fellow citizens—Negroes—the same rights and opportunities that white people take for granted. This is no more than what was preached by the prophets, and by Christ himself. It is no more than what our Constitution guarantees.

One hundred and ninety years have passed since the Declaration of Independence, and one hundred years since the Emancipation Proclamation. Surely the goals of this bill are not too much to ask of the Senate of the United States.

Enough Talk

On Monday, June 2, the Senate leadership announced that it would file a cloture petition on Saturday. For two days, the Southerners considered what to do.

Then, on June 4, they announced that they were prepared to vote on some amendments. But Humphrey and the other leaders would have none of it. He explained why to his fellow senators on that day.

. . . On March 30, 1964, the Senate began consideration of H.R. 7152 itself. In my opening remarks on this legislation, I issued the following challenge:

"We intend to seek a decision by the Senate exercising its will to vote yea or nay on every provision of the bill.

"I sincerely hope that senators opposed to this legislation will be equally willing to permit the Senate to work its will after an opportunity for a searching examination and analysis of every provision.

"We issue this friendly challenge: We will join with you in debating this bill; will you join with us in voting on H.R. 7152 after reasonable debate has been concluded? Will you permit the Senate and, in a sense, the nation, to come to grips with these issues and decide them, one way or the other?

"This is our respectful challenge. I devoutly hope it will be accepted."

The proponents acknowledged that every senator had the legitimate right—in fact, the obligation—to debate H.R. 7152 at length. We recognize the importance of this bill and the Senate's responsibility to consider it carefully and thoughtfully.

The proponents then proceeded to occupy the floor for approximately ten days and endeavored to present the so-called affirmative case for this legislation. We were prepared to discuss each and every title of this bill—and we did.

The Senate normally devotes no more than a week to floor debate on important measures. On the tax bill—the most far-reaching revenue measure ever to come before the Senate in a decade—we debated it on the Senate floor for seven days. Yet the proponents of the civil rights bill had no desire to rush the Senate's consideration unduly—we took ten days to present our affirmative case.

We then thought it only proper for the opponents of the bill to respond for a reasonable period of time, to raise their legitimate concerns with particular titles, to offer amendments, to debate and to perfect this legislation.

This we have done. Following the period of time devoted to our affirmative presentation, the opponents of the bill proceeded to debate H.R. 7152 in this fashion for ten more days.

I hasten to note that no senator spoke about cloture at this juncture. We had no desire to seek cloture under those conditions—and if we had sought it, we would have failed. . . .

The Senate had the obligation to debate the pros and cons of H.R. 7152 at this point in time. I note, however, that we had already devoted thirty-six days to the question of civil rights, including the days devoted to debating the motion to consider H.R. 7152.

On April 21, 1964, the distinguished senator from Georgia [Herman Talmadge] offered his so-called jury-trial amendment. . . . The bill came before the Senate more than twenty days prior to that, on March 26.

Again, I wish to stress that my friend from Georgia was completely within his rights in offering this amendment. Many senators have expressed concern over the question of jury trials in cases of criminal contempt arising under this bill. The leadership shared this concern and expressed no objection to giving this matter the most detailed and thoughtful consideration. With these developments, the pending business became the amendment by the senator from Georgia to extend the right of jury trials to all cases of criminal contempt arising in federal courts.

We have now been "debating" the jury-trial amendment for a full month and a half.

During the past two days, we have been told repeatedly by those in opposition to the bill that they are "ready for a vote" and that they are, for the time being at any rate, willing "to withhold further speeches on the so-called jury-trial amendments" so that the Senate could have one or more votes. The leadership has been criticized for failing to allow these votes which the opponents now so eagerly desire. . . .

[There] are good reasons for the course the leadership has chosen. The Senate deserves to hear these reasons so that there may be no misunderstanding as to the motives of those who have worked to achieve enactment of this bill.

On Monday of this week the majority leader announced that the leadership intended to file a cloture petition on Saturday next when there will have been seventy-two days debate on this bill, the longest filibuster—the longest debate or the longest filibuster, we can take our choice as to words—

in the history of the country. . . . In that period of time, the proponents will have taken [only] five days. If the senator deducts fifteen from seventy-two, he will come up with a figure of fifty-seven. . . .

I believe the only reason the Southern opponents have chosen to allow a vote or votes on "some amendments" is because the leadership has announced its intention to attempt to invoke cloture. Certain senators got cloture jitters. I think they can sense what might happen. Their strategy, which is certainly legitimate and within their rights, is, of course, designed to once again deflect the Senate's attention from the main issue of facing up to its responsibility on this entire bill, and to focus our attention, once again, on an important, though subsidiary, issue, the jury-trial amendment, which we have been considering now as I have said for well over a month and a half. . . .

[In] my opinion, the offer of the opponents to have "some votes on some amendments" is an empty offer which we have accepted before and which has carried the Senate no nearer to the conclusion of its responsibilities in this serious matter. . . .

When the cloture motion is filed it will include H.R. 7152, the proposed substitute bill, and all other amendments that have been presented and read prior to the vote on the cloture motion. That is, amendments that have been presented after the cloture motion is filed, but before the vote next Tuesday, will be covered by the cloture motion. . . .

Cloture is the last resort. I have been asked a hundred times if I have been asked once whether we have the votes for cloture. No one knows. I think the vote will be very close. I am very hopeful that we have the votes. Senators have the right to protect or conceal their own feelings as to how they will vote until the moment of decision comes. I only appeal to senators on the basis that if we are to dispose of the proposed legislation one way or the other—either vote it up or down, amend it, substantially alter it or leave it as it is, whatever the will of the Senate may be—we must come to a vote.

I wish to make it perfectly clear that the president of the

United States and the leadership of this body have said that if we have to be here until January and go over into next year we shall be considering the proposed legislation. It is that plain and that simple. . . . The will is here to do it. The country ought to know that.

These are not idle threats. These are not merely words. The statement is a commitment that has been made from the highest office of the land by two presidents—the late John Kennedy last year and Lyndon Johnson this year—and by the leadership of two political parties.

So we ought to buckle down to the task of getting the job done. . . .

I know that senators have differences on the bill. Every senator is entitled to those differences and to state his differences, and is entitled to the respect of fellow senators. . . . Every opportunity will be given to state the case, and to have an up-or-down vote on the amendments. . . .

Now, About the Native American

On June 10, 1964, the passage of the Civil Rights Act was assured. Seventy-one senators, four more than required, voted to limit debate. Eight days later, on June 18, the bill was enacted into law.

But for Hubert Humphrey, what should have been a glorious day was instead a day for tears and trepidation, a day for great sadness; for, on the day before, his son Bob was operated on for lymphatic cancer.

The father wanted to be with his son. But the public work prevented the private man from this most personal chore. He sat in his office that June 17 and cried for a while, then walked back on the floor to keep events moving smoothly. (The surgery was a complete success and Bob was cured.)

On July 2, 1964, President Johnson signed the Civil Rights Act of 1964 into law in front of a nationwide television audience.

For both men, it was indeed their "greatest achievement."

Humphrey's desire to see the act become law had to do with his desire to see equality for all people, whatever their race, color, religion or national origin. And that included the Native American.

On May 9, he took time out from the civil rights debate to address the American Indian Capital Conference on Poverty at Washington Cathedral.

Poverty is the everyday life of the American Indian. No other group in American life is so victimized by poverty.

The average income of Indian families on reservations is $1,500 a year; unemployment is seven or eight times the national average; most families live in small huts or hogans with no sanitary facilities; young adults stay in school an average of only eight years; the Indian life span of forty-two years is far short of the national average of sixty-two; Indian babies have only half as much chance as others in this country to reach their first birthdays.

I could give you more figures but these point up the problem sharply enough—the American Indian is in miserable shape and needs all the help we can give him.

To be sure, American Indians do not make up a large percentage of the 40 million persons who live in poverty in this country—but their small numbers do not diminish their importance. The Indians and their reservations must be prime targets in the war on poverty that President Johnson has asked us to undertake.

And we are going to make that move on poverty an all-out war.

There is nothing new about the evils of poverty. Its destructive toll on the human spirit—even more than its social cost in welfare and disease—has torn at our sense of justice. What is new about poverty is that it is not necessary.

We are able to do more about poverty than we ever could before. America's resources are so developed that we have the means and the knowledge to bring people into an adequate sharing of our total social and economic life.

Poverty is distributed among different groups and exists in separate pockets. The American Indian represents only one of various special situations—each will require a specially developed program.

The American Indian presents a special case in two important ways.

First, the federal government is deeply involved because it has the major responsibility for Indian affairs and is the trustee for reservations where the majority of the Indians live; and, second, Indians have special cultural problems which make it more difficult to integrate them into the economic life of a modern society with its rapid technological developments.

The federal government's authority—and its acknowledged responsibilities for Indian affairs—should give antipoverty workers an effective base from which to operate.

We know that sustained poverty breeds cultural alienation. Educators, for example, now frequently refer to children of the poor in cities as culturally deprived. One could say the same about the children—coming from poor homes and going to crowded schools—on our Indian reservations.

The American Indian, because his cultural problems are so difficult, provides a more critical laboratory in which to learn to deal with these problems. Indian reservations can become excellent pilot projects or models of what can be done—and how to do it—in the war on poverty.

Addressing the subject directly, we might ask how poverty on Indian reservations developed and why it has continued for so long.

Reservations are too small to support the number of Indians living on them. Only about 2 percent of the 52 million acres in reservations are suitable for farming and—even under the best agricultural management—this land would not provide a living for more than half of the Indian population.

Federal effort in the past has been too heavily directed to

custodial care, resulting in little development of the land and its people. A special study group pointed this out in 1961. It indicated we may have been well-motivated in the past but were poorly informed.

Indian culture has revolved around a limited agriculture and—except for hunting and fishing—has not been job-oriented. The relationship of the Indian to the land is deep and mystical. It is more than living space. It is his spiritual home and he doesn't think of it in economic terms.

Education has been inadequate on the reservations and federal policy has diverted most of the funds into preparing Indian young people for jobs away from home. Those that left permanently were torn from their people, and as a result the reservations regularly lost potential community leaders.

One word above all others describes the plight of the Indian—that word is *isolation*. Indians are isolated physically and geographically. They are isolated economically and socially. The institutions of health, welfare and education have not reached them effectively.

In recent years more has been done to deal directly with Indian poverty. The Bureau of Indian Affairs has abandoned the custodial idea—Congress has voted more money to raise Indian living standards, provide health and welfare services, and develop educational and economic opportunity—and federal policies have been focused on development of reservation resources and the Indians themselves.

These new policies mean improved housing with provisions for the Indians to build and to own homes. They mean summer work projects for young people and full-time employment for men in road building and forest programs, and on soil conservation and irrigation projects.

Reservations now are included in accelerated public works and area redevelopment programs.

These new policies mean easier credit for tribal enterprises—a change that has stimulated industrial development on or near the reservations and broadened the economic base.

At least twenty-five small industries have been developed in the past three years. Indians—using these new sources of capital—now are running small businesses, motels, canneries and sawmills. Bright economic opportunities will continue to develop if these programs are adequately funded and carried through.

These new policies have put most of the money where it ought to go—into education. The outlays for education make up about half of the expenditures of the Bureau of Indian Affairs. The bureau operates a system of elementary, secondary and vocational schools for 47,500 Indian children.

These schools have a big job in helping Indian children bridge a cultural gap between tribal life and our modern, complex society. They also are faced with the special problem of giving special attention to children considered both culturally deprived and disadvantaged by poverty.

In some other respects these schools face the same problems as school systems elsewhere: the need for more classrooms to keep up with the population, the need to raise the level of instruction, the necessity for better guidance and counseling services, the need for better libraries, and the need for new methods in teaching English as a second language.

Indian children are not the only persons requiring education. The bureau also has an education program for more than 24,000 adults—only a handful of the undereducated and undertrained on our Indian reservations.

In listing what has been done for the Indian to raise his economic status and improve his general welfare, one cannot overlook the U.S. Public Health Service. This agency, in carrying out its responsibilities for Indian health, has included hospital construction in its program.

Tremendous improvement has been made in water sanitation, although there still is a long way to go. Unsafe water has been blamed in many instances for the spread of communicable diseases that have taken such a toll on Indian reservations.

Life expectancy for Indians is far short of the sixty-two years now enjoyed by the rest of the population—but it has been increased since 1940 by eleven years. The tuberculosis rate for Indians is six times higher than for the rest of the population—but it has been cut almost in half since 1954.

It is quite remarkable how the critical economic condition of the American Indian is a mirror of the poverty problem the United States faces. It presents the whole poverty problem in miniature.

The time has come to wage all-out war on poverty in all sections of this nation. We must be certain that 400,000 American Indians no longer have to face serious unemployment, inadequate education, poor housing, disease, and income problems that have made their reservations some of the nation's worst pockets of poverty.

We must continue our best efforts until our American Indians are able to participate fully in all the benefits and opportunities of a society that fulfills their old sense of freedom in new terms.

But Not Senator Goldwater

Throughout the first half of 1964, Hubert Humphrey felt deep down that he would be Lyndon Johnson's choice for vice-president. Johnson, for his part, did little to discourage such feelings on Humphrey's part.

But, at the same time, Johnson did very little to reassure Humphrey. For the president wanted to keep his options open before his own nomination (or, at least, to appear to do so in the event he needed the bargaining power), in order to keep some amount of drama for the convention, which was to be held in Atlantic City, New Jersey, that August.

Humphrey, therefore, took no chances. He spent much of the time between passage of the Civil Rights Act and the opening gavel of the convention on August 24 lining up support from politicians, labor leaders, civil rights groups and even big business.

As the convention drew closer, any number of names were being heard as possible running mates. The more candidates there were in the speculating, the less Johnson did to indicate whom his choice would be.

Several times during July and August, Humphrey was given the signal that he was to be chosen, only to have that signal suddenly flicker out again. It was a nerve-wracking period for the senator.

After the convention opened, the president summoned Humphrey back to Washington for what the Minnesotan believed was to be the "anointing ceremony." Accompanying him, however, was Connecticut Senator Thomas Dodd, another whose name had been mentioned.

When Humphrey arrived at the White House with his colleague, and with the press corps in attendance, it was Dodd who was summoned to see Johnson first. Finally, after Dodd was escorted out, Humphrey was taken to see Johnson.

Together, the two men talked about the vice-presidency. Johnson told Humphrey that the vice-president had to remain in the background, out of the headlines and always loyal to the man in the oval office. He had been loyal to John Kennedy, Johnson said; he had done everything that was asked of him and more; and he had let Kennedy get all the glory without ever trying to steal the president's thunder. Johnson's vice-president would have to do the same.

Humphrey said he understood and was willing to abide by those rules.

Then the president informed Humphrey that bringing Dodd in with him was just a cover, to keep the drama alive. It was indeed Hubert Humphrey who would be his party's vice-presidential nominee.

On the evening of August 26, 1964, Humphrey delivered one of the most stirring speeches of his career. Before he was through, all the people in Atlantic City's Convention Hall were on their feet, cheering him on. In fact, many people throughout the nation who were watching and listening that night probably joined in; but not, one can safely assume, Senator Goldwater.

. . . I proudly and humbly accept your nomination. Will we ever be able to forget this unbelievable, this moving, this beautiful, this wonderful evening?

What a challenge to every person in this land to live up to the goals and the ideals of those who have gone before us, and have charted the course of our action.

I was deeply moved last night. I received a singular tribute from a friend and a great president, a tribute that I shall never forget, and I pray to Almighty God that I shall have the strength and the wisdom to measure up to the confidence and the trust that has been placed in me. And please let me say thank you, my fellow Democrats. . . .

Ralph Waldo Emerson once spoke of "The two parties which divide the state"—the party of hope and the party of memory. . . . They renew their rivalry, he said, from generation to generation.

This contest, between the party of hope and the party of memory, lies at the very heart of this campaign.

During the last few weeks, shrill voices have tried to lay claim to the great spirit of the American past. But they long for a past that never was. In their recklessness and in their radicalism, they distort the American conservative tradition.

Yes, those who have kidnapped the Republican Party have made it this year not a party of memory and sentiment, but one of stridency, of unrestrained passion, of extreme and radical language.

And by contrast, which is clear to all, under the leadership of President Lyndon Johnson, the Democratic Party stands today as the champion of great causes, as the party of purpose and conviction, as the party of national unity, and as the party of hope for all mankind. . . .

What great problems there are to solve: problems to control the awesome power of the nuclear age, to strengthen the grand alliance with Europe.

To continue the task of building a strong and prosperous and united hemisphere under the Alliance for Progress.

To assist our friends in Asia and Africa in preserving their freedom and promoting their progress.

And to defend and extend freedom throughout the world.

Now, my fellow Americans, these urgent problems demand reasoned solutions, not empty slogans. Childlike answers cannot solve man-sized problems.

These problems demand leadership that is prudent, restrained, responsible. They require a president who knows that Rome was not built in a day, but who also knows that the great edifice of Western civilization can be brought down in ruins in one hour.

The American presidency is not a place for a man who is impetuous at one moment, and indecisive the next; nor is it a place for one who is violently for something one day and violently opposed to it on the next; nor is it an office where statements on matters of major policy are so confusing and so contradictory that neither friend nor foe knows where he stands.

And my fellow Americans, it is of the highest importance that both friend and foe know that the American president means what he says and says what he means.

The temporary spokesman of the Republican Party— yes, the temporary Republican spokesman—is not only out of tune with the great majority of his countrymen; he is even out of step with his own party.

In the last three and a half years, most Democrats and Republicans have agreed on the great decisions our nation has made. But not the Republican spokesman, not Senator Goldwater. He has been facing backward against the mainstream of American history. Most Democrats and most Republicans in the U.S. Senate, for example, voted for the nuclear test ban treaty. But not the temporary Republican spokesman.

Most Democrats and Republicans in the Senate voted for an $11.5-billion tax cut for the American citizens and American business. But not Senator Goldwater.

Most Democrats and Republicans in the Senate, in fact

four-fifths of the members of his own party, voted for the Civil Rights Act. But not Senator Goldwater.

Most Democrats and Republicans in the Senate voted for the establishment of the U.S. Arms Control and Disarmament Agency, that seeks to slow down the nuclear arms race among the nations. But not the temporary Republican spokesman.

Most Democrats and Republicans in the Senate voted last year for an expanded medical education program. But not Senator Goldwater.

Most Democrats and most Republicans in the Senate voted for education legislation. But not Senator Goldwater.

And my fellow Americans, most Democrats and most Republicans in the Senate voted to help the United Nations in its peace-keeping functions when it was in financial difficulty. But not Senator Goldwater.

Yes, my fellow Americans, it is a fact that the temporary Republican spokesman is not in the mainstream of his party. In fact, he has not even touched the shore.

I believe in the two-party system, but there must be two responsible parties, and there must be men who are equipped to lead a great nation as the standard-bearers of the two parties. It is imperative that the leadership of the great parties move within the mainstream of American thought and philosophy.

I pledge to this convention, I pledge to our great president, to all the American people, my complete devotion to this task: To prove once again that the Democratic Party deserves America's affections, and that we are indeed the party of hope for the American people. . . .

While others may appeal to passions and prejudices, and appeal to fear and bitterness, we of the Democratic Party call upon all Americans to join us in making our country a land of opportunity for our young, a home of security and dignity for our elderly, and a place of compassion and care for our afflicted. . . .

Let us, fellow Democrats and fellow Americans, go

forward. Let us take those giant steps forward to which the president has called us, to end the shame of poverty, to end the injustice of prejudice and the denial of opportunity, to build the great society and to secure the freedom of man and the peace of the world.

We can do no less, and to this, tonight, let us resolve to pledge our every effort. Thank you.

The Candidate

Whatever possessed the Republican Party to succumb to the forces of the right in 1964, succumb they did in nominating Arizona's Barry Goldwater and New York's Representative William Miller. At a time when the Republicans needed a unity ticket more than anything else, they chose the most divisive one they could find. Even Richard Nixon, who stood pretty much for the same things as did Goldwater, would have been a better nominee as far as party unity was concerned.

The ensuing campaign looked more like a rout with every passing day. Republicans like Nelson Rockefeller disavowed their party's standard-bearer and sat on their hands. When it was all over, 43 million Americans voted for the Johnson-Humphrey ticket, while only 27 million voted for the Goldwater-Miller team.

The coattail effect of that landslide threw normally entrenched Republican senators, representatives, governors, mayors, state and local legislators out of office. Had it not been for the agony of Vietnam, the Grand Old Party might never have recovered as swiftly from that 1964 debacle.

Johnson decided that the best way for him to campaign was to stay in the White House and attend to the affairs of state. It was to Humphrey that the burden of electioneering fell.

As a result, Senator Goldwater at one point turned his guns on Humphrey and even began calling him by his full name—Hubert Horatio

Humphrey—in an obvious attempt to deride the Democratic vice-presidential nominee. It was for George McGovern to set the record straight:

"GOP presidential candidate Barry Goldwater has made what he seems to regard as a most important contribution to our understanding of the basic issues before the nation," McGovern told fellow senators on September 28. "He has discovered that the middle name of the Democratic vice-presidential candidate is Horatio.

"One gathers that in Mr. Goldwater's view, this should be considered an unbearable burden for the Johnson-Humphrey ticket to carry in November.

"Senator Humphrey has very modestly reminded us that he deserves little credit for his middle name. He attributes this responsibility primarily to his father and has expressed his pleasure that his beloved, deceased dad has been properly recognized in the campaign.

"I have known and admired Hubert Humphrey for many years. But I must confess that heretofore I have thoughtlessly failed to press him for a proper justification of his middle name. Once again, we are reminded of the value of a vigorous presidential campaign in focusing public attention on the crucial issues."

McGovern then informed the senators that his research led him to Horatio Alger, Jr., whose rags-to-riches stories had given joy to so many people.

"Indeed," McGovern continued, "the name Horatio Alger is synonymous with the ambitious, hard-working, incredibly thrifty, rugged individualist that Mr. Goldwater holds up as the American ideal to which we must return. One wonders, therefore, why the senator from Arizona would advertise to the American electorate that the enemy camp had the amazing foresight to preempt, in a humble South Dakota home fifty-three years ago, the honored name Horatio.

"Even the mythology of the ancient world offers a highly prestigious antecedent for the name Horatio. Which one of us has not been mightily stirred by the poem of Thomas Babington Macaulay, 'Horatius at the Bridge.'

"Recall brave Horatius standing at the Tiber River with flashing sword and indomitable courage single-handedly stemming the tide of the Etruscan army. . . .

"One would think that this stirring picture of a single brave patriot

*standing up to an entire army would appeal to the kind of man who has said
that what America needs is a backbone instead of a wishbone.*

*"There was certainly nothing wishy-washy about Horatius. And I
suspect that this is partly what the senior Humphrey had in mind when he
added that third H—Horatio—to an already distinguished combination—
Hubert Humphrey. . . .*

*"I share the view of the late senior Mr. Humphrey that there is a
special sweetness in the name Horatio, and I fully expect to see it adorn the
next vice-president of the United States."*

*One of the more colorful campaign stops for Humphrey came on
September 19, in Fargo, North Dakota, where he addressed an audience
gathered for the "National Plowing Contest."*

Let me congratulate you on the miracle of American agriculture.

The entire nation should know . . . that rather than being
a problem, agriculture actually is America's number-one
success story.

Long before the dawn of history, food has been a matter
of life-and-death importance in man's daily struggle to survive.

You have conquered that challenge. You have created a
revolution of abundance within the past generation.

The American farmer is the world's most efficient producer. The output of the average agricultural worker in the
last decade has increased almost three times as much as the
industrial worker's.

Farmers represent less than 8 percent of the population,
yet they produce enough food and fiber to feed the nation
better and cheaper than any place in the world.

These same farmers produce enough so that we can
provide over three-quarters of a billion dollars in food each
year to our own needy, distribute $2 billion of food around
the world under our food-for-peace program, sell nearly $4.5
billion worth for dollars abroad to increase our nation's

export earning—and still have adequate reserves for the nation's safety and a potential to produce even more. This is an amazing record.

The world has never seen anything like this. It truly is an American miracle. We should be proud of that achievement —and I am proud of you who have made it possible.

Unfortunately, we have come to take this American miracle of agriculture for granted. The American people must come to understand the great contribution that American agriculture has made to this nation, and to the rest of the world as well.

We need to know how we can improve the economic position of a numerically and proportionately shrinking group in our population.

We need to remember who takes the risks of drought and flood, hail and early frost, insects and markets, and all the uncertainties of the marketplace.

For consumers—and that is all of us—it is consumer insurance of market-basket bargains. For workers—millions of them—it is job insurance. For the nation as a whole it is balance-of-payment insurance. And perhaps most significant of all, it is our insurance of peace, plenty and freedom.

And let us remember that peace and freedom is everybody's concern, not just the farmer's. Food is power in today's world. Food is a vital force for peace and freedom, giving us needed diplomatic strength in the world as well as enabling us to exemplify the true humanitarian spirit of the American people.

Food for peace may yet prove the real path to peace.

We have scored our greatest victory over communism by the evidence of the success of our free enterprise system of American family farmers. . . .

Women Are People, Too

As vice-president, Humphrey did indeed play a low-key, backstage role to President Johnson. His main role was that of administration spokesman. The fiery speeches that set new ground had to be put aside while new ones, representing defenses of various administration policies, took their place.

This did not mean that Humphrey ceased being innovative and outspoken; it simply means that he was innovative and outspoken where it counted most—within the administration.

Nor does this mean that Hubert Humphrey gave up speaking in public or that his speeches lacked the passion of his pre-vice-presidential days; that much of a sacrifice would have been too much for Hubert Humphrey.

On July 29, 1965, for example, the vice-president spoke to the conference of Governors' Commissions on the Status of Women (there were forty-four such commissions at the time). One can see from his speech that, although the vice-presidency may have limited the scope of his speeches, it did nothing to alter their tenor or delivery.

. . . Today, more Americans than ever before, in public and private life, are committed to helping women achieve their birthright as citizens.

The talent of the American woman is an important resource in this nation. But I must be frank. All too often it is a wasted resource.

Only 14.1 percent of working women are in the profe-sions or in technical work. And only 4.5 percent are managers, officials and proprietors.

The worst of it is that there has been an almost continuous decline in the percentage of women working in these jobs.

One of the reasons, of course, why women's employment opportunities are limited is that their education is too often limited.

Women comprised 51 percent of the 1964 American high school graduating class.

But when it comes to college, the girls, their parents and even their teachers and counselors have some second thoughts. And so, looking again at the 1964 record, we find that while 51 percent of the June high school graduates were girls, in the fall, only 45 percent of the students entering college were girls.

Nor has the American woman's record in college been as high as we would like.

There has been an actual decline, since 1930, in the percentage of higher degrees earned by women.

But education isn't the only factor limiting women's opportunities.

There are restrictive hiring practices and a disinclination to promote women or to give them the same on-the-job training men receive.

The President's Commission on the Status of Women has taken the lead in opening more opportunities to women. Its work has continued under President Johnson through the interdepartmental committee and the Citizens' Advisory Council on the Status of Women. Your governors' commissions are working to improve the status of women at the state level. . . .

In 1962 the attorney general reviewed an 1870 law which government hiring officers used as the basis for specifying man or woman in filling vacancies.

The attorney general held that the old law did not give appointing officers that prerogative and that the president had authority to regulate the right of appointing officers in this matter. Immediately, the president directed heads of agencies to make future appointments solely on the basis of merit.

But it was President Johnson's talent search for qualified women which really opened the doors for women in government. . . .

Shortly after the president took office he announced that government would no longer be for men only. . . .

In the president's words: "We can waste no talent, we can frustrate no creative power, we can neglect no skill in our search for an open and just and challenging society."

Private industry is following the president's example.

One factor helping this trend is a shortage of skilled workers in such fields as engineering, science, mathematics and business administration.

Qualified women can fill these jobs. Those not today qualified can become qualified through study and work.

Private employment practices are also being affected by steps being taken by the U.S. Employment Service. The Employment Service is urging acceptance and use throughout the country of hiring specifications based exclusively on job-performance factors. . . .

But the greatest barriers are the psychological barriers.

The U.S. Civil Service Commission has done research on widely held views and attitudes. It has defined a whole series of myths—some held by men, others held by women, some by both.

I refer to myths such as "women do not make good bosses," or "it is inefficient to train women because of high turnover." These facts prove otherwise.

If we would clear the road ahead for both men and women, we must clear all of our minds of these mental cobwebs.

An open mind, like an open heart, is the prerequisite for an open door. . . .

Alliance for Progress

On March 13, 1968, Vice-President Humphrey spoke on the seventh anniversary of the Alliance for Progress.

A little less than a year before, President Johnson had met with the presidents of most of the other hemispheric nations and had pledged that a major effort would be made to economically integrate the Americas.

When Johnson returned to the United States from the Punta del Este conference, he said that this was "the decade of urgency" and that the U.S. commitment to its hemispheric neighbors must never falter.

Humphrey reiterated that message in his March 13 address.

. . . Seven years ago tonight the late president of the United States, John F. Kennedy, stirred the people of our hemisphere by proclaiming a new "Alliance for Progress."

President Kennedy was the first to admit he received his inspiration for this commitment—this broad program of action—from the Latin Americans themselves. The concept and idea of the Alliance for Progress was born in the Latin American countries.

The former president of Brazil, Dr. Kubitschek, enunciated what was known as "Operation: Panamerica." It was from this idea that President Kennedy formulated this expression of our commitment called the Alliance for Progress.

This alliance is to us a treaty, a commitment. It is every bit as sacred, every bit as meaningful as any treaty we have ever signed.

It is "a vast cooperative effort, unparalleled in magnitude and nobility of purpose, to satisfy the basic needs of the American people for homes, work and land, health and schools." These are the words of President Kennedy, outlining for you and for all mankind the commitment of our peoples in this hemisphere for social and economic progress.

Later in 1961, our nations agreed at Punta del Este "to unite in a common effort to bring our people accelerated economic progress and broader social justice within the framework of personal dignity and personal liberty."

Again, those are beautiful words of commitment, all within the democratic tradition; but they are more than words, they are a solemn obligation.

The declarations were brave ones. Our goals are bold

and audacious, for we aimed, those seven years ago, toward the broad realization of human aspirations which had gone unmet for generations. . . .

There are many who claim our declarations were empty, false promises, that our goals will remain forever beyond our reach. I call these people the perennial pessimists of history, and every generation has them. They are men of little faith upon whom no civilization could ever depend.

They point to a rising birth rate. They point to whole regions left isolated and backward. They see children growing up without adequate schooling or nourishment.

They point, most of all, to what they believe to be unshakeable characteristics of man's nature—the meaner habits—which have led to oppression, to social and economic injustice, and to the exploitation of one man for the benefit of another.

These pessimists may be right. But I do not think so. There are many facts which show that the alliance works.

The first is that we are determined that it will work. Since 1960, primary-school enrollment increased by 50 percent and secondary-school enrollment by more than 100 percent. These are no small achievements,

There is increasing net agricultural production and, more important, net food production—food beyond the growth of population.

When the alliance was conceived in 1961, the original plan was for a gross investment by Latin American participants of 80 percent. However, that investment has been 89 percent of the total.

And during this time, [we] have kept our share of the bargain by providing a total of $7.7 billion. Thus, we are keeping our commitment in money but, more importantly, keeping our commitment in determination and in spirit.

There are many other facts announced here today—new roads, telecommunications, modern industry and regional development. In implementing the Alliance for Progress we have converted the original concept of a cooperative effort into a concrete, multilateral, decision-making body: the Inter-American Committee on the Alliance for Progress.

Today the Alliance for Progress is the standard by which political leaders and governments are judged—even in those countries which do not fully adhere to the standard.

And this is perhaps the most important fact of all in rebuttal to those who doubt our capacity for creating change. It is an attempt to create change at the same time you preserve order—to have order even as you encourage the creation of change. . . .

Just how deep is our commitment to a just and peaceful revolution in this hemisphere? Just how deep is our belief that individual human freedom and dignity are worthy of our sacrifice?

If our commitment and our belief are deep enough, I have no doubt that we shall find the way to provide the other necessary things. If our belief and our commitment and will are not deep enough, no amount of tangible assets will accomplish our goal.

All of us—and I include my country—must be willing to sustain the effort and the vision, the vision we had laid before us seven years ago and reaffirmed only a year ago, the vision that will be necessary to build upon our beginnings.

In this troubled world, people everywhere are watching to see if we are capable of achieving our goals. For if we in our hemisphere, dedicated as we are to the rights of man, endowed as we are with the means to take the course of history in our hands, if we fail, what hope may others ever have?

Therefore a double duty is ours. First, the duty and responsibility of fulfilling our commitments to ourselves. And, secondly, the duty and necessity of fulfilling our commitments so that the rest of the world may take hope.

We have the chance—we have the obligation—to create the New World our forefathers talked of and sought. . . . [A] world not new in its principalities and kingdoms, nor in the glory of its monuments and its armies, but a world new in this final achievable reality: that each child—and a child always represents God's faith in the future—that each child might enter human society with the right to health, with the right to education, with the right to hope, the right to free expression and the right to human opportunity, because we of this generation willed that it be so.

I consider the Alliance for Progress our gift to those yet unborn, to people who will want, as we have wanted, to live in freedom. What we do now will determine what will happen to them in their time. . . .

Just a Few Hours More

In early 1968, the war in Vietnam took a turn for the worse. After the Tet offensive, all of the lies that the American people had been fed were exposed to them. The enemy in the North had not been weakened; the ever-increasing U.S. commitment had done nothing to bring the war closer to an end.

There were 493,000 Americans fighting in Vietnam at the start of 1968; there had already been 17,000 dead, countless others permanently maimed.

It may be easy for us to sit in judgment today and say it was a war that the United States should not have fought. It is easy because we remember it so vividly; it was, after all, the first war brought into our homes every night for years, courtesy of television news broadcasts and specials. We had a front-row seat to a blood-filled horror story that never seemed to end. It revolted us, sickened us and tore us apart.

History written fifty and one hundred years from now will have to make the final judgment as to whether U.S. involvement in Vietnam was the right thing to do. But one judgment can clearly be made today: the war in Vietnam was not our finest hour.

It would be unfair and untrue, however, to blame that war entirely on Lyndon Johnson. U.S. involvement in Vietnam began with President Eisenhower; it escalated under John Kennedy (with a great deal of prodding from the very same New York Times which later decried that involvement); it reached its zenith under Lyndon Johnson.

To many people even in 1978, Lyndon Johnson is remembered as a monster who enjoyed seeing American troops being slaughtered mercilessly in some disease-ridden rice paddy. Nothing could be further from the truth. More than anything else, Lyndon Johnson—who did more for human rights and social justice than any president before him—wanted the war to end as quickly as possible without, at the same time, causing more harm than good for the cause of world peace.

Hubert Humphrey knew that and understood it—and it cost him the presidency of the United States.

Humphrey should have known all along that Lyndon Johnson would not be a candidate for reelection in 1968, and he should have been prepared for the eventuality. Johnson had first told Humphrey that he would not run back in 1964, the day after their landslide election victory, but Humphrey did not believe him. On subsequent occasions over the next four years, the president would remind Humphrey that the men in the Johnson family did not live beyond their mid-60s and that, if he ran for another term, he would not survive in office. Humphrey ignored him. (Johnson was right. Even without the life-draining rigors of the presidency, he only lived until January 22, 1973—exactly two days beyond which he would have served had he been reelected in 1968.)

When, in January or February 1968 (Humphrey was not sure which), Dean Rusk told the vice-president not to be surprised if Johnson did not run, Humphrey ignored this, too.

That Humphrey was ill-prepared, therefore, for Johnson's announcement that he would not run for reelection and would not accept a draft was his own fault, but it was not the cause of his defeat.

Without a doubt, 1968 was the most violent year of the 1960s. First Martin Luther King, Jr., then Robert Kennedy were assassinated. Campus riots, antiwar demonstrations, racial turmoil all pointed to the mistaken notion that the United States was about to explode from within, that America could not possibly survive for very much longer.

One can only wonder whether, given the climate of the times and his ill-preparedness, Hubert Humphrey could have won the Democratic nomination in 1968 had not Bobby Kennedy been fatally shot following his momentous victory in the California primary—although it should be pointed out that Humphrey at all times led Kennedy in the polls.

But one need not wonder whether Hubert Humphrey could have won the presidency had there been any semblance of sanity left after the carnage of Chicago. For the plain truth is that, after the final vote was cast, Hubert Humphrey, who had been twenty-two points behind Nixon after the convention, had come within six-tenths of one percent of winning the presidency! As one pollster put it later on, had the election begun just eight hours later, Humphrey would have been the winner.

Hubert Humphrey, of course, could have won that election if he had come out strongly against Lyndon Johnson's Vietnam policies, even after his nomination. But it would have meant being disloyal to a man whom Humphrey considered great and to whom he owed much; and it would have meant saying things that Humphrey felt were morally unjust and untrue. Humphrey's life had been dedicated to peace and he did oppose continuation of the war, but because he would not betray what he believed, the liberal-left "forces of peace" did everything in their power to defeat Humphrey in 1968. As a result, the nation elected the man these same forces hated so vigorously, Richard Nixon.

One need only read Humphrey's words of August 19, 1968, in accepting his party's nomination for president, to understand just how misguided the liberal-left campaign against him was in that painful and agonizing year, and to appreciate the full extent of the loss the United States sustained as a result.

Mr. Chairman, my fellow Americans, my fellow Democrats— I proudly accept the nomination of our party.

This moment—this moment is one of personal pride and gratification. Yet one cannot help but reflect the deep sadness that we feel over the troubles and the violence which have erupted, regrettably and tragically, in the streets of this great city, and for the personal injuries which have occurred.

Surely we have now learned the lesson that violence breeds counterviolence and it cannot be condoned, whatever the source.

I know that every delegate to this convention shares

tonight my sorrow and my distress over these incidents. And for just one moment, in sober reflection and serious purpose, may we just quietly and silently, each in our own way, pray for our country. And may we just share for a moment a few of those immortal words of the prayer of St. Francis of Assisi, words which I think may help heal the wounds, ease the pain and lift our hearts.

Listen to this immortal saint: "Where there is hatred, let me know love. Where there is injury, pardon. Where there is doubt, faith. Where there is despair, hope. Where there is darkness, light."

Those are the words of a saint. And may those of us of less purity listen to them well and may America tonight resolve that never, never again shall we see what we have seen.

Yes, I accept your nomination in this spirit and I have spoken knowing that the months and the years ahead will severely test our America. And might I say that as this America is tested, that once again we give our testament to America. And I do not think it is sentimental nor is it cheap, but I think it is true that each and every one of us in our own way should once again reaffirm to ourselves and our posterity that we love this nation, we love America. . . !

Democracy affords debate, discussion and dissent. But, my fellow Americans, it also requires decision. And we have decided here, not by edict, but by vote; not by force, but by ballot.

Majority rule has prevailed but minority rights are preserved.

There is always the temptation, always the temptation to leave the scene of battle in anger and despair, but those who know the true meaning of democracy accept the decision of today but never relinquish their right to change it tomorrow. . . .

It is in the tradition of Franklin Roosevelt, who knew that America had nothing to fear but fear itself!

And it is in the tradition of that one and only Harry

Truman, who let 'em have it and told it like it was. . . .

And my fellow Americans, all that we do and all that we ever hope to do, must be in the tradition of John F. Kennedy, who said to us: "Ask not what your country can do for you, but what you can do for your country."

And, my fellow Democrats and fellow Americans, in that spirit of that great man let us ask what together we can do for the freedom of man.

And what we are doing is in the tradition of Lyndon B. Johnson, who rallied a grief-stricken nation when our leader was stricken by the assassin's bullet and said to you and said to me, and said to all the world—"Let us continue."

And in the space . . . of five years since that tragic moment, President Johnson has accomplished more of the unfinished business of America than any of his modern predecessors.

And I truly believe that history will surely record the greatness of his contribution to the people of this land.

And tonight to you, Mr. President, I say thank you. Thank you, Mr. President. . . .

There are differences of course, serious differences within our party on this vexing and painful issue of Vietnam, and these differences are found even within the ranks of all of the Democratic presidential candidates.

But I might say to my fellow Americans that once you have examined the differences I hope you will also recognize the much larger areas of agreement.

Let those who believe that our cause in Vietnam has been right, or those who believe that it has been wrong, agree here and now, that neither vindication nor repudiation will bring peace or be worthy of this country. . . !

Put aside recrimination and dissension. Turn away from violence and hatred. Believe—believe in what America can do, and believe in what America can be, and with the vast—with the help of the vast, unfrightened, dedicated, faithful majority of Americans, I say to this great convention tonight, and to this great nation of ours, I am ready to lead our country.

An Important Shift

The "Dump Johnson" movement, that even today claims to have succeeded in forcing Lyndon Johnson out of the White House, did no such thing. But it probably was responsible for forcing the president into announcing his retirement earlier than planned.

There is sufficient evidence to suggest that Johnson would have held up that announcement until after the California primary in June, and quite possibly right up to the convention itself. At that time, he almost certainly would have thrown his full weight behind his vice-president.

Staying in the race that long would have cut deeply into the efforts of Senators Kennedy and Eugene McCarthy, and would have probably eliminated to some degree the acrimonious nature of the convention—at least, on the inside.

But Johnson's March 31 withdrawal did enable him to pursue peace with a greater appearance of nonpartisanship, and soon the Paris peace talks were underway.

It was that pursuit of peace that prevented Humphrey from speaking out on Vietnam for the first month after the convention. He had no desire to jeopardize in any way those negotiations. On September 30, however, it was clear that nothing would come of the talks. Humphrey felt free, therefore, to speak his mind. In his first nationwide television address since the convention, broadcast from Salt Lake City, Humphrey outlined a three-point plan for peace. It represented only a minor shift from the avowed administration policy, but it was enough to bring back most of the liberals into the Humphrey camp.

. . . As president, I would stop the bombing of the North as an acceptable risk for peace, because I believe it could lead to success in the negotiations and thereby shorten the war. This would be the best protection for our troops.

In weighing that risk—and before taking action—I would place key importance on evidence—direct or indirect, by deed or word—of communist willingness to restore the demilitarized zone between North and South Vietnam.

If the government of North Vietnam were to show bad faith, I would reserve the right to resume the bombing.

Secondly, I would take the risk that the South Vietnamese would meet the responsibilities they say they are now ready to assume in their own self-defense.

I would move, in other words, toward de-Americanization of the war.

I would sit down with the leaders of South Vietnam to set a specific timetable by which American forces could be systematically reduced while South Vietnamese forces took over more and more of the burden.

The schedule must be a realistic one—one that would not weaken the overall allied defense posture. I am convinced such action would be as much in South Vietnam's interest as in ours.

Third, I would propose once more an immediate cease-fire with United Nations or international organization supervision, and supervised withdrawal of all foreign forces from South Vietnam. . . .

6

Return to the Senate

Private Life

At midnight, December 31, 1968, Hubert Humphrey went into his bathroom and flushed the toilet. It was his symbolic way of flushing away the most difficult year in his life. Twenty days later, he was a private citizen for the first time since his election as mayor of Minneapolis in 1945.

In 1969, Humphrey returned to teaching, holding positions at both Macalester College and the University of Minnesota, both in Minneapolis.

He could have remained in government, however. For Richard Nixon had asked Humphrey to serve as U.S. ambassador to the United Nations. Humphrey did not believe that the offer was a sincere one; nor did he wish to serve as a Nixon "showpiece" of unity. Therefore, he declined.

Humphrey's only connection with government that year was in his role as the first chairman of the Board of Regents of the Woodrow Wilson International Center for Scholars, established by Congress in 1968. It was Lyndon Johnson's parting gift to his vice-president, for whom Woodrow Wilson was a boyhood hero.

Humphrey talked about his hero and his own role as board chairman in an August 22, 1969, speech to the American Association for State and Local History.

. . . [The] Woodrow Wilson International Center for Scholars. . . will become a truly advanced studies institute on international relations and American government. It will become a university of universities. It's in its first year now and in the year of 1970 we will have the first forty or fifty scholars coming to this country from all over the world, having at their fingertips access to the archives of our government, to the departments of government, to the great universities and advanced study institutes to learn and to teach, to study and to tell about international relations, domestic policy, American government, to learn more about these United States.

So one of my boyhood dreams has been realized—namely, to have some identification with Woodrow Wilson.

But the Woodrow Wilson that I remember was the Woodrow Wilson of the League of Nations. We were talking here tonight about. . . my interest in international relations even as a student at the University of Minnesota, and in 1939 and 1940 when there was a bitter struggle going on in this country as to whether or not there should be a program of aid to the Allies, and particularly aid to Britain, in those difficult and tragic moments of the battle of Britain.

There was a divided America. I was one of the young men at that time that said yes, we must aid. . . . I came from South Dakota, isolationist country, and I've had many people ask me since, "How come that you could grow up in Minnesota and South Dakota, born and raised in South Dakota, your higher education in Minnesota, the center of isolationism in the United States, and still be an advocate of international cooperation, foreign assistance, foreign aid and subsequently an advocate— and a strong advocate—of the United Nations?"

I said, "Because my political hero in my adolescence, in my teenage period, in my early college days was Woodrow Wilson."

Woodrow Wilson, the man of peace, Woodrow Wilson the man of vision, Woodrow Wilson who gave his life in that cross-country tour as he fought for the League of Nations. Woodrow Wilson, who had a vision—and I still believe to this day that had we listened to his voice, had we followed his advice, we may have been spared the carnage of World War II. At least, it's my opinion. . . .

A Freshman Again

By the time Hubert Humphrey had delivered that August 1969 speech, he had already come to a less-than-startling conclusion: private life was not in his blood. Barely eight months into retirement, he yearned for the political life.

The conclusion did not hit him with any suddenness. It had been creeping up on him slowly, looking for an opening to burst through. For a while,

Humphrey toyed with the idea of running for governor of Minnesota, but Washington was where he wanted to be and there was nothing available.

Then, in August, Eugene McCarthy announced that he would not seek reelection as Minnesota's senior senator (a wise decision on his part, considering that only fifteen percent of the state's voters were considering voting for him, according to statewide polls).

The opening was there and Humphrey began touring the state in search of a return to the Senate he loved so much.

The nomination was his and so was the November 1970 election. Humphrey defeated six-term Representative Clark MacGregor by 220,000 votes—his largest victory in four Senate races. (MacGregor would go on to become Richard Nixon's post-Watergate 1972 campaign manager.)

Thus, in early January 1971, Hubert Horatio Humphrey returned to the Senate of the United States, a freshman once again. Just seven years and a few days later, that Senate, along with the House of Representatives and the entire nation, would pause to pay its respects to his memory in a manner normally reserved for presidents. But on that January day, his colleagues from both sides of the aisle rose to applaud as he took his seat.

It felt great to be home again, he thought.

On April 16, 1971, Humphrey addressed the seventeenth Constitutional Convention of the Utility Workers of America at Washington's Statler Hilton Hotel. His subject was "A New Bill of Rights for America."

"These new rights," he told his fellow senators five days later, "are, in a sense, an updating of those first ten amendments that spelled out just how American men and women shall strive to enjoy life, liberty and the pursuit of happiness."

Indeed, he told the Senate, "these new rights. . . should be a means for us to declare the primacy of man as a total being—a being of matter. . . , a being of spirit and higher purpose."

Following are portions of that April 16 address to the Utility Workers.

. . . More important than machines are men. The most common denominator that relates to all men is the rights they possess. And that's what I want to discuss today—a "New Bill of Rights for America. . . ."

By the year 2000, we will be so engulfed by transistors, computers, hypersonic speed, new energy sources and uses, that the 1960s will look like the middle ages by comparison.

These material goals are good if they stay within reason and do not destroy other values that are essential to preserving the humane and human qualities of man and the nature that surrounds us.

The first of the new rights I wish to discuss is *the right to peace.* We in America are presently at war—a war that we must withdraw from as soon as possible. Every American's right to peace is being infringed upon by this continuing act of national violence.

Actual physical violence certainly violates man's right to peace. But what about our right to be free from the threats to peace—free from fear of nuclear annihilation—free from the psychological and economic costs of an ever-increasing escalation of the nuclear arms race? Is that right any less real?

Today, throughout this nation there are well over 5 million Americans out of work. Unemployment is about 6 percent. prices continue to rise. We are in the midst of a heartless, manufactured recession. Every American has *an absolute right to a job.* Every American that is able and desires to work, should b. given that opportunity.

What good will it do us to be at peace with each other? What good will it do if we are gainfully and productively employed, if the air isn't fit to breath, if the water is too foul to drink, if food is too contaminated to eat, if the noise of technology-gone-mad deafens us, if we have paved over the country?

Clearly, each one of us has a *right to a wholesome environment*— clean air, clean water, pure food, decent housing, security on the streets, peace and quiet, and the refreshing touch of unspoiled nature.

America must build, and build soon, a health-care system that guarantees us *the right to be healthy;* not the right to be treated when we become sick. We must have the doctors, and nurses, and paramedical, technical and support personnel to make this system work. The richest nation on the face of the earth should also be the healthiest nation. . . .

There are other rights in these new amendments of freedom. Rights and responsibilities that fit new times and new circumstances.

We have a right to justice—so that man may stand before his peers and his society on a truly just and equal basis with his neighbor.

The right to free expression—so that man may speak and be heard, despite the decisions and beliefs of any temporary compact majority.

The right to search for knowledge—so that no man may remain another's slave through the denial of skill or education.

The right to public accountability—so that man may remain the master of the state, rather than the state the master of man.

The right to a meaningful role in society—so that man may follow his own cadence and live with self-respect and dignity among his fellow citizens.

The right to full opportunity—so that man may lift himself to the limits of his ability, no matter what the color of his skin, the tenets of his religion, or his so-called social status.

The right to public compassion—so that man may live with the knowledge that his health, his well-being, his old age and loneliness are the concern of his society.

The right to movement and free association—so that man may freely move and choose his friends without coercive restraints.

The right to privacy—so that many may be free of the heavy hand of the watchers and listeners.

The right to rest and recreation—so that the necessity of labor not be permitted to cripple human development.

These are the rights we seek and must realize. We must make them real for ourselves and for others.

But we must also realize that the best way to insure these rights for ourselves is to work for their enjoyment by everyone. Every right we have discussed today has its accompanying responsibility.

I want to emphasize that these rights are not outlined only in the context of helping the disadvantaged, the minority and the forgotten. These are rights that we all have in common. Adequate security, jobs, housing, health care, environment, dignity are things we all have a right to. Every American shares these rights and the responsibility to see that they are assured to all.

We have the vision to seek these rights and to make them real. We have the resources to attain and guarantee these rights. And we have the perseverance to continue the struggle to safeguard these rights from any and all who would weaken or threaten them or us.

I have faith that the year 2000 will dawn on a world not torn by dissension nor devastated by nuclear conflagration. It must and will be a world in which wisdom, humaneness, dignity and progress for mankind prevail.

The glory of planet earth is man. Let the growth and evolution of man continue—an evolution of the spirit of man, ever devising, ever seeking a higher perfection.

The Universal Killer

Hubert Humphrey knew only too well the personal tragedy that is cancer. His brother died from it; his son nearly did. He himself had a brief brush with the dread disease in 1968.

Over the years, even before this "universal killer" had claimed its first Humphrey victim, the senator had urged an all-out war on cancer. At first, he had joined in West Virginia Senator Matt Neely's crusade to win approval for massive funding for cancer research; when Neely himself succumbed to the disease, Humphrey picked up the banner and made it one of his crusades.

Now, in 1971, President Nixon was also urging that sort of massive government program. Congress, however, did not seem any more convinced that year than in any previous year. Its members in both houses debated the suggested appropriation.

On June 18, 1971, Humphrey made an impassioned plea to the Senate to stop debating and start appropriating the needed funds. "How much longer must we wait?" he cried.

. . . Man is blessed with tremendous powers and one of the most omnipotent of these is science, but even the force of scientific knowledge is finite and its horizons limited in the context of time. Time is the element which science, especially medical science, is in constant conflict with.

After all, what is the cure of disease other than forestalling the ultimate stoppage of time, or death?

But in another context, time is equally elemental, and that is to acquire the knowledge and create the tools to speed the cure of diseases before they take their toll. For if we cure today, we save a life today; if we cure tomorrow, we lose all of those who will die today.

With the present institutions and financial means available, the enigma of cancer will eventually be solved, but these resources and agencies are not constituted to meet the urgency of the problem.

There is an overriding sense of urgency that we must face up to. Congress must mobilize our health resources in an all-out battle against cancer.

We cannot hesitate, for time is the enemy in seeking to lift this devastating burden from the minds and bodies of mankind—and we have the means to shorten this time.

Nearly a thousand people perish every day from cancer in this country alone, and every day we delay we have to ask ourselves, "Had we speeded up our work, had we tried to do a better job of administration, had we concentrated more attention, how many lives would we have saved?"

Now we are not dealing with an ordinary disease. . . . It is one thing to be ill from other diseases, but the agony of cancer is indescribable. Those that linger with it are a pitiful sight—strong and healthy people, stricken and literally demolished and devoured by this disease. . . .

More than four decades ago, the late Senator Matthew Neely of West Virginia, who died in 1958 of the very disease he had been fighting legislatively for more than thirty years. . . , noted that cancer was then taking 125,000 lives a year. . . . Today. . . , the death rate from cancer [is] at 325,000 a year. . . .

He called for a $100,000 initiative against cancer that year, but Congress was not fully convinced of the threat and finally voted only $50,000.

How different things might be if the Congress had listened to Matt Neely in 1928, or in 1937, when he succeeded in getting Congress to establish the National Cancer Institute but failed to win for it the money he felt it needed to do the job.

In 1946, Neely, then a member of the House of Representatives, introduced a bill to appropriate $100 million to launch a large-scale offensive against cancer.

That was twenty-five years ago—twenty-five years before President Nixon called for a $100 million cancer initiative.

How much longer must we wait. . . ?

Let me point out that more Americans died of cancer last year than were killed in action throughout the Second World War.

And in the past six years of fighting in Vietnam, 44,000 Americans have been killed. At the same time, back home, cancer killed 2 million persons—that is more than forty-five times as many human beings destroyed by cancer as by the war.

And of those 2 million, 35,000 were children. That is about 312 youngsters a week.

I do not wish to dwell in the past and on the lost battles of Matt Neely, for "of all the words of tongue or pen, the saddest of all are these: it might have been."

But we should not ignore his prophecy, for those who forget the lessons of history are doomed to repeat them.

Of the 200 million Americans alive today, 50 million will die of the disease unless better methods of prevention and treatment are found.

About half those deaths will occur before the age of 65. Cancer today causes more deaths among children under the age of 15 than any other disease. . . .

In the race against cancer, time is important. And the time that we use in bureaucratic red tape means time that is lost and lives that are lost.

We do not know whether the critical experiment in cancer research has yet been done. Cancer is not a simple disease with a single cause that will be subject to a single cure of a single immunization, as was the case with polio. Cancer comprises many diseases and results from a variety of causes that will have to be dealt with in a variety of ways. . . .

We urgently need a continuing commitment of adequate funds, starting with a minimum $400 million and building by 1976 to $800 million or even a billion dollars a year.

These are small sums when placed against our national resources or the human suffering and economic loss attributable to cancer.

Pain and sorrow cannot be measured in terms of dollars. The economic loss in jobs and earning power of persons stricken with this disease is conservatively estimated at $15 billion a year.

Major advances in the fundamental knowledge of cancer have been made in the past decade. They have opened up promising areas for intensive investigation. They must be explored vigorously if we are to exploit the opportunities that lie before us.

Just thirty years ago, only one in five cancer patients survived. Today, one patient in three is cured. That number should be reduced to one in two and finally to the point where all patients survive. . . .

A dozen years ago, I was chairman of the Government Operations subcommittee on reorganization and international organizations. After extensive study and research, including travel and visits to medical centers in Western Europe, Poland and the Soviet Union, we published a document entitled "Cancer: A Worldwide Menace."

I said in my 1959 report and I repeat today:

"The evidence is clear that cancer is a world problem, best solved by research on a worldwide basis. The combined efforts of scientists throughout the world should be applied to developing and exploiting leads wherever they occur. . . .

"Against a universal killer, mankind must offer a universal defender—scientific cooperation. Against an enemy which strikes irrespective of politics or ideology, mankind must strengthen teamwork in a manner which transcends these or other factors.

"At stake is triumph in a human adventure of highest drama.

And with triumph, will come the prize of a lessening of human suffering and of premature death throughout the world."

I believe the United States, with the greatest medical and scientific community in the world, should take the lead in this historic effort.

Frankie Retires

Frank Sinatra's announcement in June 1971 that he was retiring sent shockwaves throughout the entertainment industry that were felt even in the hallowed halls of the Senate.

On June 30, 1971, California's Senator John Tunney rose to bemoan the great loss. When he was done, Hubert Humphrey joined in the tribute.

. . . I am very pleased today to have the opportunity of associating myself with the remarks of the distinguished junior senator from California and others concerning. . . a noted American and a man of great personal talent and achievement, Francis Albert Sinatra. . . .

The measure of a man is interpreted in different ways. Viewed by close friends, casual acquaintances, or those who become aware of his purpose in life by chance, he may often appear to be many things to many different people.

Without a doubt, those rare individuals who emerge as stars of the entertainment world are unique in our society, inasmuch as they have been cast in a role that is in many ways bigger than life.

As professionals, their highly developed talents have provided the most delicate link for a most personal communication to our hearts, our minds and our emotions.

The term *star* itself is indicative of the honors we have given to such a gifted personality. Webster defines *star* as "a person of brilliant qualities who stands out preeminently among his fellows."

The definition is highly applicable and exceedingly accurate in this case. But one is prompted to wonder if this explanation is at times a bit too generalized to cover everyone privileged to wear this mantle or this title of star.

It is of great credit to the entertainment industry that on many occasions one of their members rises beyond stardom to become. . . a legend in his own lifetime. . . .

When a person becomes a legend in his lifetime, he typifies the fabled American success story which has been repeated around the world since the days of our Founding Fathers. He is a legend, because he has displayed a sincere interest in humanity which drives him to use his talents, prestige and unrelenting trust to stretch out a hand and help his fellow man whenever he encounters a need.

This, without question, is a noble extension of stardom in the performing arts and far too often such generosity goes unrecognized and, indeed, without thanks.

Like many Americans, I was saddened to learn of the retirement of Frank Sinatra because this man is so vigorous, so vital, so much a part of the American scene; he is a remarkable man and a star in his own right, and a legend whose touch reached far beyond the footlights.

Sinatra gave and continues to give, and will continue to give for years to come, far more than the abilities with which he was blessed.

His talent was a magical instrument with the power to help the unfortunate and the infirm as well as to mark the memorable milestones in the international world of entertainment. . . .

Battling Child Abuse

In early January 1973, Chicago newspapers and Time *magazine reported the death of a six-year-old boy.*

It had been no ordinary death. The boy had been given up for adoption by his parents some years before. He had been staying with foster parents and living a happy, normal life. Then, his natural parents decided they wanted him back.

The boy did not want to go, however; he was afraid of his father's violent temper. Nevertheless, the courts ordered the foster parents to return the youngster to his natural parents.

A few months later, the six-year-old was so severely beaten by his father that he had to be taken to a hospital. Four weeks later, he died from those injuries.

On January 23, Humphrey called upon the Senate to help bring child abuse to an end.

. . . Each year more children are killed by their parents than die of any one disease.

Dr. Vincent Fontana, director of pediatrics at St. Vincent's Hospital in New York and chairman of Mayor Lindsay's Task Force on Child Abuse, has said that abuse and neglect is the number-one killer of children in this country.

At least 700 children are killed annually and 50,000 to 200,000 children suffer serious physical abuse.

It is estimated that the number of child abuse cases is increasing alarmingly. In New York City, for example, the number of reported cases increased 549 percent between 1966 and 1970. And only a fraction of the total number of neglected and abused children are recognized as such and given proper medical attention. . . .

Child abuse is an ugly disease and in many ways a symptom of other deep problems of our times such as poverty, pollution and congestion. Some evidence suggests that parents who mistreat their children are usually psychopathic or are reacting to feelings of anxiety.

In many cases, the parent was once a victim of child abuse. In 1971, Dr. Fontana's task force reported that battered children, if they survive and approach adolescence, begin to show signs of psychologic and emotional disturbances reported as irreversible in most cases.

All of us have a moral responsibility to break this vicious cycle. Physicians and social workers need to become more aware of their responsibility to report abuse. Legislators have a moral responsibility to make available any legal tools which might help to reduce the incidence of abuse.

Child abuse has long been ignored because it is something we would all like to pretend doesn't exist. And child abuse has been ignored because children have no political muscle, no effective way of articulating their needs to those of us who write the law.

While the causes of child abuse may not be reached by law, I believe we must face the fact that the law is very weak in this area. The lack of children's rights in court is matched by the lack of laws restraining their parents. There is no federal effort to protect child abuse victims—and state legislation is not adequate.

Child abuse certainly will not evaporate with the passage of new legislation, but a federal child abuse law may be necessary because of the many inadequacies of state laws.

Let me outline briefly some new directions we might take on the federal level to protect our children from abuse. Through federal legislation we can:

Simplify the reporting process so that reporters of abuse are exempt from further involvement after filing a report;

Designate a central reporting agency in each state to be responsible for any necessary follow-up reports;

Make it mandatory for doctors, social workers and other professionals to report abuse;

Reduce the maximum penalties for abuse and reclassify the crime as a misdemeanor so that people will be encouraged to report abuse. The emphasis must be placed on the need for psychological rehabilitation of battering parents;

Help provide the states with funds necessary for the implementation of their programs.

I have outlined just a few suggestions for federal child abuse legislation. Much work remains to be done on this problem, for the seriousness of child abuse has too long escaped our attention. We must work to build a sound-thinking and emotionally stable adult society by protecting our most precious resource, our nation's children. . . .

A Man of the People

On December 26, 1972, at the age of 88, Harry S. Truman died. What Humphrey felt for Truman has been reported in other pages of this volume; there is no need to repeat it here.

But we would be remiss if we did not repeat the words Humphrey spoke to the Senate on December 6, 1973, when that body in which the man from Independence served paid tribute to his memory.

. . . The life story of Harry Truman is America at its best—patriotic, self-reliant, courageous, simple and uncomplicated, forthright and loyal, a partisan and a patriot, a devoted husband and father, and a great president and statesman.

He was a builder in a world ravished by war. He was a healer in a world beset by disease, pestilence and poverty.

He was a giant of a man who lived in troubled times and had the courage to make difficult decisions. . . .

He has served America and all mankind with humility, dignity and greatness.

I recall when the Humphreys first came to Washington in

1948. I was elected to be the freshman senator from Minnesota. Harry Truman was our president.

My parents came to visit me during those first few months. Concluding that even a freshman had the right to make at least one request of the White House, I phoned the president's appointments secretary, Matt Connelly, to ask if my parents could meet the president. My father was a lifelong Democrat and a strong supporter of President Truman. Not long after, my parents and I were escorted into the president's office.

My father and mother had never been in the White House before and for them and for me it was an exciting experience. The president was kind and gracious, particularly to my mother, who admitted she was "scared to death" to be in his office. Truman gave her a hug and said, "Oh, we're just folks here."

The thirty-third president of the United States then took my parents on a personal tour of the White House. I shall never forget it. And I know that to my father in particular it was the high point of his life.

So, as a human being we remember Harry Truman for his uncomplicated, direct and friendly appeal. He truly was a man of the people, from the people, and for the people.

As president, we remember him for courage, frankness and principle, in the face of monumental decisions which had to be made and which he did make:

The atom bomb and the peacetime uses of atomic energy;

The Potsdam Conference and the diplomatic and military follow-up to World War II.

The creation of the United Nations and the guarantee of U.S. participation in it;

His timely and firm response to the threat of communism in Greece and Turkey; the Marshall plan in Europe; the Point Four program;

His combat of disease and pestilence and poverty worldwide;

The North Atlantic Pact;

The Berlin Airlift;

Resistance to communist aggression in Korea; and

The maintenance of civilian control over the military.

And then his pioneering in so many areas of domestic policy. We should never forget that it was Harry Truman's administration that laid before the nation and the Congress proposals for the improvement and expansion of our health care system, including the proposal of Medicare.

Nor should we ever forget that it was President Truman who appointed the commission that came forth with a monumental study on race relations in America and recommended the shaping of a program for reform.

For these and so many other acts of leadership in the world, President Truman won our admiration and gratitude. He established the basis for postwar peace and the survival of human dignity.

For most Americans, President Truman was not a president whose greatness would be recognized only after the passage of time. He was recognized—as a great and democratic president.

A Sense of Purpose

In 1976, the nation was celebrating its 200th birthday.

Much had happened over the past few years. The chaos of the 1960s had given way to Watergate. For the first time in history, both a president and a vice-president resigned from office in disgrace. Other men now held those offices who had never been voted for by the people of the United States.

The Bicentennial, therefore, was more than just a birthday celebration; it was a time to reassess where we as a nation were going, what our future held in store, what our role should be.

Hubert Humphrey had much to say in that year, particularly about the nation's young people.

On February 18, 1976, he told the Senate, "The vitality and strength of our democracy are sustained by a politically informed citizenry, capable of maintaining accountability and demanding effective performance of their elected officials. . . .

"We could make no greater mistake than to ignore the new spirit of political awareness which is building in our land. It is idealistic, yet pragmatic—tempered by the active participation of millions of young Americans in our political parties, campaigns, government and citizen groups.

"I am greatly encouraged by the strong desire on the part of this nation's young people to claim responsibilities, to harness the vast potential of American industry and creativity in the cause of social justice and human dignity, and to restore our American commitment to the basic rights of life, liberty and the pursuit of happiness for every citizen."

Several days earlier, Humphrey had addressed the graduation banquet of A Presidential Classroom for Young Americans, a week-long program held in Washington to acquaint young students with the workings of their government.

On July 2, 1976, he made another address to the Senate on the subject of the Bicentennial and the need to revive the spirit that made America great. Following are excerpts from those speeches.

. . . The fifty-six men who signed the Declaration of Independence on that hot, humid July day in Philadelphia were effectively putting their names to their own death warrants.

During the War of Independence, nine of those men died of wounds or hardships, five were captured as traitors, twelve had their homes ransacked or burned, and the sons of many others were killed, wounded or captured.

But the job they did was worth the price they paid, for they had set in motion the most powerful force of human freedom of all time. They had lighted for the world a beacon of hope that still shines today.

I continue to be impressed over how relatively young these men were. Nineteen of the fifty-six signers of the Declaration of Independence were in their 40s. Sixteen were in their 30s. Two were only 27.

In 1776, Thomas Jefferson was 33, James Madison was 25, Alexander Hamilton was 21.

George Washington held the position of public surveyor of Fairfax County, Virginia, at age 17. When he was only 20, he was sole manager of a 4,000-acre tobacco plantation, while simultaneously holding a commission as a major. . . of one of the four military districts of Virginia.

At 21, he was entrusted with a critical diplomatic military expedition to the French positions in the Ohio Valley. The report which he wrote was published in Virginia and England and helped alert the British government to the encroachment of the French into the Western areas of the colonies.

At 22, Washington was a lieutenant colonel, and a year later he was made commander-in-chief of all Virginia militia.

When Alexander Hamilton was 20, he was an impassioned and effective pamphleteer in defense of colonial policies. A year later, he was a lieutenant colonel on George Washington's personal staff.

Two hundred years ago, we the people came together to form a more perfect union. We took a risk that never had been taken before in the history of mankind.

It was not the risk of rebellion, for many rebellions had been tried and failed. Rather, it was the risk of a grand experiment in democracy—of forming a government under which all the people were sovereign as well as subject, rulers as well as ruled.

The risk was that of union, a union of persons who—whatever their station in life, their level of income, their education, or their background—were to be regarded as equal in creation and in their protection under the laws.

The document which those fifty-six men took a risk in signing—the Declaration of Independence—affirmed that there are certain God-given, inalienable rights, including life, liberty and the pursuit of happiness. And, to secure these rights, a government was instituted, deriving its just powers from the consent of the governed.

But it was President Franklin Delano Roosevelt who effectively translated for our time the demand for a new pioneering leadership to make the promise of the Declaration of Independence a reality.

"I do not believe that the era of the pioneer is at an end," he said. "I only believe that the area for pioneering has changed." He then went on to say that "our country needs bold, persistent experimentation. It is common sense to take a method and try it. If it fails, admit it frankly and try another. But above all, try something!"

Those who are young ought to have a great sense of purpose and idealism as they step forward to explore the future. And traditionally it has been part of the American character to be optimistic—to have faith and confidence in the future.

That is why I am deeply concerned when I see some of our young people reflecting a more pessimistic, negative mood—when they seem unwilling to take a risk on the future.

Our whole history is filled with adventure and pioneering. Americans through the years have opened up a continent—developed a new nation. We have showed the world new technologies in agriculture, medicine, education, transportation —yes, in every aspect of life.

You are in the very spring of life. Today, you are better equipped to challenge old assumptions and the traditional ways of doing things than any generation in human history. Now is the time to question and to probe—to gain new understandings and to live each day to its fullest.

I sense a new spirit dawning in America. I find it no matter where I travel. A long nightmare of confusion and dashed hopes for all too many Americans is going to end, because at the root of the American experience is a determination *not* to lower expectations, but to engage in bold experiments.

We are not a nation that seeks the certainty of sure stability. No, we are a people who thrive on exercising free choice.

So, test your knowledge and your ability to the utmost. Continue your education and your political involvement throughout your lifetime. Trust in your own judgment and remain open to new ideas. You *can* make a difference if you take the risk of becoming informed and involved.

In closing, I want to remind you of what that great philosopher, Victor Hugo, said: "The future has several names. For the weak, it is impossible. For the faint-hearted, it is unknown. For the thoughtful and valiant, it is ideal. The challenge is urgent. The task is large. The time is now."

... America faces a paradox this year. It is the 200th anniversary of our system of government—the greatest force for freedom in the history of civilization. It is a time for celebration and a time for reflection—on what we have become and what we want to be.

Yet it is also a time when Americans feel far from their government. It is a year in which our most hallowed institutions are the objects of suspicion and mistrust—a year in which our representative form of government and many of its achievements are being called into question.

We seem to have lost our traditional optimism and our perennial self-confidence, and with them our will to pioneer, to experiment, to take a risk in the hope of something better.

Our people seem to lack a sense of accomplishment, a feeling of dedication to a common purpose and a cause larger than ourselves.

Throughout our history, it has been the government, expressing the will of the people, which has acted as the voice of a united citizenry.

But we have ceased to hear that voice in recent years. And as a result, each of us carries with him a small emptiness, a hollow place in ourselves which is the sense of something unsatisfied—a sense of something that is best in our character going unused.

Americans are an independent people. We are a nation of individuals who are jealous of our own prerogatives. We are a nation of many distinct regions and groups.

And we can be proud of that tradition—it is a part of our character. Indeed, the respect we give to individual freedom and the diversity of our ethnic, cultural and geographic backgrounds have contributed immeasurably to the progress and richness of our society.

But there is another, more profound, part of our character as well, and it is not being fulfilled. It is that element in us which wants to be part of a greater whole. It is our sense of community and our deep reserves of compassion, courage and self-sacrifice.

We have drawn on those reserves before. America's greatest hours have come, not when each of us was simply working on his own behalf, but when we were motivated by a common purpose and achieved our goal. . . .

Those were great days for America, days full of courage and commitment. They were days when we showed what was best in us. They were days when we proved to the world that Americans are not afraid to make a promise or to get a tough job done, that Americans do not run away from a fight.

I believe that we can revive that spirit in these times—to bring back our great days as a nation and our pride in our accomplishments.

In this famous year of our history, America needs national goals. We need ideals to match our strength. We need challenges to match our imagination.

And sensing that need, Americans feel out of touch with their government. They are ready to work. They are not afraid to put their talent to the test. They are prepared to meet any eventuality.

They know that human beings need goals and promises to give their lives meaning and purpose.

They know that no challenge is too great for this country— no fight is too hard, no problem too complex and no sights too high for the American spirit.

They know that we have the greatest accumulation of human energy and talent in the history of the human race ready and waiting to go—and yet we are not putting those resources to work.

Our forebearers from every part of the world fought the wild lands of a new and unmapped wilderness, and out of it created cities which were miracles of human invention.

They stretched our borders to the Pacific Ocean and beyond

and made the world our market. They showed an unbelieving globe how to build well and to build plentifully.

They turned our unforgiving landscape into a garden, and our broad and level plains into the most abundant producer of food and fiber the earth has ever known.

What can we do to share their tradition? What special challenges remain to us in our own time, in the beginning of our nation's third century?

The answer is reflected by the broken glass and echoed from [the] concrete of our cities.

It is glistening in the tears of a hungry child and it is standing in the stillness of the unemployment line.

The challenge is whispered by the dying man whose disease we could have cured and echoed by the family whose home we could have saved.

It is running in the refuse in our lakes and streams and carried in the air around us.

The challenge is waiting wherever bigotry or injustice still survive and wherever a man or woman is prevented from becoming the best that it is in them to be.

The answer is that we still can become what our forefathers shed their blood for, what they staked their lives and their fortunes on.

The answer is that we can keep the promise made 200 years ago by men who saw a vision—a vision of a people committed to protecting every person's right to life, liberty and the pursuit of happiness; and a promise of a firmly united nation determined to establish justice and to promote the general welfare.

Those promises must be kept. They are a sacred trust, and we cannot rest until we have seen them through—until we have built the kind of nation which will preserve them inviolate for generations to come:

—A nation which is dedicated to life—not survival, not subsistence, not wealth for a few only, but the good life for each and every person;

—A nation which is committed to liberty—not anarchy, but real liberty which comes from duty and responsibility; and

—A nation which offers the pursuit of happiness—which holds out the hope, unfettered by poverty, that every American can achieve to the limits of his ability.

Thank You, Mr. President

On January 19, 1977, Gerald Ford served his last full day as president of the United States. The first man ever to hold that office by appointment rather than election, he took command at a time when the very fabric of our democratic system was being torn apart by the excesses of Watergate and the fury of a nation that had been deceived.

Hubert Humphrey was a Democrat and he had little use for what he considered to be basic Republican philosophy.

But he was also an American and, as such, he stood on the Senate floor that day to deliver a moving tribute to the departing president—a tribute that was tinged with more than a little bit of personal reflection about a very warm human being.

. . . With the inauguration of President Carter, one of our honored public servants will become a private citizen again. Of course, I speak of Gerald Ford. . . .

Gerald Ford became president at a time when the presidency had become characterized by presidential excesses and wanton abuse of power. . . .

He became president at a time when this country was divided, disillusioned; when cynicism was abroad in the land.

He assumed the awesome responsibilities of the presidency at a time when people were beginning to lose faith in the institutions of government. He came into the White House as our president at a time when that distinguished and noble office had been tarnished. He took the reigns of power and authority in the presidency and has served us with honor, with ability and dedication to this very hour.

His actions as president have helped to heal the wounds caused by the previous administration. . . . He helped reunite this nation and renewed the needed confidence in our government. . . .

After I had returned from the hospital, having been there for some three weeks, I received a call from the president's secretary. The secretary asked: "Would it be possible for you and Mrs. Humphrey to join the president and Mrs. Ford for a little dinner at the White House on the night of Wednesday, November 17. . . ?"

Well, we came to the White House, and I said to Mrs. Humphrey, "I suppose that there will be a small group there, Muriel."

I had just been recuperating from surgery and was not feeling too strong. But I said, "It will be a delightful evening and we will have a chance to meet some of President Ford's friends and, most likely, some of his associates in the office."

We arrived at the White House and went up to the second floor of the White House, where the president's private living quarters are. I looked down the hallway and there was the president, sitting by himself—no one else. He came to greet us. The first thing he said was, "Betty will be with us in just a few moments."

I looked around and no one was there. I said, "Mr. President, maybe we are a little early." He said, "Oh, no. Betty and I just wanted to have a chance to have dinner with you and Muriel."

I consider that one of the nicest tributes I have ever received and one of the nicest and kindest acts of any man in public life. I have not always been exactly the tribune of praise for Mr. Ford's policies. . . .

That was one of the most interesting and exciting evenings of my long public life. We had a chance to talk very privately. The president was only a few days away from the election results. It was a very close election. He could have been morose, he could have been bitter. I read in the press that he was, which, of course, is not true. He was neither morose nor bitter. He had accepted the results as a man of character and quality would.

We just talked about what took place in the campaign, joked a little bit about it. I said, "I don't know, Mr. President, if you have extra connections up there in the divine heavens, but I had intended to be out on the stump doing a little campaigning against you, but I was immobilized."

Of course, that might have been all to his benefit, had I been out on the stump, campaigning against him. But as some of you know, he had come to pay me a visit in the hospital and during the time of my illness, both President and Mrs. Ford were most attentive, calling Muriel, my wife, many times, seeing how I was getting along, sending me a little note, paying me a personal visit. These are acts of a good man, of a very decent man.

That evening, I found it to be even more so. . . . We had a great time. I want to repeat here what I said to him there:

"Mr. President, you and I have had many disagreements, particularly on some of the economic policies. I have scolded you about some of your vetoes."

He took this all in good humor. But, I said, "History will not remember those things. You will be remembered not because of what economic policy you advocated; you will be remembered not because of the bills that you signed or the vetoes that you made. But you will be remembered in history for having restored to the office of the presidency, the decency, the honesty, the integrity, the honor, the nobility which that office must have."

And I said to him right then, "I would have given five years of my life to have had two weeks, two months, in this office, and you have had two-and-a-half years. You lost an election, but you have not lost the love and the respect of the American people."

That is exactly the way I feel about Gerald Ford. I think that, with all of his limitations—and we all have limitations, do we not? If anybody does not think he has some, he ought not to be in this body—with all of his limitations, this man has served this country well. . . .

I take this moment to express very sincerely my thanks to a fine and good man who has served as president of the United

States. I say to Gerald Ford, in every office that he has held, he has shown himself to be a man of good character, honesty, decency and fairness. He has shown wisdom at times and restraint at all times. He has demonstrated personal integrity and a sense of humanity in his actions. In all of this, he has gained the respect of all of us who have had the privilege and the honor of knowing him.

President Ford has had a long and distinguished career in public service. I say today that he will be missed, but he will be around, too. He is a healthy man and he is a vigorous man. He is leaving office on a wave of good feeling. What better thing is there than that? That wave of good feeling comes not only from his friends of many years in Congress but from all of the American people. . . .

So, Mr. President. . . , I wish you well. You have been a long-time friend and you are going to continue to be as long as I have the opportunity of living and a chance to know you and to see you.

7

The Last Year

He Cried That Day

Hubert Humphrey believed at the beginning of 1977 that the surgery he had undergone had cured his cancer. By midyear, however, he was to learn that a new cancer had developed. This one, he was told, would take his life.

For most people, that would be a death sentence. For Humphrey, it was a sentence of life. He would fight to keep on living and working for as long as possible. When he died, he would die with dignity.

In his first public appearance after leaving the hospital, Humphrey spoke to the Minnesota AFL-CIO on September 20. Much of what he said that day came from his heart; it was not part of any prepared text.

Hubert Humphrey cried that day, and America cried with him.

. . . I think I know how you feel, and I know how I feel about you, and that expression has been clear this morning. . . by your wonderful reception. . . .

Now, I ran off without my glasses, without my Kleenex. I am a little more sentimental after some period of what you might call physical trauma than usual, but I guess we will make it through anyway. . . .

The first thing I want to say to you as individuals and as a movement: If you are going to be something, if you are going to do something, you have to be proud of yourself and you have to be proud of your heritage, or your religion, or whatever else it may be. . . .

I told the president of the United States at a private luncheon that we had not long ago, I said:

"Mr. President, you just have to understand in our discussions, there is just a couple of things that I may be slightly prejudiced on amongst others. . . .

"I never would have been in the United States Senate had it not have been for my friends in the labor movement, and, please, don't ever ask me to do anything that would in any way cripple or injure or weaken that movement.

"Secondly, I have got to tell you, I had a lot of help from my friends in the Jewish community. They have been generous, they have been my friends and, please, don't ask me to do anything that would betray their legitimate interests and their deep concern over their role in American life, American politics and in the state of Israel."

I said, "Other than that, you can ask for almost anything."

But I have some loyalties and I have some priorities. . . . [One] of my loyalties has been to this great movement and I will tell you why. Not because you are perfect, not because there hasn't been a scoundrel now and then, because none of us are perfect. We have all made mistakes—and God only knows some of us have made too many.

But we judge a movement like this by its overall record and we judge the labor movement on what it has done to lift the standard of living for millions and millions and millions of plain American citizens who today can have their own home, who today have decent working conditions, who today can send their children to a good school. . . .

Be proud of it, dear friends, be proud of it!

Just remember this. [Pause as Humphrey wipes tears from his eyes.] Mom said they will take your picture if you wipe your eyes with the Kleenex. Well, that's all right. Take it. The fellow that doesn't have any tears, doesn't have any heart.

The history of the labor movement needs to be taught in every school in this land. We need to know what our roots, as they say—we learned about roots, didn't we, in 1976?—we need to know who we are, what we are, where we come from, how we got here.

You have heard me say that before. It is imperative. It is part of American history. This great nation wasn't built just because somebody sat behind a table and finagled and even financed—important as finance is, and it is important; important as planning is, and it is important; important as design is, and it is important.

Ultimately, it is the worker. It was the worker that built the railroads, that dug the tunnels, that dredged the rivers, that built the ports, that built the huge skyscrapers, put in the highways and built the homes.

America is a living testimonial to what free men and women, organized in free democratic trade unions, can do to make a better life—and we ought to be proud of it. Just remember that.

The first thing that any authoritarian or any two-bit dictator does is abolish free labor. That is the first thing. Long before they get to expropriation of land, long before they get to even putting into jail the so-called political prisoners, they abolish a free labor movement. . . .

That is the first sign, and in America, thank God, instead of abolishing it, abolishing our labor movement, we are going to strengthen it, and workers today that are not organized. . . , workers today that do not have the working conditions that they ought to have, are going to have a better chance.

Nobody is going to give it to them on a platter. It is not going to be easy, but they are not going to have everything set against them. . . .

Thank God for collective bargaining, what it has meant to the income of our families, what it has meant for working conditions, what it has meant for grievance procedures, what it has meant for job security, what it has meant for recreation and vacation so that families can get together and travel across this country, what it has meant for pensions and what it has meant for health.

Millions of Americans today have health care—not because the government has passed it, because we haven't had the guts to do it—but because negotiators have sat down at the table with their employers and have worked out a health-and-welfare pension program, commonly called "fringe benefits," which makes it possible for you as union members to have good health care with the best of doctors, the best of hospitals and not have to go broke during the whole process. Isn't that a marvelous statement?

Now, who does that hurt? See, we need to tell people about

this. The doctors get their money, the hospitals get their money, the family still survives, the community is better off.

What is all this nonsense about when you get a little wage increase for a worker, [that's inflation]?

[The] American worker—and let's get this down straight now—the American worker is the most productive worker in the world, the most productive worker in the world.

I can hear somebody say, "Yes, you can expect that from Humphrey."

Don't expect it from me. That is the official record. We have the best labor relations in the world, fewer work stoppages than any other industrialized country. Not bad. . . .

Let's take a look at what is ahead. . . . [One] of the things that has got to be done is for the government of the United States by official declared policy to state that the goal and the objective of all of [its] policies. . . is full employment and economic growth.

And that is what the Humphrey-Hawkins Bill is all about. . . . I don't want you to be deceived by these letters to the editors. I don't want you to be fooled by these ill-informed editorials that appear from time to time. I want you to take a look at what we are really trying to do. . . .

The whole purpose of the Humphrey-Hawkins Bill is to utilize the resources of the government in coordination with private enterprise to maximize private enterprise, to see that private enterprise has the credit, the money, the resources, the trained workers that are necessary to keep this economy of ours growing, so that as the labor force grows, we can absorb the new ones and that we can pick up the millions that have been left behind.

The second part of the Humphrey-Hawkins Bill is merely what we are doing today, but not enough: emergency public works, the comprehensive educational training program known as CETA, the special aid to our cities, the Job Corps, the Youth Employment Program of which I was coauthor. . . , but we need to do more of it.

Ladies and gentlemen, the greatest enemy America has

today is the fact that there are 7 million [people] capable of working that ought to be working, that are unemployed, and of those 7 million, 3 million are youths between the ages of 16 and 22, and many of them never had a job, many of them have never known work discipline, many of them know nothing of parity that comes from work. . . . [They] have learned how to live off the street and I am here to tell you that as long as you have that many people unemployed, you will never cut the crime rate, you will never get at dope addiction, you will never solve the social and economic problems which you read about which plague our cities and move into our countries.

Solving the problems of unemployment is not only an economic necessity, it is a social necessity. We need to wage war upon unemployment. . . .

Take a look at how long it has taken us to even set up a job corps center. So many people have got to pick at it, and we have to go through so many different little rules and regulations.

Let me tell you, Franklin Roosevelt set up the Civilian Conservation Corps back in the '30s. . . . He put one man in charge. He called him in in March and he said to this gentleman, "By the end of June, I want 500,000 young men in camps out in the forests at work, clothed, with the tools and ready to go to work."

From March until June. And by June 30, 530,000 young men were at work in the camps out in the forests, doing the job.

It can be done. You have just got to make up your mind to do it. . . .

We have got things to do in this country. . . . [We] have gone along here piddling along, and we have been spending billions and billions and billions. We have never made up our minds that America needed something: forests to be replanted; cities to be rebuilt; railroads. . . . that need modernization and rebuilding. . . ; over 30,000 bridges in America that are out of date that slow up our transportation system; ports that are too old and too small to take care of modern shipping. The list is unlimited.

We are fifteen years behind in reforestation. . . . By the

way, we ought to have an urban forestration program, too. Plant trees in our cities just as we do now in our countryside.

We have got things to do in this country and I want the labor movement to start demanding that they be done. That is the way we get things done. . . .

We have got a job to do to clean up our cities. We can't afford to let them fall apart. . . .

When are we going to wake up? If we can have a World Bank that can loan money to Chile, if we can have a World Bank that can loan money to Afghanistan, and many of us don't even know where it is, then we ought to be able to have a national domestic development bank that can loan money to Minneapolis and St. Paul, and New York and Rochester, and Los Angeles and San Francisco. . . .

I have only been at this now fifteen years. . . , but it has got to come, because we have got to save the cities, because the people that live in those cities have to be saved and it does no good to pass out food stamps. . . .

We need to tear out whole sections.We need to build parks and playgrounds and modern transportation. . . . No nation ever went bankrupt building.

You go bankrupt in wars. No nation ever lost its life trying to save life. You lose your life when you take life, and I ask the labor movement to really, once again, become the idealistic conscience of American politics.

Too many people in politics today are afraid. They are afraid, they say, "Oh, they won't go for this."

Well, I knew they wouldn't go for civil rights in 1948, I knew they wouldn't go for Medicare in 1949, I knew they wouldn't go for the Peace Corps in 1958 and I knew they wouldn't go, if you please, for the arms control and disarmament agency in 1959. But, ultimately, they did.

If you are going to be a man in politics, you have to be like a soldier in the battlefield. You know, there are risks, there is no guarantee of your life, but as somebody once said, I would rather live fifty years like a tiger than a hundred years like a chicken.

Thank you very much.

The Greatest Gift

On October 25, 1977, Hubert Humphrey returned to the Senate for the last time.

As he entered the Senate chamber, senators and guests rose and for several minutes applauded.

Senator Robert C. Byrd, the majority leader, rose when the applause stopped to address his colleagues:

"The Senate is a special body," he said, "whose character and actions are shaped not only by its official nature but also by the personalities and commitments of those who serve in it at any given time. The presence of Hubert Humphrey in the Senate enhances the greatness that already inherently belongs to this distinguished chamber. . . .

"George Santayana, the philosopher and poet, wrote:

"'It is not wisdom only to be wise,

"'And on the inward vision close the eyes,

"'But it is wisdom to believe the heart.'

"Senator Humphrey is one of those great political leaders who have combined the best of mind and soul, wisdom and inward vision. He has indeed believed his heart. . . . He has always had a vision of what America can be and he has sought to give reality to that vision throughout his career. . . .

"Some men attempt to alter the course of history, or bend the direction of their era, through thunder and threat; they launch armies, marshall forces and fester plots. Hubert Humphrey has changed our own time through the impact of his personality, the exertion of his energy, the vibrance of his spirit, the exercise of his intellect and the compassion of his heart. . . . [He] is a man whose influence will reverberate for generations, in America and around the world. . . ."

Senator Herman Talmadge told his colleagues: "As the nation and, indeed, the world have come to learn, Senator Humphrey is one of those rare leaders who sets his sights high and upon whom you can always depend to get the job done. . . .

"Hubert Humphrey has built a record of great accomplishments in many areas—human rights, agriculture, rural development, child nutrition and education, and in virtually every area of human endeavor.

"In all of his undertakings, Senator Humphrey always has been a man of dignity, honor and the highest sense of duty. He has given himself totally to the *service of his country without regard to any self-interests. He has dedicated his life to make this nation a better place to live for all of us, and for generations yet to come. . . ."*

Other speeches of praise followed. Finally, Humphrey rose to address his colleagues.

. . . Gentlemen, most of you know me as a sentimental man, and that I am.

Today is a very special day in my life, not only because I feel strong enough to come to this historic chamber, back to the U.S. Senate, the greatest parliamentary body in the world, but more significantly because of the genuine friendship and warmth that has been exhibited here today by my colleagues.

The greatest gift in life is the gift of friendship and I have received it. And the greatest healing therapy is friendship and love, and over this land I have sensed it. Doctors, chemicals, radiation, pills, nurses, therapists, are all very, very helpful, but without faith in yourself and in your own ability to overcome your difficulties, faith in divine providence and without the friendship and the kindness and the generosity of friends, there is no healing. I know that.

I have been going through a pretty rough struggle. But one of my doctors back home said: "Hubert, we have done about as much for you as we can for a while. Why don't you go back to Washington where you want to be, where your colleagues in the Senate are to be and and where you can be with your friends, those whom you love so much?" And I said: "Doctor, that is good advice. . . ."

[And] I followed this advice. I waited, however, because I am a frugal man, until I could get a free ride. . . .

Well, for at least twenty years I have been trying to get on Air Force One. I realize it was not a prolonged experience, but just the thought of it, the vibrations, gave me new hope and new strength. . . .

It was a beautiful trip. I had a chance to visit with President

Carter and to express to him some of my concerns and my hopes.

I want to put it just this way: I have been known in my life to be an optimist—some people say a foolish optimist—and I suppose at times I have ignored reality and had more than the usual degree of optimism. But I said to the critics that I am optimistic about America and that I rebuke their cynicism.

The reason I do is because history is on my side. We have come a long way in this country. More people today are enjoying more of what we call, at least in the material sense, the good things of life in every form. We have made fantastic strides in science, technology and engineering. Our agriculture is a wonderful world but, most significantly, we are a heterogeneous population, and we are trying to demonstrate to the world what is the great moral message of the Old and New Testament: namely, that people can live together in peace and in understanding because really that is the challenge, that is what peace is all about.

It is not a question of whether we pile up more wealth; it is a question of whether or not we can live together, different races, different creeds, different cultures, different areas, not as a homogeneous people but rather in the pluralistic society where we respect each other, hopefully try to understand each other, and then have a common bond of devotion to the republic.

I have a blind devotion to the Senate. . . . What a wonderful place this is, where we can argue, fight, have different points of view, and still have a great respect for one another and, many times, deep affection. . . .

[When] it comes to the Senate and to what this body means, it is not Democrat or Republican. It is citizen, which I consider to be the highest honor that can be paid to any person in the world, higher than emperor or king or prince, to be citizen of the United States and then, as a citizen, to be elected and selected by our own constituency to represent the citizenry in this body. What a great honor.

May the Good Lord give each of us the strength to never in any way besmirch that honor, but in every day of our lives, as we see what we believe to be the truth, as we dedicate ourselves to what we believe to be best for our country, even though we may disagree, let us conduct ourselves in a manner that future historians will say, "These were good people. They were good men. They were good representatives, at a time when the nation needed them." And our nation does need us now.

Now, my plea to us is, in the words of Isaiah, as a former president used to say—and I mean it very sincerely—"Come, let us reason together." There are no problems between the different points of view in this body that cannot be reconciled, if we are willing to give a little and to share a little, and not expect it all to be our way. Who is there who has such wisdom that he knows what he says is right? I think we have to give some credence to the fact that majority rule, which requires the building of an understanding and the sharing, at times the compromising, is the best of all forms of rule.

Well, I got wound up. I did not intend to be that long, but that has been the story of my life. You would want me to be natural. Thank you very much. Thank you very, very much.

The Speech He Never Gave

On the evening of Friday, January 13, 1978, Hubert Horatio Humphrey died after lapsing into a coma.

He had been scheduled to speak at "A Tribute to Hubert Humphrey" on the following day, January 14, as part of the tenth annual Martin Luther King's Birthday observance. When his weakened condition prevented him from attending in person, he designated his sister, Dr. Frances Humphrey Howard, to appear in his place.

He died, however, less than twenty-four hours before the speech was to be delivered. Following is the text of that address.

Fourteen years ago, Dr. Martin Luther King, Jr., shared with us his dream for America. That cherished dream of what our nation could and should be became our dream as well. Today, we come together to celebrate the forty-ninth anniversary of the birth of this champion of the rights of all people. We come together to recommit ourselves to the struggle to reach the promised land which he described from the mountain top.

I am deeply moved by the tribute bestowed upon me tonight. To be linked to Dr. King in the battle of equal rights is a distinct honor. My only regret is that I cannot be with all of you tonight to share in your warm friendship.

Your work, your sacrifice, your vision, your determination and your commitment to an equal chance in life for all of our people have made great progress possible. Because of your efforts we have rewritten the nation's laws to clearly recognize equal rights for all Americans. And, don't let anyone sell this achievement short—it is monumental. Without it, equality of opportunity is not possible in education, in employment, in your neighborhood, in any important aspect of American life.

Today, life is better for most black Americans than it was for their parents or grandparents. Incomes are better, political influence and representation has increased and much more.

That is progress. Progress which reaches into the homes of millions of our fellow citizens and directly affects their lives. It is real progress and we must not forget that it has occurred.

But, we cannot be satisfied in measuring our progress solely by the distance we have come from the abominable conditions that existed in a period of gross injustice. We must face the facts. For despite our progress, a huge valley of shame separates black and white America:

—Black family incomes average only 62 percent of white family incomes;

—Less than half of all black people over age 18 have a high school diploma;

—Unemployment rates for black Americans have been double the rates for white Americans for two decades;

—27 percent of our black families still struggle to survive on incomes below the poverty line.

These are only a few of the facts, but the point is clear. We are a long way from our goal of a society with equal opportunity and justice for all. In moving toward this goal, our focus today must be on jobs—decent jobs, good-paying jobs, jobs with a challenge, jobs with a future.

That is why my first priority, and I think it should be yours, as well, is passage of the Humphrey-Hawkins Full Employment Bill. This bill will commit the government to full employment in a politically accountable manner that has never existed in the past. It will make full employment the central focus of our nation's economic policy. It will result in a new and unparalleled push for full employment in America.

Don't listen to those who say this bill is watered down and not worth fighting for. Most of these people have no idea how national economic policy decisions are made. Many of these "instant experts" have never taken the time or trouble to read the bill. Some of these commentators are trying to kill the bill by convincing its supporters that it is meaningless.

I will never deceive you and I believe you know it. This legislation is a must. It is no miracle cure, but it is an indispensable step toward economic justice. We must keep up the fight. If we do, I assure you, it will be well worth every effort you make.

A Humphrey Eulogy

When Lyndon Johnson's portrait was hung in the National Portrait Gallery, Hubert Humphrey delivered a moving tribute to the late president. That was in May 1974.

We are printing it at the conclusion of this volume because much of what he says about Lyndon Johnson we feel applies equally to himself.

. . . Mortality is a strange phenomenon. And when reflecting on the life of a great or historical figure, the temptation is always to want to enlarge and exaggerate the qualities of the one who is remembered so fondly.

But I'm going to level with you. I think it's impossible for any of us here to grasp at this hour and this time the full meaning of Lyndon Johnson's life. This will require the refinement of time, the refinement indeed of historical perspective, to filter out the dust of the minutae, so that we can find the solid rock of character and of accomplishment that really symbolize and represent the man, his politics, his administration.

What we can and do know is that he was a unique man. . . , a giant of a man. When he embraced you, you were embraced. And when he chastised you, you were chastised! There was no doubt, no ambivalence, no indifference. . . .

He was touched by the disparities of great wealth and cruel poverty, by the arbitrary divisions of the North and of the South, and between the privileged and the deprived, and between the great and the mean.

Lyndon Johnson worked his way, fought his way, earned his way to the pinnacle of political power. . . . But. . . he never once lost sight of who he was, what he was, who he was for, and what he was for—in other words, his mission.

Rooted firmly and squarely in the best traditions of our nation, this man had a clear and sensitive understanding that people, not institutions, are the foundation of our government.

He knew the first three words of the Constitution—"We the People." He never got them confused.

He understood that the whole objective of government is what Thomas Jefferson said it was to be. . . : The health, happiness and well-being of the people.

And that, indeed was the guiding philosophy of President Johnson, who wanted to be remembered as the man who made great contributions to education, and wanted to be remembered as having opened the doors of opportunity for every American and even extending his great strong hand and arm to help people walk through those doors.

He was keenly aware of the worth of every person and the responsibility of government—and particularly the president—to speak to the needs and aspirations of those who are deprived of the opportunity to enjoy the promises of freedom. I guess that's what drew me to him more than anything else.

And looking on the life of a fallen leader, we are sometimes inclined to speak of the achievements that he left behind, as I have here for this moment. But Lyndon Johnson's legacy is not the past. It is a living one. It is here and now—and that legacy is found in the face of a black child who will never again be forced to live in a society that has been divided on the basis of race.

It is a legacy of universal suffrage for all. I think that the one moment that he was happier than any time that I witnessed him in the legislative process was that moment in the joint session of the Congress when he addressed us on the voting rights—voting rights for everybody, and said, "We shall overcome!" That was a moment of tremendous emotion and also of great purpose.

It's a legacy that he's left us for elderly Americans, hope for their greater security in their final and their dwindling years.

It is a legacy for every American boy and girl. Can't you just hear him say that he wanted every American boy and girl to have all the education that they could take, all that they could absorb.

And it's a legacy for economic opportunity for hundreds of thousands of disadvantaged citizens. I'd like to say here that the one war that this man really wanted to win, and the one that he wanted to wage, was the war on poverty—not just the war on the poverty of the purse, but the poverty of spirit.

The list is endless, but most of all Lyndon Johnson left us with hope for the survival of our precious democracy. He showed us that the most diverse elements could be brought together. He understood the preamble of the Constitution—that we were required to form a more perfect union, to establish justice, to insure domestic tranquility; to provide for the common defense; to promote the general welfare, and to secure the blessings of liberty for ourselves and our posterity.

And he believed that these things could be done in the

political process—with reason and debate and decision. He defined for me and for you the challenges, and he showed us a way to meet them—upright, head-on, and not to retreat. . . .

I invite all Americans to remember not just the president, but to remember the man, Lyndon Johnson. Be proud of his accomplishments, for he was truly one of our own. Let's not look to his achievements as a static history of his period, but view them, rather, as a challenge to tackle the tough jobs that remain —just as he did, with a fierce, at times, and an uncompromising hatred for injustice, bigotry and poverty which you and I know and which he knew sap the life of our people and taint the blessings of liberty. . . .

God bless you.

Epilogue

[*This introduction is a reprinting of excerpts from the two eulogies delivered by Vice-President Mondale: the first on January 15, 1978, in Washington, D. C.; the second on January 16 in St. Paul, Minnesota. We reprint them with permission of the vice-president, who said he could not improve on what he had already said because Senator Humphrey's death had so totally drained him emotionally.*]

January 15, 1978, Washington, D.C.

. . . There is a natural impulse at a time like this to dwell on the many accomplishments of Hubert Humphrey's remarkable life, by listing a catalogue of past events, as though there were some way to quantify what he was all about. But I don't want to do that, because Hubert didn't want it and neither does Muriel.

Even though this is one of the saddest moments of my life and I feel as great a loss as I have ever known, we must remind ourselves of Hubert's last great wish: that this be a time to celebrate life and the future, not to mourn the past and his death.

But, Muriel, I hope you will forgive me if I don't entirely succeed in looking forward and not backward, because I must, for a moment.

Two days ago, as I flew back from the West over the land that Hubert loved and to this city that he loved, I thought back over his life and its meaning, and I tried to understand what it was about this unique person that made him such an uplifting symbol of hope and joy for all people.

And I thought of the letter that he wrote to Muriel over forty years ago, when he first visited Washington. He said in that letter:

"Maybe I seem foolish to have such vain hopes and plans. But, Bucky, I can see how, some day, if you and I just apply ourselves and make up our minds to work for bigger things, how we can some day live here in Washington and probably be in government, politics or service. I intend to set my aim at Congress."

Hubert was wrong only in thinking that his hopes and plans might be in vain. They were not, as we all know. Not only did he succeed, with his beloved wife at his side; he succeeded gloriously and beyond even his most optimistic dreams.

Hubert will be remembered by all of us who served with him as one of the greatest legislators in our history. He will be remembered as one of the most loved men of his time. And even though he failed to realize his greatest goal, he achieved something much more rare and valuable than the nation's highest office: he became his country's conscience.

Today, the love that flows from everywhere, enveloping Hubert, flows also to you, Muriel. And the presence today here, where America bids farewell to her heroes, of President and Mrs. Carter, of former Presidents Ford and Nixon, and your special friend and former First Lady, Mrs. Johnson, attests to the love and respect that the nation holds for both of you.

That letter to Bucky, his Muriel, also noted three principles by which Hubert defined his life: work, determination and high goals. They were part of his life's pattern when I first met him, thirty-one years ago. I was only seventeen, fresh out of high school, and he was the mayor of Minneapolis. He had then all the other sparkling qualities he maintained throughout his life: boundless good humor, endless optimism and hope, infinite interest, intense concern for people and their problems, compassion without being compromising, energy beyond belief, and a spirit so filled with love there was no room at all for hate or bitterness. He was simply incredible.

When he said that life was not meant to be endured but, rather, to be enjoyed, you knew what he meant. You could see it simply by watching him and listening to him. When Hubert looked at the lives of black Americans in the '40s, he saw endurance and not enjoyment; and his heart insisted that it was time for Americans to walk forthrightly into the bright sunshine of human rights.

When Hubert looked at the young who could not get a good education, he saw endurance and not enjoyment.

When Hubert saw old people in ill health, he saw endurance and not enjoyment.

When Hubert saw middle-class people striving to survive and working people without jobs and decent homes, he saw endurance and not enjoyment.

Hubert was criticized for proclaiming the politics of joy, but he knew that joy is essential to us and is not frivolous. He loved to point out that ours is the only nation in the world to officially declare the pursuit of happiness as a national goal.

But he was also a sentimental man, and that was part of his life, too. He cried in public and without embarrassment. In his last major speech in his beloved Minnesota, he wiped tears from his eyes and said, "A man without tears is a man without a heart." If he cried often, it was not for himself but for others.

Above all, Hubert was a man with a good heart; and on this sad day it would be good for us to recall Shakespeare's words:

"A good leg will fall; a straight back will stoop; a black beard will turn white; a curied pate will grow bald; a fair face will wither; a full eye will wax hollow; but a good heart is the sun and the moon; or, rather, the sun and not the moon; for it shines bright and never changes, but keeps its course truly."

Hubert's heart kept its course truly.

He taught us all how to hope and how to love, how to win and how to lose. He taught us how to live and, finally, he taught us how to die.

January 16, 1978, St. Paul, Minnesota
Yesterday, our nation honored Hubert Humphrey in a wonderful outpouring of affection. Hubert would have liked it. But today is an even more special day—the day Hubert comes home to Minnesota for the last time, to rest in the place he loved best and the place which gave him spiritual and political sustenance.

While he was an international figure and a national figure, as we in Minnesota well knew, he was always a Minnesotan and always a son of the prairie. There was something in this land and its lakes and especially its people that fed the springs of love, the streams of ideas, the torrents of enthusiasm and which nurtured the special genius and the immense humanity of Hubert Humphrey.

There was a kind of unity, of integrity in this love affair with the people of Minnesota that permitted Hubert's idealism to flower. He was a special man in a special place and I knew he would want me to say today, "Thank you, Minnesota."

That mutual affection was important, for in a democracy, a leader can only pursue greatness if the people will let him. The people of Minnesota not only let him, they encouraged him, and are in a true sense a part of his greatness. . . .

Carl Sandburg once said of another American hero, "You can't quite tell where the people leave off and where Abe Lincoln begins." What was true of Lincoln was surely as true of Hubert. He could not be separated from his people.

Muriel, you've heard words of praise for Hubert from many people and places. They are genuine and they reflect the deep affection for your husband and our friend. But beyond words, I think last night when we went to the state capitol and saw masses of people, who stood for hours in severe cold and burst into spontaneous song of celebration when you arrived, that this confirmed if there was any doubt—and there's none —that this state loved Hubert in a very special way.

Yesterday, I spoke to you about Hubert. Today I would like to say: Hubert, your memory lifts our spirits, just as your presence did. And though these days have been especially long and emotionally draining, you would have been very proud of Muriel, who has received in your absence the gifts of love with dignity and courage and strength. With her here, your spirit, your joy, your good heart remains with us.

Muriel, you have been an immense part of the life we celebrate today. For forty-one years of marriage and before that, you were the force and the infinite resource which sus-

tained this wonderful man. You have shared his triumphs and
his disappointments. And you have been equal to his overwhelming love and returned it to him in a way that made
it possible for him to be the buoyant creature he was.

As usual, Hubert said it best, when he dedicated the story
—his basic book on his life—to Muriel. He said this: "To Muriel:
my partner and sweetheart, who has made my way easier, my
life fuller, and without whom I could not have reached out to
be what I wanted to be."

What the people of Minnesota have been to him in a
general way, you have been in a personal and specific way.
Without you, Hubert would have had to struggle far harder to
reach the esteem he did. Ultimately, the nation has learned
what we who were privileged to know him longest and best,
knew first. That Hubert was an incomparable creator of great
plans and grand designs, but that the big picture, the master
program never, never replaced what was the essence of Hubert
Humphrey. The ability to touch an individual's life, often the
life of a stranger—if there were any strangers in his life—
and make those lives better and more joyous.

Hubert loved people in the mass, but he also loved each
human being in an almost saintly way. He had time for everybody, which is why he was always late. There was an article in
the *Washington Post* yesterday that said it nicely. He instructed his
staff not to schedule him so tightly. When he walked through
the halls of Congress, he wanted to be able to spend as much
time as possible with ordinary people. He said, "I can rush by
people or I can go by and be good and gentle. Maybe say a little
word to somebody and take a little time. Don't be worried if I am
a little late or something like that, I am going to take some time to
say hello to some kids."

The mayor of Waverly said this weekend, "If he met someone, the next time he saw him he'd remember his name. He had a
fantastic memory. My children met him at his home and when
he went to visit the school he remembered them by name."

It was really more than a fantastic memory. It was a will to
reach out and say I know you, you are an individual. And people

knew he felt that way. A politician may fake it for an hour, or maybe a day, but you can't fake it for a lifetime.

To Hubert it didn't make any difference who you were or where you came from. Hubert was the ultimate ecumenical spirit. He was the Pope John of American politics. He accepted no distinctions which denied humanity in each individual. Race, age, religion, ethnic origin, color, economic class, sex, made no difference to Hubert Humphrey. He never found a person who was not worthy of his time, concern and love. Where others wearied, he took strength. Where others turned aside, he embraced. Where others snarled, he smiled. Where others spoke in bitterness, he spoke in love.

He was a universal man and that is why he struggled with problems of world hunger and poverty, education and medical care, of basic human conditions. That's why he worried, as few others did, about the issue of arms and nuclear holocaust. Hubert may have been wrong sometimes; he never claimed to be perfect. But when he was wrong, it was never a matter of the heart, because Hubert was a man of great and good heart.

I have tried since yesterday, to find a conclusion that was different, to say in another way what I felt about Humphrey. But I couldn't, so I would like to repeat it again:

Hubert taught us all how to hope and how to love, how to win and how to lose. He taught us how to live and, finally, he taught us how to die.

Eulogy to Hubert Humphrey Delivered by
President Jimmy Carter

At critical times in our history, the United States has been blessed by great people who, just by being themselves, give us a vision of what we are at our best and of what we might become. Hubert Humphrey was such a man.

In a time of impending social crisis thirty years ago, his was the first voice I ever heard, a lone voice, persistently demanding basic human rights for all Americans.

It was a most difficult moral and social issue that my own generation would have to face in those early days. His was a clear voice, a strong voice, a passionate voice, which recruited others to join in a battle in our country so that equal rights of black people could be gained—to vote, to hold a job, to go to school, to own a home.

I first met Hubert Humphrey when he was vice-president —torn because his heart was filled with love and yearning for peace, while at the same time he was meticulously loyal to a president who led our nation during an unpopular war.

I also remember him in a time of political defeat, courage-ously leading a divided Democratic Party, losing his uphill campaign for president by just a few votes.

But he was a big man; and, without bitterness, he gave his support to the new president and then came back later to the Senate to serve his nation once again.

For the last year of his life, I knew him best, and that is when I needed him most. Despite campaign disagreements and my own harsh words spoken under pressure and in haste, it was not his nature to forget how to love or to forgive.

He has given me freely what I need: the support and understanding of a close and true friend, the advice of a wise and honest counselor.

When he first visited me in the oval office, I felt that he should have served there.

I know that he has been an inspiration and a conscience to us all, but especially to the leaders of our nation: to Harry Truman, to Dwight Eisenhower, to John Kennedy, to Lyndon Johnson, to Richard Nixon, to Gerald Ford and to me. We and our families are here today to testify that Hubert Humphrey may well have blessed our country more than any one of us.

His greatest personal attribute was that he really knew how to love. There was nothing abstract or remote about him. He did not love humanity only in the mass. You could feel it in the scope of his concern, in his words, in the clasp of his hands, in the genuine eager interest in his eyes as he looked at you.

He always spoke up for the weak and the hungry and for the victims of discrimination and poverty. He never lost sight of our own human possibilities. He never let us forget that in our democratic nation we are a family, bound together by a kinship of purpose and by mutual concern and respect. He reminded us that we must always protect and nurture the other members of our national family.

Yesterday, as messages poured in to me, as president, and to the members of the Humphrey family from throughout the world, I realized vividly that Hubert Humphrey was the most beloved of all Americans and that his family encompassed not just the people of the United States but all people everywhere.

He asked, as the vice-president has said, that this service be a celebration; and in a way, that is what it is. Even as we mourn his death, we celebrate because such a man as Hubert Humphrey was among us.

The joy of his memory will last far longer than the pain and sorrow of his leaving.

Index